EDUCATIONAL
RESEARCH

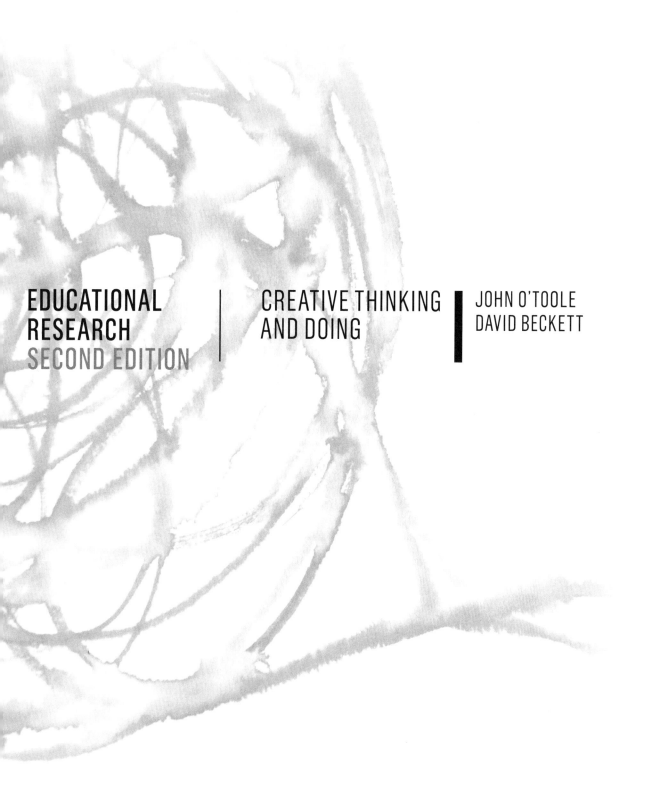

EDUCATIONAL RESEARCH
SECOND EDITION

CREATIVE THINKING AND DOING

JOHN O'TOOLE
DAVID BECKETT

OXFORD
UNIVERSITY PRESS
AUSTRALIA & NEW ZEALAND

Oxford University Press is a department of the University of Oxford.

It furthers the University's objective of excellence in research, scholarship, and education by publishing worldwide. Oxford is a registered trademark of Oxford University Press in the UK and in certain other countries.

Published in Australia by
Oxford University Press
253 Normanby Road, South Melbourne, Victoria 3205, Australia

National Library of Australia Cataloguing-in-Publication entry

Author: O'Toole, John, 1941– , author.
Title: Educational research : creative thinking and doing / John O'Toole; David Beckett.
Edition: 2nd edn.
ISBN: 9780195518313 (paperback)
Notes: Includes bibliographical references and index.
Subjects: Education—Methodology—Research.
          Education—Research.
Other Authors/Contributors: Beckett, David, author.

Dewey Number: 370.7

Reproduction and communication for educational purposes

Edited by Anne Mulvaney
Text design by Polar Design
Typeset by diacriTech (P) Ltd
Proofread by Naomi Saligari
Indexed by Jeanne Rudd
Printed by Markono Print Media Pte Ltd, Singapore

Links to third party websites are provided by Oxford in good faith and for information only. Oxford disclaims any responsibility for the materials contained in any third party website referenced in this work.

CONTENTS

PART B Doing Research   89

ACKNOWLEDGMENTS

Our first acknowledgments must go to Drama Australia, the national association of drama teachers, for its timely recognition that a book like this was needed, and for providing the original opportunity to write and publish its precursor, *Doing Drama Research*—as we explain in the Introduction. Our thanks go to Chris Sinclair, officially the editorial assistant to that book but much more than that really, for her energy and care, and The University of Melbourne for making her assistance possible.

We also want to thank and honour the original editorial committee and those other co-researchers of the Australasian drama research community who contributed directly and indirectly to that book, with no thought of reward or recognition. Many gave written advice encompassing many pages; others gave copies of documents and course outlines, references and exemplars. All gave considerate and considered contributions of the highest standard. A few of those we have acknowledged in the text, but many have become absorbed in the intellectual dialogue that informed both that book and this successor: Michael Anderson, Penny Bundy, Bruce Burton, the late John Carroll, Kennedy Chinyowa, Christine Comans, Kate Donelan, Julie Dunn, Robyn Ewing, Kelly Freebody, Janinka Greenwood, Brad Haseman, Janet MacDonald, Mangeni Patrick, Tarquam McKenna, Tony Millett, Tiina Moore, Morag Morrison, Tim Moss, Angela O'Brien, Peter O'Connor, Jo O'Mara, Robin Pascoe, Anna Plunkett, Ross Prior, Jo Raphael, Tracey Sanders, Richard Sallis, Heather Smigiel, Madonna Stinson, Philip Taylor, Prue Wales and David Wright.

Doing Drama Research has undergone many changes to turn it into *Educational Research*, and then some more in preparing this second edition. In this process, we are particularly grateful to Brad Astbury for his advice on methodology, to Wu Chao-Kuei for insisting on clarity for non-Western researchers, and to Philippa Moylan for her meticulous counsel and unfailing care towards us, as to all the fledgling researchers whom she supports. For the second edition, we are grateful to David Forrest for permitting us to play some more with our agony column, Dr Sophie, who first appeared as 'Dr Phil' in one of his edited books, and to OUP's Belinda Leon, for firmly keeping us up to the mark and the schedule. In addition, we are grateful for the useful and informative discussions with lots of teachers and educators, community workers and friends, other practitioners and workers in arts and education, here and overseas, who have given advice and shown interest. Our heartfelt personal thanks also to Robby Nason, and to Denise, James and Sophia Beckett for their unfailing patience and help.

And then of course not least there are the research participants, those mainly young people whose involvement in all the research projects has provided us with most of the knowledge and understanding that is in these pages.

John O'Toole and David Beckett
February 2013

INTRODUCTION

'When I use a word', Humpty Dumpty said in rather a scornful tone, 'it means just what I choose it to mean—neither more nor less.'
'The question is', said Alice, 'whether you can make words mean so many different things.'
'The question is', said Humpty Dumpty, 'which is to be Master—that's all.'

(Lewis Carroll, *Through the Looking-Glass*)

'Curiouser and curiouser', said Alice.

(Lewis Carroll, *Alice's Adventures in Wonderland*)

▦ truths and meanings

Lewis Carroll is on to something very important for anyone coming to research in an educational context: getting a handle on the right question is tricky in itself. Who is to be the master of meaning? Whose 'meanings' count? And why?

There is a slipperiness about the basics that can make new researchers wary and suspicious of any claims to establish anything significant. And in education, there is a lot at stake—equally for students, teachers, administrators, and their trainers, facilitators and professional development experts of all kinds. In words as in actions, not just any meanings will do, so Humpty Dumpty is wrong: words and actions, with their meanings, do not mean just what he chooses them to mean. Education is all about what things mean, in all their complexity: some of its parts we call 'sciences' and 'social sciences' because we maintain that we can 'know' what they mean and verify our knowledge or at least agree upon what works. On the other hand, the parts that we call the 'arts and humanities' encourage exploration of human experiences at such levels of intensity and ambiguity that meaningfulness resides in the social, the personal and, even sometimes, the idiosyncratic.

▦ neutrality

Those of us who work in education are all familiar with the truism that there is no such thing as 'neutral' subject matter, still less a 'neutral' teacher. Teaching is a political, cultural and ideological act in which we are all situated very specifically. That's just as true of research. This is why we, as the authors, feel it is important to come clean, right up front, about our own positioning, which is also part of our reason for writing this book, that will be useful, we hope, for beginning researchers right across the spectrum of education. We both come from the arts and humanities—and claim those two words as our home territory: one of us is a philosopher, and the other a drama educator—and the book has been further informed by the collective wisdom of the growing research community in drama education, for reasons we will explain. There are quite a few textbooks on educational research already, informing many research methods courses in universities. Most of these books have been written and the courses taught by scientists and social scientists—inevitably, as they have a long-standing research tradition and dominance in almost every aspect of systemic education. This 'situatedness' of the leaders in our scholarship traditionally has not always been acknowledged, but just taken for granted.

Taking another old truism about teaching, that the good teacher 'starts where the students are at', those authors' positioning is thus fine for students with a scientific bent, comfortable with the *object world*, with numbers and facts, the verifiable and the quantitative. However, as a result, although there are many inspiring educational research methods courses, we have noticed for many years that arts and humanities students—more comfortable with the *subject world*, with words, human relationships and imagination—often struggle, especially at the start, when they are immediately confronted with what appears to be an alien landscape. By the time the intricacies and ambiguities of qualitative research are introduced, too often the daunted would-be arts or humanities scholar is imbued with a sense of defeat and some have already fled the world of research. That's what used to happen, anyway, all too often; and we don't intend to set up that process in reverse, frightening off the scientifically inclined! One thing we have noticed, for instance, is that educational research in science and social sciences is changing its emphasis. The studies we see our colleagues investigating tend to be much less focused on content than they would have been once. Just like research in the arts, the emphasis in education research is much more on reinforcing the importance of context in research—moving from researching the content and how to transmit it, towards considering the learners' contexts, the use of experimental or radical pedagogies, and the values being exchanged and engaged (rather than transmitted) with the knowledge.

▨ positioning
▨ object world

▨ subject world
▨ content and context

Once upon a time, it was mandatory to believe that any research report was authoritative and entirely objective, written by a neutral and invisible hand in the third person. Nowadays, that is quite outdated and inappropriate. Instead, the research writer usually identifies his or her position in relation to the research and articulates it up front. So, to be quite explicit about this, the book you are holding in your hands has been written by two arts and humanities academics, who take very seriously the location of 'education' in the academy as a social science (which, formally, it is), but who want to contribute to the 'subject' world of social science research, while fully acknowledging the traditional strengths of the 'objective' world of research in the social sciences. In this book we seek to provide a balanced view of the full range of approaches to research in education, as a *social* science, by giving greater prominence to the 'subjective' world, presently under-represented in education research methodology publishing. We are delighted that this second edition is possible because the first edition hit this target in the academic marketplace so well.

Let us develop that aim a little. In the past fifty years, there has been an explosion of interest and involvement in new approaches to research, which are now quite 'scholastically responsible' and which encourage creativity. For all sorts of reasons, traditional and usually 'objective' physical and social sciences research methods seemed too remote or too narrowly focused to throw light on such complex and evanescent phenomena as the breadth and intensity of meaningful human experiences. Within that pursuit of meaningfulness, arts and humanities practitioners, in particular, just got on with doing (for example) drama, literature, music, philosophy or history without much regard for the methodological niceties of 'high-status' positivistic (or quantitative) research. There was a much narrower and less appealing range of qualitative approaches to research, then, too.

▨ new approaches

'Two Cultures'

ways of seeing

magnification

refraction

Like the best of contemporary research methodology courses, we shall be questioning, and to some extent dismantling, that unhelpful divide between 'quantitative' and 'qualitative' research, which really harks back to the mid-twentieth-century polarisation between 'arts' and 'science' satirised by CP Snow as 'the Two Cultures' (1963). Our book is addressed to all would-be educational researchers, but we're just alerting you to where we are coming from, which will, of course, show in our arrangement of the material and the use we make of it. And that, dear beginning researchers, is what you'll do too—that is, start from where you're at, just as the learners in your schools, colleges and workplaces should be helped to do! Any good educational study refuses to take the world as it seems—this is what Lewis Carroll's Alice learns in Looking-Glass Land—so any book about educational research has to deal centrally with the ways we 'see' the world, in doing research, and what these ways of seeing mean for claims on knowing. Rather than flip-flop between, on the one hand, the merely arbitrary meanings of words, and, on the other hand, the mastery of all words, as Humpty Dumpty would have it, we set out a more creative and scholastically responsible approach in this book.

Researchers of any kind—in the physical sciences, the social sciences, the arts and the humanities, and anywhere in between—would agree that what we take for granted is constantly re-examined, sometimes reassuringly, more often discomfortingly. Research is about getting at truths, so there are assumptions in all research about what reality is, and what will be scholastically responsible ways of knowing this reality. In deciding to research some aspects of 'reality' (whatever that is taken to be), we are rather like Alice, choosing to step back and forth through her looking-glass, in and out of personal experiences. The arts and humanities give us particularly creative lenses for that looking-glass in education; the sciences and social sciences give us particularly systematic ones. Whichever lens is inserted, the glass becomes one of *magnification*, bringing into focus the complex and unique context that is any educational setting: the personal, the social and the idiosyncratic—and of *refraction*, changing the perspective and the appearance, giving us new, provisional and changing views of what we thought we knew to be solid and unchanging. But because our overall focus is educational research, this looking-cum-magnifying-glass has ultimately to generate 'ways of knowing' from these diverse 'ways of seeing'. Our book is trying to make sense of both 'ways', and locate a research reality that beginning education researchers with any of an arts/humanities, social sciences or scientific background will find equally accessible. Scholastically responsible research in Education (where the capital letter indicates a faculty or formal discipline, of 'education'), both for schooling (involving curricula and pedagogy) and non-school contexts (such as adults' workplaces, or projects involving community or social activism) needs to make a difference. Do small class sizes make for better learning? Does a variety of teaching or training strategies engage a variety of learning styles? How do marginal groups affect, and get affected by, resourcing decisions in hospitals, prisons and rural areas? These sorts of questions have underlying assumptions of meaningfulness and truths—and of realities experienced by real people—which insightful Education researchers need to have laid bare.

Science and mathematics can identify and codify what is happening, collect and analyse the basic data and statistics, in order to make or prove hypotheses. The social sciences, which are based on studies of people and communities and what motivates them, draw on collection and analysis of human data to make assumptions and inferences about our very complex needs, desires and drives. The arts and humanities make possible creative 'ways of seeing' these assumptions, and make feasible creative and responsible 'ways of knowing'.

This book has unusual origins for a research textbook: in an earlier volume, in a particular community of arts and humanities practitioner/researchers: drama teachers, a book which was written for them—and to some extent by them. Drama has long been on the edge of the curriculum as an interesting, tempting and sometimes bewildering art form and pedagogy. The art form of drama itself rather obviously fulfils some of those conditions we have noted above, of being able, at least momentarily, to change our perceptions of reality and let us inhabit a looking-glass world of new possibilities. The idea of that book, and quite a bit of the content, came from the national drama teachers' association, Drama Australia. The members of this organisation characteristically are passionate teachers, wrestling with the complexities of a very embodied practice and a new pedagogy in often inflexible and sometimes hostile classrooms. They recognised that they needed, more than anything else, ways to reflect on their practice, to evaluate it and compare it and experiment with better practices … in other words to research, though the word was one that seemed quite foreign to many. A nascent drama education research community started to develop in Australia, as overseas, helped by the new research methods for the arts and humanities that have emerged in the last generation. Drama Australia approached one of the authors of *this* book, to write it for them. Somewhat daunted by the task, he promptly emailed every member of that fledgling research community, inviting them to give him their best ideas on all the key issues (and he identified over one hundred of these that they might address), their hottest tips and their best stories. These he would use or not as he felt like it, rewrite them as he wished, and give them not a cent for it except a minimal acknowledgment. This scintillating offer amazingly received positive replies from almost everybody in the community, and nearly a hundred thousand words of their most precious copy. That kind of generosity is not untypical in educational communities, but would be quite astonishing in some of the more adversarial traditional research disciplines. With this assistance, the author put together *Doing Drama Research*, which was published by Drama Australia in 2006. ▪ drama Many of the ideas and structures, and some of the text of that book, we have retained either in whole, in part or in spirit. This book, therefore, is not just written by the named ▪ research authors, but like an increasing amount of contemporary educational research, by a broad collaboration collaboration of interested and knowledgeable colleagues, in this case Drama Australia and its research community, to whom we are deeply grateful, and most of whose names at least appear in the acknowledgments.

Although the momentum of this book is towards formal research (albeit the experientially intense, that is, 'meaningful'), we need to acknowledge the tradition of informal, practitioner-led research of which that community of drama educators,

■ praxis

and all of us, are inevitably part. The preconditions for at least informal research and investigation—for 'praxis' as Paolo Freire (1974) called it—were present, and had been for some years. They were preconditions that dictated what *kind* of research educators would start doing, what our concerns and motives were, and, to some extent, where our strengths and weaknesses as potential researchers lay. This laid the foundation for teachers to see their schools as communities of reflective practice, and themselves as reflective practitioners, phrases which have become part of the landscape of schools today. A number of externally driven changes in our fields of practice and in the scholastic environment would be added to these preconditions, and this would impel a quite rapid move towards formal research.

■ university changes

That movement in drama education is just one tiny exemplar of the way that educational research has democratised over the last few decades. Research used to be the prerogative of universities—and obviously, universities are still the main centres of research activity. When the authors finished school, they were part of a fortunate 5 per cent of school leavers who attended university, and few of that small number engaged in any of the research that went on there. Most undergraduate degrees taught the content of specific academic disciplines or liberal studies; then graduates interested in teaching went on to do a practically focused Education diploma. Other teachers trained at colleges that were entirely focused on practical training. Then they were all immersed in a schools system that was equally focused on the day-to-day. Few teachers went on to do a research degree in education, even if they were ambitious, for that was rarely, if ever, a promotion criterion. How the numbers, and together with them the research landscape, have changed, for undergraduates, and even school students, for teachers seeking a better understanding of their workplace or promotion through improved qualifications and for the PhD prospector and beyond.

However, Australian education systems have historically been readier for these democratising changes than some education systems in parts of Europe and Asia, for instance. First and foremost, we shared with the United Kingdom and USA a tradition that placed students as practitioners and participants of their learning, rather than as the audience. Scholarship was practical rather than theoretical, with workshops rather than lectures the norm for teacher training and school classrooms. We shared a number of other more general factors in Education, such as the arts versus sciences dichotomy and a postwar move from a mechanistic curriculum favouring sciences towards a more progressivist one. This was especially so in humanities education, with child-centred, experiential and discovery learning inspired in the USA by John Dewey (1956) and his followers; process learning inspired by the UK's Newsom Report (1963) and educationalists like Jerome Bruner (1977); and here in Australia by Garth Boomer's (1982) 'negotiated curriculum'. Many school-based educators shared a strong ethos of education for social justice and change. In the United Kingdom, this was often consciously tied to specific socialist ideologies, while in Australia, it was perhaps more associated with generic egalitarian sentiments. At the same time, mainly in the USA, curriculum theorists were breaking out of the constrictions of top-down curriculum—such as Tyler's 'objectives-based' classroom planning (1949)—to propose more radical notions of curriculum-as-lived, dynamic and negotiated curriculum, and even 'aesthetic curriculum' (Eisner 1985, pp. 33–5). The last of these concepts would, incidentally, have been quite familiar to traditional Chinese educators, since Confucius thought the aesthetic was one of the five basic pillars of education. During the 1970s and 1980s, Australia led the world in wide-ranging reforms in school-based curriculum, pedagogy and assessment: the 'democratic schooling' agenda. This in turn resulted in some anti-intellectualism and scorn for elitist scholarship—especially that associated with traditional university sources.

▪ progressive education

▪ curriculum reforms

Exponents of the reforms had to prove themselves equal to the challenge of new disciplines and pedagogy, and, in fact, to make it manageable daily in classrooms. We saw the refinement and demonstration of curricula and assessment practices as the way of advocacy, in favour of social and educational reforms, as Western societies became more multicultural. This has revitalised the purposes of schooling, and, more recently, lifelong learning, and also demanded more of teaching, training and facilitating.

As curriculum design became more inclusive, and the timetable more crowded, new disciplines and knowledge bases have crowded into what became known, after the 1991 National Curriculum initiative, as Key Learning Areas (KLAs) and more recently just Learning Areas. The 'integrated curriculum' has been both a blessing and a danger. As these new subjects—creative, artistic and technological—have been increasingly recognised in the West as part of what a 'clever' or 'smart country' requires (since 'cleverness' is closely linked to 'creativity') so, paradoxically, has the deliberate dedicated timetabling and resourcing of such areas been under threat. The vocationalisation of both secondary schooling and of adults' post-compulsory learning (that is, beyond the age of 15 or 16 years) has reinforced fears among practitioners of those disciplines not immediately contributing to workforce skills—in schools, community colleges (or Technical and Further Education institutes) and even in universities—that their expertise is under threat. What is the point of research, when even *practising* is futile? This attitude has appeared in both the traditional disciplines and among the newcomers.

▪ Key Learning Areas
▪ Learning Areas

Yet 'practising' is, in our view, fundamental to the formation and development of successful practitioners everywhere, and more is now expected of practitioners: practices should have impact (such as improving literacy and numeracy), achieve outcomes that are valued (by schools or hospitals or a bank), and be underpinned by theoretical and ethical considerations that society regards as worthwhile. In this book, we refer to this as 'praxis'—the valuable integration of theories in significant practices. Chapter 1 explains further this approach to research.

Now, at the time of writing this second edition, yet another competitor for the attention and time of teachers has entered the lists: the Australian Curriculum. In many ways, we suspect that it does not, and will not, change the educational landscape very much, or the focus and substance of educational research. For one thing, the Australian Curriculum's purpose is not to supersede state-governed curricula, but to provide all students with common entitlements and reference points. The curriculum

■ Australian
Curriculum

will be delivered through the various state and territory systems and schools, usually in conjunction with or embedded in what they teach now and how it is taught. The new imperatives of the Australian Curriculum, however, will demand a more reflective and integrated approach by teachers, to incorporate the new materials, content and expectations into their current practice, to ensure that the new generic curriculum goals are achieved along with what their context demands for effective practice.

The Curriculum has been designed and written on quite old-fashioned lines, with a range of subjects that (partly fortuitously) mirrors the historically dominant subject divisions and 'key learning areas' operating in most states. However, some new factors do exist. For instance Geography and History now gain (or regain) separate subject status, having in most states been subsumed in subject areas with titles like 'Studies of Society and Environment'. English has been a heavily contested area for decades nation-wide, with linguists, literacy teachers, critical literacy specialists and literature buffs all vying for dominance, and the pendulum swinging wildly from decade to decade. Now, Literacy, Language and Literature all have to be honoured in the English curriculum. The Arts now carry an entitlement for all pre-school and primary students to have an introduction at least to all five component subjects (Dance, Drama, Media Arts, Music and Visual Arts).

Research has not been a feature of the Australian Curriculum design process, and the authority responsible has neither a mandate nor the resources to generate any research to underpin the design, monitor and document the process, or track the implementation of the new Curriculum. However, the lead writers who devised the subject areas are well-established research scholars in their discipline, and their advisory panels have been chosen to include research expertise as well as teachers, educational administrators, and industry and community representation. At the time of writing this edition, the roll-out and implementation of the Curriculum is, in fact, an area ripe for research, so if you are picking up this book looking for ideas for a research project ... start there!

We want to convince you that 'research' has changed. As we have stated at the outset, your own and others' subjective experiences can be deeply and creatively trawled for scholastically responsible knowledge. Practitioner-led research is now much more prominent, although it is not displacing theory-led research, which is still quite properly a feature of academic life. Innovations in pedagogy, curricula and assessment in a variety of educative contexts (not only in schools, by teachers) are now ripe material for rigorous research, of a formal nature.

Australia's particular politics also eventually created the conditions and the imperatives for *formal* research. For example, in the competition for drama to become established as a subject within the Arts, and then for the Arts to be fully accepted as a Learning Area, arguments had to be compelling, not just passionate. Economic rationalism reinforced this with demands for 'accountability' in education and an increasingly specialised society with macro-social pressures producing a need for 'experts'. These conditions applied equally to all 'new' or contemporary arrangements of knowledge into learning areas, such as Health and Physical Education, Legal Studies and Technology. The binary tertiary system was 'unified' into a single university system in 1990, and for a while, the Colleges of Advanced Education's honouring of practice and praxis was lost in endless rounds of institutional amalgamation. It was replaced by research as the prime—sometimes the only—indicator of worth.

▪ tertiary unification

Simultaneously, action-based and phenomenological forms of research were becoming more 'respectable' as research paradigms and tools, perhaps partly to cope with the influx of practitioners. We were aided too by a major convergence in social science and humanities research. Pioneer arts researchers, particularly in the USA and Europe, had already been drawn towards the discipline and scientific characteristics of sociology, psychology and anthropology. In 1983, the influential anthropologist Clifford Geertz (1983, p. 19) drew attention to a new tendency of sociologists to mix genres in their writing, deriving analogies and metaphors from the humanities. This indicated a change in their thinking too, looking less for immutable laws of behaviour, 'the sort of thing that connects planets and pendulums, and more for the sort that connects chrysanthemums and swords' (Geertz 1983, p. 19). This tendency Geertz labelled 'blurred genres', and it has been enthusiastically taken up and greatly expanded upon by critical theorists, constructivists, feminists and post-structuralists. Together they (we) have ganged up on the positivists' assumptions in orthodox research about the permanence of knowledge, and the authority of its authors. (This same convergence of thinking and blurring of genres is often referred to in the literature, somewhat alarmingly, as 'the crisis of representation'.)

▪ blurred genres

By the end of the twentieth century, large chinks were even appearing in the hegemony of science and scientific-friendly funding structures for research. Response in the new 'unified national systems' of universities, appearing in many Western countries, was quite swift and pro-active: the arts and humanities started tooling up for the new culture of research, first by the lecturers getting themselves credentialled with PhDs and publications.

Some systemic factors and changes on the eve of the millennium actually helped formalise practitioner-led research cultures. For example, there was and is a growing emphasis on teachers who were reflective practitioners, as Donald Schön called them (1983; 1987). But not only teachers: social and community workers, psychologists, nurses, and lately even corporate managers and human resource experts are likely to talk the language of Schön. The idea of lifelong learning at and for work, for adults, has seeped in to myriad daily workplaces. Practitioners-as-researchers are popping up everywhere!

▪ reflective practitioners

A highly significant change in the tertiary education landscape at the time of writing this second edition is the onset of substantial revisions to the Australian Qualifications Framework. These changes at Masters level affect entry levels and professional development across Australia, bringing new demands for 'integration' and 'capstone experiences' involving theory and practice, and the ability to reflect critically on

▪ Australian Qualifications Framework

complex problems. In other words, to begin to read both practice and research together, as part of your professional formation at point of entry to, say, teaching, nursing, accountancy, law or medicine. And if you don't understand that sentence, don't worry, because we will clarify it for you in Chapter 1. If your motive for perusing this book is that you need help in making sense of a 'capstone' project, take heart! All that follows will be relevant to a formal, but small-scale, research project, as much as it more obviously relates to a thesis, or dissertation—that is, a larger project.

Teachers and trainers naturally reflect upon their practice, perhaps more than most: the shared and negotiated components of group-work, whether in school or in community groups, demand constant, ongoing rethinking. Schools are organisations set up for learning; the same is not necessarily true for a hospital, a lawyers' office or a factory. These workplaces have learning as a desirable, but not core, activity. Of course, the 'Learning Organisation' push of the 1990s (Senge 1990) changed that, and helped legitimise the 'reflective turn' in such non-school practice settings.

Another important contextual change apparently gives arts/humanities and social sciences teachers and workers an inbuilt advantage in educational research, but scientists need to discover their own heritage here too: there has been a growing requirement for school and university students to learn generic human skills. These 'General Capabilities', as they are known in the Australian Curriculum—previously known as 'Key Competencies'—involve, across Western societies, collaborative skills such as 'teamwork', 'communication', 'problem-solving' and 'conflict resolution', for example, which are relational, and deeply personal and usually simultaneously so. That is, they are not atomistic, residing only in a solitary, competitive individual. Add to these generic skills, or capacities, the spectacular comeback in the business and commercial community of a devalued and denigrated word, 'creativity'. These were all qualities that we have always known the arts and the humanities could grow, but this organic potential has now moved to the front and centre of the national and international 'lifelong learning' wish-list—where 'creativity' is found alongside 'employability' as a desired attribute of the new global citizen.

■ capabilities

Creativity is, nowadays, vigorously claimed by sciences, social sciences, humanities and arts as core business and parts of their territory. Despite all this, for many arts and humanities teachers, trainers and facilitators, the word 'research' still carries the traditional connotations of fear and awe of a powerful, uncontrollable and rather alien beast. For many science teachers, the word 'creativity' implies 'unscientific' and we are very aware that, for many scientists and teachers of the sciences, confronting the words 'arts' or 'humanities' for the first time conjures up a similar fear: too deep, too meaning-full!

For all educational researchers, reassuring signposts and pathways are needed. This book should exorcise fears, domesticate the beast and generate new confidence—as you move through the looking-cum-magnifying-glass—in doing research in Education that is both creative and scholastically responsible.

How to approach this book

The format of the book is designed to be helpful in finding your way around the labyrinth of research. The book is divided into two parts, as indicated:

- Part A (Chapters 1 to 4), 'Thinking Research', deals with the generic concepts and concerns of research in our field.
- Part B (Chapters 5 to 9), 'Doing Research', gives practical advice from what is likely to be the chronological beginning of a research project, to the end.

Perhaps the first thing to notice about the book is that the form of address throughout Part A is the first person plural: 'we'. This occasionally causes grammatical infelicities, for which 'we' apologise. However, it denotes and serves to remind us all that you and the authors are in fact a community of researchers, all engaged in the same business, and those of us who have more experience and write handbooks like this are also still learners, researchers in our own research practices. Equally importantly, it denotes that this is not just the work of the named authors on the cover; many of Australia's expert researchers in one discipline have contributed some of its most salient points, as we have already noted. For Part B of the book, 'we' have decided to move mainly to the second person address, as this is the 'how to' section and it gets to be both artificial and patronising not to acknowledge that 'we' are giving 'you' advice. However, readers, if you are new to research, please read the whole book, and do not just dive in recklessly at Chapter 5 'Making a Start' and work on from there. You will most certainly need Part A to help you think, in advance, about some of the ethical, philosophical and methodological issues that are raised here. Before you actually do 'make a start' you will also need to have carefully considered the later chapters of Part B, such as data collection, analysis and how you are going to report the research.

You will note that the main text is accompanied, beside virtually every paragraph, by a word or phrase in the margin that acts as a label for the key concept or main topic of that paragraph. Many paragraphs also contain other important keywords and phrases, which you might need for quick reference. These are all tabulated in alphabetical order with a page reference in the Index, so that when you want to look up a concept or term or key author quickly, you can seek it there. To further help you, in Chapter 2 we list key concepts with some brief definitions. With these various devices—and of course the list of Contents—you should be able to find what you want quickly and painlessly.

Each chapter begins with a list of Objectives, and concludes with central references for wider reading, and some Reflective Questions. We are thus deliberately trying to extend both your depth of scholarship, and your depth of practical reflection, as a beginning Education researcher.

We have tried throughout to incorporate many directly useful stories of practice, and examples and anecdotes from the field—some of which are hypothetical, or amalgams of real stories. Some of these examples are less than a sentence long, some are real narratives, others still are exemplars or pro-formas that you might like to follow. They are denoted throughout in boxes, so they are easy to pick out. Sometimes we tell a story from research practice. Most of these refer to real research projects.

The book is an introductory text, and we have tried to be thorough in addressing or touching on all the components and aspects of research that you are likely to need on setting out. We have deliberately tried to keep the direct references in the book to a helpful minimum. This may seem strange, as there is a colossal amount of literature about research, in Education especially; much of this, researchers will certainly need to access. However, we want the book to be easy and accessible to read, and as readers will know from some other research texts, a wealth of referencing can easily weigh down or slow up a good read.

In the Contents and section headings, as any researcher must, we have tried to indicate clearly and concisely the logic of the book's structure and the signposts.

PART A: Thinking Research

This part consists of four chapters that outline the basic principles of doing research and raise the most important issues and considerations before you start.

- **Chapter 1** is an introduction to research, its nature and why we do it.
- **Chapter 2** discusses some of the underlying philosophical considerations and some of the responsibilities that being a researcher entails, and leads directly into key definitions, so that in the rest of the book you can feel confident about understanding how research unfolds: terms and theories make sense if pinned down in advance, we suggest. You can come back here as you feel the need.
- **Chapter 3** explores research and the practitioner. No matter where you are in the education world, you will need to give thought to your practices, and those of others. In fact, such thinking is a solid basis for moving research forward.
- **Chapter 4** unpacks three different approaches to research that readers are most likely to find useful (which we identify towards the end of Chapter 3) by setting out commonly used research methodologies and methods in Education, within that trio of approaches.
- **Postscript to Part A** deliberately provides a little trap in order to offer a helpful warning.
- **Epilogue to Part A** takes a light-hearted look at some of the common issues and problems that beset those setting out on research journeys; though tongue-in-cheek, the stories are all true, and our attempts to address them are quite serious, too.

PART B: Doing Research

This part, in five chapters, is more of a practical handbook.

- **Chapter 5** addresses the tasks that researchers must undertake before they start any project.
- **Chapter 6** suggests how researchers might approach the 'literature' or what is already previously known about the subject of the research.
- **Chapter 7** deals with the 'data', the material that researchers must collect for processing.

- **Chapter 8** deals with what must then be done with the data to make useful sense and new knowledge out of it: the analysis and synthesising.
- **Chapter 9** discusses the outcomes—ways in which the research can be documented, reported and disseminated.
- **Postscript to Part B** offers a sincere valediction and wishes good fortune to the new researcher.
- **Epilogue to Part B** rounds off the book with another ironic glimpse, this time of the problems and issues of actually doing the research.

These are the general topics of each chapter. What we recommend is that you look through them to decide what you might need from this book, and then consult the full Contents list, which provides a more detailed breakdown of the sections.

Finally, please remember that just as many readers are novice researchers, the authors ('I' and 'we') are novice writers of textbooks for researchers. This is no tablet of stone, nor is it comprehensive; it represents what we have discovered in our own ventures into Education research. You will come across other methods, paradigms and good advice, sometimes conflicting with ours; you will come across things we have omitted either through our different priorities or our sheer ignorance of them. In this book, as in the process of research itself, there is much that can be illuminating and useful, and enjoyable too, we hope—but no universal truths. Just as older readers will remember that in the *Hitchhiker's Guide to the Galaxy* (Adams 1978) the answer to Life, the Universe and Everything (forty-two) doesn't mean a thing if you don't know the question, it is exactly the same in Educational research, so remember the immortal invocation on the front cover of that classic: *Don't Panic*.

Wider Reading

Davis, S. H. 2008. *Research and Practice in Education: The Search for Common Ground.* Rowman & Littlefield Education, Lanham, Maryland.

de Landsheere, G. 1999. 'History of Educational Research', in J. P. Keeves and G. Lakomski (eds) *Issues in Educational Research*. Pergamon, Elsevier Science, Oxford. Chapter 2.

Schön, D. 1983. *The Reflective Practitioner: How Professionals Think in Action.* Maurice Temple Smith, London.

Walter, M. 2006. 'The Nature of Social Science Research', in M. Walter (ed.) *Social Research Methods: An Australian Perspective.* Oxford University Press, Melbourne.

PART A

THINKING RESEARCH

'SEEING' RESEARCH

☑ CHAPTER OBJECTIVES

After reading this chapter, you should be able to:

- discern why 'research' is systematic investigation, and how its purposes and contexts vary
- understand that perspectives—'ways of seeing'—will point towards 'ways of knowing'
- learn how to find out about some main traditions of scholarship in research.

↘ WHAT IS RESEARCH?

Let's begin by defining some of the basic terms we use in research, through the rhetorical device of going to textbook definitions of 'research' itself, so that we are on common ground. The *Concise Oxford English Dictionary* defines research as:

> n. & v. Systematic investigation into and study of materials and sources, in order to establish facts and reach new conclusions.

Of course, a simple definition cannot explicitly encompass such a complex noun, so to start our 'systematic investigation', let's examine the sentence more closely. Take 'new conclusions', for instance: a pretty flat and bland phrase, as it stands, to define what we may discover in the arts/humanities about human behaviour, the imagination and the shifting and dynamic forms of our experiences. Most universities, in their research degree instructions, make the demand for 'new knowledge', and leave it to the researchers to define what they mean by that and justify how they have achieved it. With arts and humanities researchers, 'gaining new insights' is popular, implying that 'in-sights' (or 'ways of seeing') are as important as 'out-sights' like facts or conclusions. This is in contrast to research into pharmacy, or engineering, which we expect to be entirely verifiable and objective—we don't want pills or bridges that are open-ended, dynamic and ambiguous. But to stay with such a distinction is too simple.

Our approach to educational research in this book needs to acknowledge that many of the facts we discover—whether through 'in-sights' or 'out-sights'—and the conclusions we draw from both these ways of seeing are not objective, nor are they certain truths. In this book, we are drawing attention to the manner in which both of these ways of

definitions

new knowledge

seeing occur, in the 'subject' world, because we believe that research methodology books tend to overlook this, at least for beginning researchers. In the Introduction, we made the point that the 'object' world is very well served—research is what happens 'out there'—and we do not wish to belittle those activities or the achievements that result. There are great truths to be found. We are looking within the 'subjectivity' of research for both in-sights and out-sights. Accordingly, as educators, and as human beings, one of the very joys of the arts—of the fictions we construct to make sense of our individual and social existence through literature, media, painting and drama—is their evanescence, their vivid impermanence—in Eugenio Barba's lovely phrase 'a fistful of water' (1995, p. 100).

▦ in-sights and out-sights

The dictionary phrase 'materials and sources' needs expanding, too. Many of the most basic products of our mind and spirit, and what for instance is important about those arts mentioned above, are not material at all. Our artfulness exists as a dialogue between abstract ideas and their bodily and linguistic manifestations. Arts and humanities experiences often work indirectly and obliquely, through metaphor, through irony, through allusion and analogy—that is the very basis of fiction, and experienced most powerfully subjectively. Research in these areas at least, and in some areas of social and health sciences, and even medical research, must take the power of this experience as central to research design, and thanks to contemporary developments in research methods and tools, it can do so.

▦ non-material

▦ subjectivity

The one part of the dictionary definition that must be allowed to stand is the phrase 'systematic investigation'. Research always starts with a need to know, which is framed into a question that can be investigated, consciously and methodically. The outcomes of research may not always be anything as simple as an answer to that question—they may be more questions or other questions, or other answers. The idea of systematic investigation is very present in the USA's National Research Council's (2003) criteria for 'high quality scientific research in education'—that a study must:

▦ systematic investigation

1   pose significant questions that can be investigated empirically
2   link research to relevant theory
3   use methods that permit direct investigation of the question
4   provide a coherent and explicit chain of reasoning
5   replicate and generalise across studies
6   disclose research to encourage professional scrutiny and critique.

Those of us engaging in arts and humanities or social science research need not be afraid to apply that word 'scientific' to our research! Although we may find later we need to modify these criteria, particularly the third and fifth, they will do pretty well for a start.

 WHY DO IT?

Most people engage in research in Education with mixed motives and purposes, some of which are academic, some personal and some professional. One of the first tasks of the researcher is to try and identify and separate these clearly and honestly. Although there is inevitably some overlap, here are some of the main motives.

To create new knowledge for its own sake

We are all driven by *curiosity*, and as educators we are also usually driven by a passion for our calling that gives us a powerful desire to know, deeply, more about how it works, why we do it and what effects it might have. There are, surely, 'ways of knowing' that excite us. Can we 'create' new knowledge? Creativity in itself is a wonderful and wonder-inducing phenomenon. But ways of knowing start with the perceptual: there are creative 'ways of seeing'. What can this mean? Consider the famous contemporary representationalist painter Lucian Freud (grandson of Sigmund), who has expressed his curiosity and passion for the writing and artwork of John Constable. He noticed that Constable 'knows' from what he 'sees':

■ curiosity

■ creative ways of seeing

> I love to read them [Constable's letters]—there's something so sympathetic about him. And very interesting things that look as if they're made up, except you know they aren't. People saying 'Why are you using that thick paint and sploshing it all over your canvas? You're just doing it to show off'. To which he replied: 'No, I'm not. I realise it looks awkward and rough and coarse, but in time the paint will settle down and it will become part of the landscape'. Incredible! Because when you look at them, actually the paint is so thick. Just amazing. (Freud 2006, p. 14)

To this curiosity about 'ways of seeing' as ways of knowing, we might add *to test and/or seek verification of established knowledge*—of what we think we know. This might be to test a belief or assumption that the researcher holds, or an ideological tenet, or some aspect of the accepted lore of education that perhaps might need challenging, or is unhelpful or untrustworthy. This is what we mean by being 'scholarly responsible': not all experiences will count as research. In fact, Lucian Freud goes on to affirm that his own creativity deliberately isn't 'researched', as we understand it in this book:

■ testing assumptions

> *Interviewer (Sebastian Smee):* You've always said you wanted to avoid the look of having 'composed' your pictures. Why is that? What is it you're resisting?
>
> *Freud:* It's the idea of adopting a way of doing things. Or doing things that have been done before. All those things (at least this is how I feel in my head) would work against me doing something which was disturbing, by which I mean alive. (Freud 2006, p. 15)

In researching creatively, we must 'adopt a way of doing things', and respect what has 'been done before'. While our passion and curiosity can and should drive creative research, systematic investigation is the key to success, and to credibility. Creative research should generate knowledge for its own sake, but it has to be grounded in investigation that tests or seeks to verify what is already established. Even Freud, when he reflected on his own learning from Constable, was, as we saw, respectful of what had gone before.

■ respect for old knowledge

To create knowledge in context

■ educational
purposes

As practitioners in educational or workplace community contexts, we are working in complex and as yet very fluid disciplines. We still have lots to learn: in general, and about every classroom or adult's learning context. Sometimes we conduct research to create new knowledge that we need for our *educational purposes*:

> Rod's teaching of senior school civics and citizenship led him to design and publish textbooks that looked more like comics (Wise 2000). Cartoons, old newspaper clippings and pop culture references enlivened his teaching, and these books were then filtered as fieldwork through a PhD that critiqued Australia's national policies in these curriculum areas.

■ case study

This may often take the form of a *case study*, where we choose a particular person, group of people or teaching context to investigate a phenomenon we have noticed, or a hypothesis we would like to test. Sometimes this is just to *solve or at least investigate an ongoing problem* or issue in our educational systems and schools:

> Gayle's concern with the quality of adult literacy learning among Somali women refugees in Melbourne led her to get their migration and settlement stories down on tape, as a way of provoking new pedagogical approaches more sensitive to the trauma of the past and the opportunities of the present (Morris 2004).

■ evaluation
■ verification

It may involve *evaluation* or *verification* of how we think education happens in our context, or what and how children of different ages and adults learn through our practices:

> Wendy was curious about the reasons for enrolees undertaking inner-city community arts classes in drawing or dancing or singing (Hopkinson 2012). Her agency, a prominent inner-city Christian church, professed a desire to know if its view of 'mission' was matched by the participants' reasons for signing up.

■ artistry and
research

For all constructivist educators, we and our students are constructing our culture, and making cultural products, and so (especially but not exclusively if we are arts and humanities educators), either explicitly or implicitly, we are also artists. In the grown-up art world, research is of course an essential part of making an artwork. A production or artefact has to be researched, particularly one that is historical or foreign to one's own culture, for its social and cultural context, its manners and mores and styles. Any creative piece or event, especially if documentary or based on facts or stories, or interviews with witnesses, also has to be carefully and properly researched. This 'making' can be intensely personal, as Matisse wrote:

> Suppose I set out to paint an interior; it gives me a sensation of bright red—and I put down a red which satisfies me; immediately a relation is established between this red and the white of the canvas. If I put a green near the red, if I paint in a yellow floor, there must still be between this green, this yellow and the white of the canvas, a relation that will be satisfactory to me … I must organise my ideas. (In Chipp 1968, p. 134)

Our book takes this 'relationality' very seriously, as the Introduction has made clear: there are 'ways of seeing', such as Matisse experienced, and wrote about, and these lead to 'ways of knowing', or understanding aspects of the world in particular ways. Teachers and trainers across the educational sector are rightly, in our view, encouraged to 'see' themselves within their practices. In TESOL (Teaching English as a Second or Other Language), for example, 'only recently have scholars begun examining the everyday contexts in which policies are interpreted and negotiated in ways that reflect local constraints and possibilities' (Ramanathan and Morgan 2007, p. 447). So for us, contexts are crucial, and we discuss this next.

▦ TESOL

To create knowledge for a particular context

Our need for research may spring from some very immediate contextual demand or problem. This includes analysing and *critically reflecting on our own theory and practice*, or that of colleagues, and of course improving it:

▦ contextual problems
▦ critical reflection

> Stephanie wanted to recommend changes to undergraduate nursing curricula, because Australia's ageing demographic is generating more nursing experiences in hospital contexts of grief caused by death and suffering (Lockhart 2008). By exploring through narrative enquiry how nurses have constructed accounts of these experiences, she was able to improve teaching programs for younger nurses.

We may have a *particular problem or issue* in our class or our community that defies our everyday attempts to solve it, and clearly springs from the deeper agendas and structures of our teaching context: for this we need *action research*.

▦ action research

> Leadership can be tricky in a community organisation, where everyone is a volunteer. 'Heroic' men and women no longer have the credibility they once did (Byrnes 1999). As part of her DEd, Jenny worked in such an organisation on an action research basis for over one year, to install a model of participatory leadership that was built up by and 'owned' by the volunteers as an expression of their vision.

personal agendas   We may have a personal need for research that has nothing to do with the issues within our classrooms or professional settings. Perhaps a professional promotion or increased esteem in the establishment one works for relies on a history of active research, as is increasingly the case in university settings.

To create knowledge for reimagining or reforming society

Research into human behaviour, and the social behaviour of humans, is part of the very nature of education, especially in the arts and the humanities: there is always that intensity of human experience to draw upon. Novels, poetry, theatre, films, sculptures, some computer-generated environments—that grow from increasingly sophisticated gaming technology (de Freitas and Maharg 2011)—are ways of creating realistic models reimagining society   of not only how we are and how society works, but also how we and society might be. Through such fictions, we create possible worlds and behaviours that we can compare with and use to test the realities we perceive, which have no consequences in the real world unless we wish them to: worlds of fiction disappear as soon as we wish, and importantly, 'this insubstantial pageant faded, leave not a rack behind', as Shakespeare explained (*The Tempest*, Act 4, Scene 1). The arts offer some of the best and safest ways of investigating—even critiquing—society and speculating on possible new societies.

social reform   For many teachers, trainers and facilitators, some *participation in social reform* is part of our *raison d'être*, either at the level of helping to improve the social understanding, communication skills and interpersonal relations among our students, or making inroads into the greater injustices of society. If you are intending to change society, you need to know in depth what you are up against, and to monitor and evaluate your success in achieving the changes … or what other effects your activism produces.

> Neighbourhood Houses are sites of adult education, but are lowly in status compared to TAFE institutes and universities. Allie was keen to bring to prominence the emancipatory work done in such Houses—normally by underpaid women, and for many less advantaged learners—in literacy and basic education (such as introductory IT) (Clemans 2005). Her PhD, based on recording the 'whole-person' experience, goes to the heart of humanistic research, and led to state-wide recommendations for reforms to the provision of adult learning.

↘ CONTEXTS OF FORMAL RESEARCH

support   Whatever the initial motivation, anything beyond the most basic and informal research needs a context where it will be sufficiently supported. Finding an appropriate base camp can be the hardest part of the mountain climb, and it is certainly crucial: many well-meaning research studies have faltered because they were not underpinned with support. Usually this takes the form of *time, money, facilities and resources* or *access*.

Some climate of encouragement and approval is usually also necessary for the researcher to carry on, particularly if the uphill going gets steeper, the views more tedious, and the hoped-for outcome constantly seems to recede, or disappear entirely; in research, as in mountains, it often does.

University study

For many, the sensible entry point is the institution whose primary traditional function is research—the university—and usually it is through one form or another of postgraduate study. Australian universities have lecturers to help us learn how to research, facilities to help us to do it, and usually a range of courses tailored to our need and level of expertise. We should not be afraid to be picky, right from the start, but make sure that the courses and the teachers suit our needs and research focus. And of course, *caveat emptor* (buyer beware!): universities need students as much as we need their services, and occasionally offer more than they can effectively provide.

postgraduate study

Most first degree courses in education are concerned primarily with producing professional practitioners, not researchers. However, the best of these encourage students to take a reflective and critical approach to all their studies, which provides at least an attitude and a viewpoint amenable to future research. Moreover, new 'capstone' regulations recently introduced to all Australian undergraduate courses require at least a preliminary research approach, or 'pre-research' focus, in the latter stages of the course. A few—and most honours courses—provide formal introductions to research methods. But because these one-semester starter packs usually have to be designed generically for maths and social sciences as much as for humanities, they are not always conducive to more subjective kinds of research. They can be off-putting initially, especially for people to whom abstracted numbers, diagrams and statistics are a mystery. Most useful are those that are tailored towards the most common forms of educational research. These programs tend to *investigate the quality and complexity* of human behaviour rather than *quantify what is measurable*—which is often the emphasis of introductory research methods courses. This is a distinction commonly made between *qualitative* and *quantitative* research, which, as we shall see, is not always useful or productive to us. However, the great British educator Dorothy Heathcote's truism that you must 'start where the student is at' (1971) is just as important in research as it is in the classroom: we must feel comfortable and confident before we sign the contract. And we must not be put off—we will be able to find a method of research that is comfortable and that fuels our enthusiasm to engage in study.

capstones

methods courses

quantitative and qualitative

A quite gentle introduction to research is usually to be found in the coursework degree sometimes called a graduate diploma, and sometimes a masters. A few of these do not offer any research training, but most combine research methods with other generic coursework to broaden our background, and a dissertation where we dabble in a basic research project. Some universities (and even a few TAFE colleges) offer courses—often 'vocational training' credentials—combining practice and research, which we can be sure are absolutely tailored to our employability. Many others offer a generic MEd or equivalent, where we will find that we can spend virtually the whole time on topics and tasks entirely relevant to our context and our passions. So we should not feel bashful about shopping around and pestering the course convenors—remember, they are often looking for students.

shopping for courses

external study

A very important corollary of this is the question of internal or external study. We may be geographically disadvantaged, or we may prefer remote study anyway, in which case we look for a university with a web-based or distance mode. In many fields, these are sometimes accompanied by a summer school, for that valuable face-to-face engagement that is at the heart of all educational experience.

research higher degrees (HRD or RHD)

Nearly all universities offer masters and doctoral degrees that are principally or totally research, and project-based. A research masters is usually two years full-time or four years part-time, and a doctorate (normally called Doctor of Philosophy or PhD) three and six years respectively. In Australia (unlike America and many European countries), the PhD normally has no coursework attached, with other nomenclature for degrees where coursework leads into a dissertation, such a Doctor of Education (EdD, or more unfortunately, DEd). These nearly always require some prior experience of research methods, and consist of an independent research project, with the assistance of one or more personal supervisors. If we think we qualify for a research higher degree, there are two crucial considerations. The first must be answered by looking to the university: finding a supervisor who is not only effective, but congenial. For the second, we researchers must look to ourselves: can we commit the time, energy and focus necessary for study spanning several years? This is not a question to be taken lightly.

supervisors

commitment

grants and scholarships

If we qualify for research higher degree status, we may be eligible for a scholarship or a grant, and we might even be just the person that a research team is looking for. As well as teaching students, university lecturers are involved in research projects, many of which need *research assistants* (providing some useful preliminary experience). Some offer special scholarships, usually through the Australian Research Council, and the university research team will be looking for scholars to fill them. When we start doing the rounds of universities enquiring about research study, we should always leave a calling card—let the universities know who we are and what our research interests are, and we might find we fit a research team's profile.

Sponsored research

university funding

As we have indicated, universities are the natural home of research, so if we are associated with a university, either as a staff member or as a student, we will have access to other funds. Some of these funds the university itself provides and some come from outside bodies and government agencies that nevertheless work through the university system. We will need to apply for these. Competition is always intense, with previous experience and a track record of successful research a prized commodity. New researchers should look for an experienced and successful mentor before applying for most of the grants. In recent years, however, universities and even the Australian Research Council (ARC) are actually encouraging new researchers with specially categorised grants.

mentors

Which brings us to the 'big end of town'. For science and social science educators, this has usually meant the ARC. Up to the late 1990s, the ARC was virtually closed to arts and humanities educators, arts especially—out of twelve subject categories, of which 'Maths' was first, the whole of 'Humanities' (including everything from philosophy to musicology and languages to literature) came a very poor twelfth. Just as research methods have changed to become inclusive, so has the ARC, and educators right across the board have the same sporting chance of ARC grants. Moreover, our eclectic pursuits as educators are not, as sometimes, a disadvantage, as cross-disciplinary research is encouraged.

■ Australian Research Council (ARC)

Our own bias is now briefly on display, quite deliberately, as the next few paragraphs are intended specifically to encourage the arts and humanities researchers among our readers—for whom some of the research opportunities and even the literature have not always been kind historically, as we have seen. The ARC is not the only source of statutory funding. More specialised bodies such as the Australia Council for the Arts currently acknowledge a responsibility for both research and education, and many state ministries such as Arts, Social Services and Health can be approached to come to the party, providing they can see some outcome that will or may ensue from the research that is profitable to their own interests.

■ Australia Council for the Arts

■ government ministries

In terms of profitability, the arts are at some disadvantage in our society. However much they may contribute to its social and cultural capital, in terms of GDP (gross domestic product) they are very small beer (apart from the astronomic salaries paid to a very few film stars and novelists, and the massive investment in the real estate business known as art-collecting). Just compare the money available to artists with that for pharmaceuticals, for instance, or ICT—but that's not unreasonable in itself, as those may need much more expensive equipment. Not many industries directly need artists' help, maybe, but they can use their shape-shifting wiles. A lot of money is spent on training, for example, and industry trainers are constantly looking for effective and efficient pedagogy—which is part of the core business of artists and all educators. Believe it or not, a majority of businesses actually use the arts in their training already (by performing 'role-play' or 'simulation', sculpture and art-making and even music, movement and dance), and as the research already shows, some of those use it execrably badly (e.g. Smigiel 1996; Taylor 2000), which is a very good reason for research.

■ GDP

■ industry training

Non-government organisations (NGOs) might provide both an outlet and some research funding for the highly developed sense of social responsibility common in the arts and education industry. Overseas, in the 'developing world' particularly, NGOs like UNICEF have, for many years, been ploughing millions of dollars into the arts. This is to help them communicate with villagers on health and environmental issues in remote areas without access to electronic communication or literacy. Not all the money has been wisely spent and only belatedly are these organisations realising that more research is needed in the discipline. Australasia has its own 'developing worlds' of disadvantaged communities with poor communication, and NGOs are making interventions of all kinds, from forum theatre to founding radio stations and rock groups, with visual arts, music and sport very prominent in Indigenous and human services settings.

■ non-government organisations (NGOs)

■ systemic priorities   Obviously education systems and the schools they operate need research, and may appear to be an obvious source of funding for the arts and humanities. In fact this is rarely so. For one thing, education systems are not really funded to deliver research, and there is always enormous political pressure on them to provide services, immediately and in the classroom. Money 'siphoned off' for the indirect and uncertain benefits of research is an easy target for populist criticism. Some educational systems have neither a research section nor any capacity to undertake research. These organisations can be included as an industry partner in applying for those statutory grants. Here again, arts and humanities teachers need to be doubly clever because we work from a position of disadvantage. First, education systems invariably have declared priorities and areas of special need, and they will be favourably disposed to consider partnering research that feeds into those areas of special need. Conversely, the arts and the humanities are, with the sole exception of literacy education, rarely among those systemic priorities. The arts, in particular, are still in the process of being established as valid curriculum rather than a marginal attraction. But we do have a spectacular pedagogical advantage, of which the systems are becoming dimly aware. Arts students and teachers fight way above their weight in pedagogical performance indicators, in schools, staffing and promotion rounds, excellence in teaching awards and university graduation statistics. (Or do we? There's an assertion based on our perceptions, anecdotal evidence and inadequate statistics, which would be well worth researching.) If so, that is the opportunity for artists to shape-shift again. At the moment, bullying in schools (O'Toole and Burton 2006) and the pedagogical implications of Information Technology (Carroll et al. 2006) are two high priorities where enterprising drama educators are collaborating with education systems in research projects.

■ multi-literacies   Another area of massive potential barely touched by the arts is that of literacy, or rather the newer nomenclature of 'multi-literacies', to which the arts have plenty to offer in the classroom. Languages other than English, English as a Second Language, Studies of Society, Health and Physical Education, as well as generic issues such as gender in education, are all areas where arts already make strong interventions in practice. These can sometimes be high official educational priorities and fertile ground for seeding research. Educational and governmental priorities in education often include innovative practice (particularly when allied to a high-status area like literacy), and there is also plenty of untapped potential for research in innovation and teacher in-servicing of the kind mentioned above, evaluating the effectiveness of a range of arts-based interventions. The problem is that grants for innovative practice are usually tied to practical implementation and professional development, and it takes persuasive talking and submission-writing to coax out extra money to demonstrate the praxis, that is, how the research component emerges from the practice.

Self-funded research

Particularly for those engaged with universities, it is easy to get into a 'grant-welfare-dependency syndrome'—in other words, to forget that research is possible without either a grant or a scholarship. The admirable practitioner is constantly reflective and self-critical, and seeking new ways of making their discipline and their pedagogy more effective. But a word of caution: all research, especially formal projects, makes two demands: *time* and *care*. Reading the background literature and finding out what research has already been done, gathering data thoroughly and carefully analysing it, and then recording or documenting it—the basic tasks of all formal research—are time-consuming and labour-intensive, especially if we are personally involved as a participant researcher and have no assistants. Our research capacity will depend on our level of passion combined with our ingenuity in finding indirect ways of poaching time: the exceptionally lucky may pull off some kind of scholarship, fellowship or sabbatical for study; the super-dedicated may choose to give up long-service leave or even go on half-pay for a while; the quite dedicated may elect to give up another activity like sports coaching for a year or two … but we can't just fit it in with what we are already doing in our spare time. Sacrifices must be made.

▦ time constraints

Whether we identify with the world of arts-humanities with its concentration on the subject world, or that of sciences with more focus on the object world, we need to map ourselves within the existing scholarship, including the 'how-to' scholarship. Clearly, all beginning researchers should become aware of the depth and extent of the scholarly work on how to do research well. Encyclopaedic efforts to do this are readily available. For example, the third edition of John Creswell's *Educational Research: Planning, Conducting and Evaluating Quantitative and Qualitative Research* (2008) is a monumental contribution to such mapping. He makes the wise note, in listing changes in the third edition, that:

▦ research scholarship

> Quantitative and qualitative research approaches are no longer seen as two completely separate different approaches, but as forms of research that lie along a continuum … Often in educational research, the studies … contain some elements of both … mixed methods and action research reinforce this emerging trend in research. (p. vi)

He goes on to also note that

> ethical issues have been expanded … [and such] discussions now frame our introduction to research, and … in both quantitative and qualitative data collection. (p. vi)

Stepping outside Education for a moment, we also note the justified popularity of intensive analyses and surveys of qualitative approaches (e.g. Denzin and Lincoln 2005), of specific approaches (e.g. on action research: Zuber-Skerritt 1996), and then, combining specificity within Education (e.g. qualitative research in Education: Freebody 2003). We list a couple more on page 14.

In conclusion, we support a particular curiosity about research scholarship that is open, eclectic and even somewhat promiscuous. Those starting out should immerse themselves in the broad traditions, then situate accordingly their values and 'ways of seeing' and therefore of knowing, and finally move into their own researcher space, underpinned by scholarship as it is assembled by them, for their own purposes.

◼ eclectic approaches   Lyn Yates (2004) has written superbly on 'political and paradigm disputes' in education research and her work is most helpful for beginners. Keeves, in his 'Overview of Issues in Educational Research' (in Keeves and Lakomski 1999, p. 3) states: 'The research enterprise in education draws upon many disciplines and employs a wide variety of approaches to investigation … it is argued that the choice of procedures to be employed depends on the nature of the problem under investigation.' We fully agree!

? REFLECTIVE QUESTIONS

1   How would you go about researching creativity in your own field of educational practice?

2   What could the field gain by such close scrutiny of 'ways of seeing' and 'ways of knowing'?

3   On the other hand, suppose that 'curiosity killed the cat'. How amenable to systematic investigation is your field of educational practice? Would *you* survive it?

WIDER READING

Creswell, J. 2009. *Research Design: Qualitative, Quantitative and Mixed Methods Approaches*. Sage, Thousand Oaks, California.

Keeves, J.P. and Lakomski, G. (eds) 1999. *Issues in Educational Research*. Pergamon, Elsevier Science, Oxford.

Somekh, B. and Lewin, C. (eds) 2005. *Research Methods in the Social Sciences*. Sage, London.

WHAT DOES RESEARCH ENTAIL?

2

☑ CHAPTER OBJECTIVES

After reading this chapter, you should be able to:

- become familiar with the Western traditions of thinking about 'systematic investigation'
- identify some main tensions and challenges these traditions raise for research
- locate convenient definitions of key concepts used in this book.

SOME PHILOSOPHICAL CONSIDERATIONS

Questions, logos and logic

In the beginning was the word (*logos* in Greek), and in the beginning of Western research were the ancient scholar-monks who withdrew from the world into monasteries, to spend their time seeking the truth (singular and absolute) through the words of Holy Writ, passed down by even more ancient scholars. These early university scholars, undertaking the world's first literature reviews, thought that all worthwhile knowledge had already been revealed in a past golden age. Their zealous excavations cannot be scorned, as they produced a wealth of interpretive research. Besides, a literature search still forms an important early stage of most research projects. Before embarking on finding new knowledge, we must be sure we are not actually reinventing the wheel, and the work of earlier writers often helps us find our direction.

That was not quite the beginning, actually. The word 'academy' derives from an ▣ the academy
institution founded by the even more ancient Greek philosopher Plato (c. 350 BC), originally to maintain the brilliant method of enquiry of his own mentors, Pythagoras (remember his theorem?) and Socrates. This consisted of doggedly pursuing not answers, but questions: the technique known as Socratic method consisted of asking hard questions about philosophical, ideological and moral issues, and then interrogating the answers to those questions, and so on, taking nothing for granted, looking for logic ▣ logic
and what we would now call reliability. For this dangerously destabilising practice, Socrates was put to death, but his inspiration led to the more cautious reasoning

tradition of Plato and his own student, Aristotle. Aristotle focused his studies on the natural and social worlds: physics, politics and ethics, and poetics, including, incidentally, a fine analysis of the structure of poetry and drama (c. 330 BC). Plato's own relationship to the arts was contentious. On the one hand, he wanted to banish the artists from his ideal republic because they were dangerous. They presented, or rather, re-presented Truth, and since their work was at least one remove from reality, the truth was distorted (especially in fiction or legend), which might destabilise the rest of the population. On the other hand, Plato was the one of the Western world's first and greatest humanists: his belief that through the study of philosophy some (fortunate and very few) people can achieve knowledge of profound Truth lies at the heart of our intellectual traditions. This is a momentous idea, even if we disagree with its elitism.

The works of the Greeks and the tradition of logical questioning were, in fact, lost to Western society for a thousand years, though preserved and brilliantly built on by the Islamic scholars of the Arabic and Moorish empires such as Averroes. Then came the Renaissance (literally, re-birth), not only of art, but of science and logic. Listeners to Australia's ABC will probably be familiar with 'Ockham's Razor', the informal research program named in honour of William of Occam, one of a group of Western Renaissance scholars who defied the church and risked their lives (remember Galileo too?) by seeking knowledge in natural phenomena, and the evidence of the senses.

- Islamic scholars
- Renaissance

William of Occam lived in the fourteenth century and died in the Black Death—a time for reassessing traditional thinking if ever there was one. His most famous principle—his 'razor' or 'principle of parsimony': *Pluralitas non est ponenda sine necessitate*—can be summed up in a rather more contemporary phrase as 'K.I.S.S.' (Keep It Simple, Stupid!) when you're investigating the natural world, that is, doing research.

- Occam's razor
- K.I.S.S.

Modern research really started in the seventeenth century with René Descartes, sometimes known as the 'founder of modernity' (of whom more in Chapters 3 and 4). 'The Age of Reason' and 'the Enlightenment' followed, with new traditions of scientific logic and empirical discovery established that were epitomised by Isaac Newton. These have been dominant ever since. These are the same traditions that are summed up in the six principles of scientific research that formed our original definition in Chapter 1.

- reason
- the Enlightenment

This approach has brought us, among other things, the fruits of modernity: the Industrial Revolution, modern medicine and the internet. Much of what we now know depends on a reality that is solid, verifiable and positively reliable: skyscrapers and bridges that don't fall down; cars, pills and computers that work. Modernity is closely connected to positivism: the view that truths, and therefore research towards the Truth (note that there is normally an assumption in modernity that 'truth' is singular), is best established by getting the tightest fit between the human senses and what is 'given' in the world. The cornerstone of such Truth is the pursuit of rigorous causal relationships between us and the world. Science, traditionally, and all similar research in the humanities, has been based on this view of the role of reason in human life—that truth is its purpose. Modernity and 'progress' are bedfellows. We move forward, and, through rigorous scientific reasoning, are the better for that.

- modernity

- positivism

Dynamic and provisional knowledge

However, just when it all looked firm and clear—God's immutable laws replaced by Science's inevitable progress—along came Albert Einstein, suggesting that matter, time and space were relative. About the same time, around eighty years ago, philosophy had made great innovations. Karl Popper, in *The Logic of Scientific Discovery* (1935), argued that scientific (or positivist) method was not constituted by the traditional formation of generalisations based upon experience. This 'problem of induction' (how can any law apply when it's only ever built up from experiences?) is resolved, claimed Popper, by formulating bold hypotheses about the world which are then tested through experience (that is, experiment) subject to 'falsification', not to confirmation. As the *Oxford Dictionary of Philosophy* (ed. Blackburn 1996) puts it: 'Many thinkers accept in essence his solution to the problem of demarcating proper science from its imitators … the idea encapsulates many people's objections to such ideologies as psychoanalysis and Marxism' (p. 292).

■ relativity

All knowledge thus looks more fragile: science because it may be only provisionally true, and non-science because it is not true in any empirically convincing way (Marxism, for example, may be 'true' but held as an article of faith). Then came the chaos theorists, suggesting that even the immutable laws were subject to contingencies (e.g. Gleick 1987). Now notions such as 'the butterfly effect' (e.g. Stewart 1989) and 'fuzzy logic' (e.g. Kaehler 2006) impinge on our consciousness, attached to objects as apparently embodied and permanent as washing machines.

■ chaos theory
■ contingency

At the beginning of Chapter 1, we hinted that the word 'knowledge' can imply very different things—there are ways of 'knowing'. The scientists have wrestled to make room in their thinking for what is still beyond our ken, but the unfixing of Newton's universe has been a great opportunity for people like us, scholars interested in studying human behaviour. We've been given a pretty hard time, in some ways, by science and logic. The 'social (quasi-) sciences' like sociology, psychology and anthropology have emerged, certainly. Until recent years, however, research in human behaviour has been as subject to Occam's reductionist structures of scientific investigation as the physical sciences, and education systems have been constructed round them. Think, for instance, of the power and influence that the simplistic, quaint but amazingly useful notion of a single, unchanging, measurable human IQ (now at last under siege) has had on education systems. But new philosophies have gradually gained ground, which suggest that human behaviour needs to be, and can be, studied in all its complexity, holistically. How can 'experience' count? In Chapter 3 we explore the details of this question, with reference, among others, to Dewey, the great educational philosopher.

■ social sciences

Experience is elusive, but ubiquitous; we all have it, almost all the time. For instance, 'constructivism' suggests that each human constructs his or her own reality, based on their perceptions of their experiences within society. These constructions can change as our experiences change, and so does the social context we perceive, as numerous contemporary educationalists such as Bruner (1990) point out. Humberto Maturana, a frog-dissecting scientist turned educator, used his scientific understanding of the way frogs perceive the world to show that some of our perceptions are actually hard-wired

■ constructivism

into the brain, but paradoxically that means that nobody can be coerced into learning—that teachers can only work within what any learner is able, programmed and ready to learn (Maturana and Favela 1987).

■ propositional knowledge

But new experiential ('postmodern') approaches to learning contrast with the traditionally Truth-driven, modernist approach where knowledge is 'propositional', that is, it shows a change in brain state/understanding within the mind. We memorise propositions such as facts, theories and arguments, and thus understanding is literally 'in' the mind (and can be written down). Examinations are instances of educational 'progress' in propositional learning, but are underpinned by unhelpful assumptions about the static nature of whole-person experience, as we explore in Chapter 3. Because the arts and humanities are normally exactly about such whole-person learning, they have been, until recently, regarded as of lowly educational status: what they call educative is not 'really' Truth. To draw upon our Introduction again: we may say that we have come from a single research tradition of an 'object world' as the focus of ways of seeing and knowing into a new perception that the 'subject world' is actually worth researching as well. Not only that, but the two worlds are not necessarily dichotomously opposed

■ subjective-objective reality

(i.e. either 'objective' or 'subjective') but intricately interrelated, where the objective and subjective perceptions of our reality constantly interact and reshape our knowledge.

What we know is provisional, shifting and dynamic, and research methods have emerged to take account of this. This gives a wonderful opportunity for Education researchers such as ourselves to give priority to a kind of informal research into human behaviour. In the arts and humanities, in particular, and also in the social sciences, we look for, and often create, experimental models of how humans behave and the consequences of their behaviour, sometimes explicitly framed 'as-if' scientifically, sometimes in metaphorical and symbolic terms (that's the arts' core business). Central to all such research is the development of understandings of 'subjectivities'—of self and

■ praxis

of others. Most research into experiential intelligent action (called 'praxis') shares this focus and there are common elements in the practices of most of the arts and in the doing of research right across the spectrum of human activities, not just in Education but also in community development, and, dare we say it, in the corporate world (there are now experts in the spirituality of business!).

Pure and applied research

Traditional scientific researchers have been used to dividing their disciplines into 'pure' or 'applied' research. *Pure* is that which is undertaken for the new knowledge itself, such as finding undiscovered galaxies, proving a hypothesis through a new mathematical relationship, or gaining a better understanding of Dante or Shakespeare. *Applied* research is that which is undertaken for a practical purpose: to find a cure for an illness; to find a reliable economic theory that can help anticipate boom and bust cycles; or to provide authentic period data to an actual production of a Shakespeare play. But what is 'pure research' in any educational setting? It's an oxymoron. However,

■ usefulness

the question of 'usefulness' is relevant. It is helpful to make a distinction between short-term pragmatic or utilitarian uses for the research, and long-term social, philosophical or epistemological relevance.

Advocacy

That should ring an alarm bell! Usefulness is a dangerous weapon. Even within Education, as well as the workplace and professional communities in which we find ourselves, many subject disciplines are still held by many to be too 'soft'—or too intensely idiosyncratic—to establish reliable 'research' proof that they are worthy of respect. Many educators in such communities or workplaces are, however, exceptionally dedicated practitioners, passionate advocates for our subjects. For this, we need arguments and statistics that will convince administrators, colleagues and competitors (as well as the children, their parents and the community, and political leaders) of the worth of those subjects in a variety of settings and for a variety of purposes. One of the most useful outcomes of research, therefore, is to provide data for our advocacy—to help argue for inclusion, or to fight exclusion. That sounds like a good 'applied' reason for doing this kind of research, and in one sense it is. In another way, however, it is the very antithesis of research. We make many claims for these 'soft' fields: as subject world, as a pedagogy, as a tool of social and expressive development, as communication tools, as promoters of good health and fitness. It is tempting to look for evidence that will back up our claims (as advocates, that's our job). But, whatever our subject area, even if to look for evidence for our claims is the reason we embark on research, it should not be our immediate goal, otherwise we are in great danger of setting up the research just to prove what we want it to prove, and particularly of avoiding, overlooking or silencing any data that might contradict or contest that conclusion. And that's not sound research!

'soft' subjects

supporting evidence

Inconclusive or contradictory research

If we embark upon our research honestly, we cannot guarantee the results. For many reasons, the results may be inconclusive, or worse, contradict what we hoped they would deliver. This may be because of a fault in the research method, which cannot always be prevented. There may be factors in the complex web of relationships and dynamics that characterise human behaviour as manifested in educational settings, which we could not reasonably take into account prior to the research, but which emerge as crucial. Some research methods can take account of this, but not all. Alternatively, the context of research or the research site may change irrevocably and unexpectedly.

> One of the authors was put off research for many years, partly because of the experience of a friend who was an economist. This scholar embarked on a PhD charting the reasons for the success of the then flourishing United Arab Republic. Three weeks before he submitted his thesis, the UAR collapsed, quite unexpectedly, and mainly for economic reasons! The scholar was, however, awarded his degree, though the main conclusions of his thesis were now discredited, and so they could hardly be called 'useful'!

This kind of concern should not put you off research. Invariably, providing you have done your research well, if you don't discover what you are expecting, you discover something else that can be and will be useful *even if you were wrong about the conclusions.* At the least, the next researcher will learn from your negative results. This is where the notions in the title of this book, 'research' and 'creativity', first meet. Creativity can only emerge in a context that permits trial and error—because, of course, not every creative invention works. It is the same with research.

▪ negative
conclusions

▪ trial and error

 # SOME RESPONSIBILITIES

All the above is focused on the researchers, and our own power to investigate—our powerfulness, in fact. Particularly as we work in Education, and deal with vulnerable people in 'captive' situations, we need to look at the people and customs that we are investigating. These people are usually known as research 'subjects'—which can give a useful clue about the power relationships between the researchers and the researched in a 'subject world'. Subjects, subjectivity and subjection have more than just a grammatical affinity in educational settings!

Power in research

The research process is not a neutral act. Research studies and their researchers have power and status because they can interrogate the lived behaviour of students, teachers and their communities who constitute the subjects of the research. The politics of research is now a contested area and the social dimensions of the power relationships operating within research have become clearer. This asymmetrical power relationship between researcher and subject has to be considered in terms of outcomes. Who will benefit from the research? Will it only be the researcher or can the subjects of the research benefit from their participation in it? As Foucault makes clear, 'power is crucial in the construction of reality' (1980, p. 109). It is no longer tenable to engage in research that takes the outcomes out of the hands of the research participants in a way that leaves them disempowered by it.

▪ power

▪ beneficiaries of
research

Through the exercise of cultural power, Education researchers have evolved a range of discourses that are accepted by our culture as producing truth about the experiential events we participate in and report on. As Foucault further points out, 'everything is dangerous, nothing is innocent' (1980, p. 33). By this he means, in our own case of educational research, that we reflect some value judgment or ideology. However, the very nature of the interactions that make up learning-by-doing—the shifts of role and point of view that we can make in the models and fictions that we construct, in every subject area—allows such researchers to accommodate some of our concerns about what constitutes acceptable research in the arts.

▪ value judgments

One way is to use the development of 'critical theory' as a research model. This methodology deals with *interpersonal relationships, role, power* and *context* as central

▪ interpersonal
relationships

to a consideration of research outcomes. These very words are, of course, central to Education. In research, transformations happen in the negotiation between relationships, role, power and context, and these require the researcher to engage in attitude change, emancipation and collaboration along with the subjects of the research. This research process refutes the distinction between researcher and researched by classifying all those involved in the process as researchers. The purpose of critical research, as identified by Patti Lather (1992, p. 87), is to get below the surface of social relations and disclose the myths and rituals of social relationships. In almost all educational research, the participants are knowing subjects within their cultural context and they can construct research narratives about the world drawn from their personal experience and imagination—and this includes young children.

▓ role

▓ power

▓ context

An understanding of power relationships operating within the research will enable the participants to be actively engaged with the researcher in generating the research knowledge, and in an exploration of the relationship between power and knowledge and of the value systems involved in the research.

Whatever our topic, our research can explore the power of the genres in which we work. We can also examine the relations of power, both institutional and interpersonal, that define the discourses of contemporary schooling and of many adults' workplaces, such as the corporate world, where, it can be argued, we are 'complicit in our own surveillance' (Usher and Edwards 1994; cf. Foucault on the Panopticon, the nineteenth-century prison designed by Jeremy Bentham, so that prisoners complied with their implicit, not explicit, surveillance). Dorothy Heathcote put it pungently: 'I am always interested in social politics in the sense that I get fed up with the way we don't let children take any important decisions about their lives and we totally leave them out of power politics of any kind' (1997, p. 89).

▓ complicity

Given the post-September 11 'surveillance' we all seem to have signed up for, it is easy to overlook or undervalue that we are workers in some underlying system entailing social control, whether school or youth club or prison or sports club, and our context always contains all the genres of interaction and all the power relationships that underlie the real context, whatever our specific subject matter. Whether or not we choose to model our research on critical theory, fully or in part, we are privileged researchers within such systems, and we need to take note of David Deshler's comment: 'what we decide to research and the way we conduct our research is a political statement about who and what is important to us' (Deshler and Selener 1991, p. 9). This is neatly bookended by Beth Graue's view (2006) that a writer 'performs' their identity (see Chapter 9, p. 179).

▓ social control

▓ politics and privilege

Ethical issues

Next, some crucial ethical and legal issues need to be addressed. Research of any kind today raises issues of the rights of others—even market research, such as those pesky 'cold calling' phone approaches over dinner, which have generated a national database of citizens who do not want to be involved. As the 'object world' has been joined by the 'subject world', ethical considerations have multiplied. Almost every possible kind

▓ ethical and legal responsibilities

of relationship is researchable, so it is entirely justifiable that those actually doing the research should be well acquainted with, and indeed sympathetic to, the rights of both 'objects' and increasingly of 'subjects'. Failure to be so will incur enforcement of legal compliance in one's institution or organisation, and the risk of litigation from outside it.

We can orient ourselves ethically by drawing upon existing lists of 'principles'. Here, we draw upon six from within action research, which is a good place to look. By its nature, action research invites broad participation and ownership of the research process, so it possesses a finely drawn ethical sensibility. Richard Winter (1996, pp. 16–17) proposed these:

- Make sure that the relevant persons, committee and authorities have been consulted, and that the principles guiding the work are accepted in advance by all.
- All participants must be allowed to influence the work, and the wishes of those who do not wish to participate must be respected.
- The development of the work must remain visible and open to suggestions from others.
- Permission must be obtained before making observations or examining documents produced for other purposes.
- Descriptions of others' work and points of view must be negotiated with those concerned before being published.
- The researcher must accept responsibility for maintaining confidentiality.

In Part B, we set out some ways to ensure these principles are carried through. For the present, beginning researchers, especially if they are also practitioners, would do well to reflect on how these principles would be upheld, or played out, in their own workplace. Having one's colleagues as 'subjects' brings with it not just the immediacy of experiences worthy as 'data'. It may also bring their expectation that you will regard them in a particular way—even compromising the integrity of that same data, because your colleagues may merely placate you with easy responses, or, worse, tell tales about their buddies. Various contexts and purposes of research will bring differing ethical challenges. No set of 'principles' comes with a single application. The integrity of research is thus intimately bound up with the location of the researcher, the value-ladenness of the site(s) of practice and research, and the 'reading' all participants give the research. Ethics is a prime focus for the 'ways of seeing' and 'ways of knowing' we mentioned in the previous chapter. We like to think we perceive the values we expect to see; but equally, we may not be aware of how we are perceived by others, or what the site itself does to our perceptions of those who occupy it.

Turning now to legal aspects, we need to ask: whose intellectual property (IP) is the knowledge generated, especially when through collaborative research? How do we exercise or safeguard the IP of our research? In times past, before we were so conscious of the power relationships and the rights of the research subjects, researchers could claim the IP without qualms or much acknowledgment, except on an 'honours' basis, and the main disputes were among the researchers themselves, or between them and their institution. Now we live in more responsible times—and more litigious ones, too.

■ action research

■ ethical challenges

■ intellectual
property

There is always an ethical component in the 'subject world', particularly where it involves a documentary element, for example, collecting information or witness statements from people. Tapping the fountain of oral history is a delicate process. The subject may know what was true for him or her, but cannot know what use will be made of it: the recorder, in changing the context, must inevitably change the original, and may well dishonour the original intention.

▧ documenting witnesses

> Running an art studio for adults with intellectual disabilities presents daily challenges, but when these are also meant to be the stuff of PhD fieldwork, the challenges multiply (Daye 1998). Cheryl needed to 'pin down' the aesthetic understandings that painters with such disabilities may have, yet, by definition, her learners could not be expected to articulate these in regular interviews. This 'outsider art' is, however, very amenable to honourable articulation once an extensive array of photographs, visits, wider opinions and immersion in the life of the studio is set up. Cheryl was able to balance the constraints and opportunities of her studio to provide an ethical and insightful account of this new aesthetic, and its educational significance for program design.

Here another couple of key questions arise:

- Who is responsible for whatever uses are made of research knowledge or findings?
- What happens if the research leads to unforeseen consequences?

Again, the ground has shifted in recent years. In times past, those labels 'pure' and 'applied' came in very handy. If the research was 'applied', then by definition, any direct application was a valid outcome, and the researcher got the credit if it worked, or had to wear the opprobrium if it didn't. If it was 'pure', the researcher could rarely claim to have any interests in the uses that might be made of it, or any responsibility for maleficent uses. Nowadays, research outcomes are more various and diverse. We are much more aware of indirect effects, including those unforeseen or indirect consequences, and outcomes where the research might have been a contributing factor but not the sole one. In our approach, there are neither easy calls nor generic or authoritative answers. It is up to the researcher to try and take into account any possible effects, positive or negative. As one of the first steps in any research project, it is wise to try and identify in advance all the possible stakeholders (those who might be affected directly or indirectly by the research) and examine whether the effects will be likely to be beneficial, neutral or deleterious, or perhaps perceived to be so by the relevant stakeholder. When weighing up the benefits as against the possible counter-effects, 'do no harm' is a pretty good mantra, especially where children are concerned, although informed adults may like to be taken into the decision process themselves. Even, dare we suggest it, children perhaps ought to be taken into the decision-making process, if we are to consider them as already sentient beings, rather than as citizens-in-waiting.

▧ responsibility

▧ consequences

■ risk management

■ compliance

For legal reasons, virtually all formal research projects have to meet some basic 'risk management' demands, for compliance and clearance. These, based broadly upon the ethical principles above, include considerations such as explicitly transparent planning and management of a project, confidentiality and disclosure, and informed consent. These considerations involve systematic practical procedures, as we detail in Part B.

Cultural issues

Many of the subjects of research belong to populations who are well used to being the object of research and rarely see any benefits from their engagement in the process. Linda Tuhiwai Smith, documenting the exhaustive and recolonising process of much research undertaken on Maori people, states: 'Years of research have frequently failed to improve the conditions of the people who are researched. This has led many to believe that researchers are simply intent on taking or stealing knowledge' (1999, p. 176). Smith

■ cultural appropriation

suggests a range of models for culturally appropriate research by *Pakeha* (non-Maori) in Maori settings, which are useful ways of thinking about research with any marginalised group including indigenous groups and other select populations whose stories have become the lifeblood of researchers.

Researching within specific cultural groups requires more than sensitivity to their needs. (Those groups, incidentally, includes not only groups recognisable by their racial distinctiveness, but the smaller subcultures and territories of our students: the distinctiveness of age, political geography, social class, sexual preference, shared

■ cultural practices and protocols

popular culture and so on.) It requires knowledge of appropriate cultural practices and protocols and a willingness to verify this knowledge with cultural experts. It requires recognition that the stories we research are not ours, but that we are engaging with our subjects in open and honest communication about what and why we are researching. The benefits of this are twofold: we can verify what is available for taking away and we can return the results of our findings to the communities we took them from. The research should create some benefit for those who have been researched, as well as for Education communities elsewhere and for the career of the researcher.

> Julia understood training practices within the Australian franchise industry (e.g. convenience stores, fast food outlets), since she has her own consultancy in that field. Her DEd thesis was thus embedded in the commercial culture of small-business operators (Camm 2012). Yet she was convinced that a more rigorous approach to training franchisees was necessary, so her thesis fieldwork explored ways workplace learning could be better used in that training. Her 'way of seeing' this better 'way of knowing' was Foucauldian because that theoretical lens brought to prominence power-knowledge relationships between franchisors and franchisees.

> Sumera works in community development in Pakistan. Her PhD studies social development in six villages, not to investigate its impact as such, but as a means to evaluate the 'unintended outcomes' of development programs (Jabeen 2013, in progress). Her research will generate an innovative approach to understanding the significance of unintended outcomes in evaluation practices, and in their theorisation. Her expertise in program evaluation, as well as her intimate knowledge of Pakistani culture, are thus intertwined in this PhD project.

In working with individual stories within research, it is sometimes appropriate not merely to check with participants on the accuracy of statements, but for them to be a part of shaping how the story should be told. There are other connected issues, such as the use of pseudonyms to describe individuals, and what personal identifying details remain in the research, which need to be clearly defined during the research process and verified before publication. On occasion, participants may rightfully retain vetoing rights until publication.

▪ pseudonyms

▪ right of veto

DEFINING THE KEY TERMS

Research does involve specialised terminology, so we'll need to get serious with the jargon. There are key general terms that are sometimes used loosely or variously, and if we are doing research we need to be precise about what they mean.

▪ terminology

There is actually a hierarchy of terms that is worth clarifying, which applies to any research. These include the following words and phrases, which we regularly come across in the course of our research, most of which are probably already familiar to you, so we will keep the list and the definitions as short as possible: *paradigm*; *topic*; *site*; *subjects*; *Research Question*; *methodology* and *method*; *positioning*; *literature*; *fieldwork*; *procedures* and *instruments*; *quantitative* and *qualitative*; *data* (and *data collection*); *statistics*, *metrics* and *variables*; *longitudinal study*; *reliability* (and some synonyms) and *contestation*; *analysis*, *inference* and *synthesis*; *documentation* and *dissemination*; *thesis* and *dissertation*. Some terms, unfortunately, can only be defined using other terms in the list, but we'll try to be helpful and clear!

▪ hierarchy of terms

Not many years ago, *quantitative* and *qualitative* would have been at the top (most generalised level) of the hierarchy, presented as an incompatible dichotomy with all research from the outset divided into one or the other. This still lingers in traditional thinking, but Chapter 1 closed with clear evidence that most thinking on the subject has changed.

- Research is *quantitative* when the researchers think they can answer their Research Question through some form of measurement.

▪ quantitative

- It is *qualitative* when they need to collect, interpret and make judgments about data that cannot be measured—such as what people say and do, how they say it and why.

▪ qualitative

Drawing this distinction at the beginning of an educational research project is actually very unhelpful. There may be aspects of the Question that can be measured, and others where evidence has to be interpreted and judged for relevance or importance. Accordingly, we are putting this old polarisation way down the list, where it can actually be helpful.

Top of our hierarchy is the word *paradigm*, which, confusingly, has two applications in research, which we've already had to use in this chapter.

philosophical paradigm

- A *philosophical paradigm* is a world-view that underlies the theories and methodologies of the researcher's practice and research. Whatever topic we choose or are driven to research will be subject to this world-view, our basic philosophy and point of view, whether of art or education.

research paradigm

- This in turn will guide our particular *research paradigm*, which is the theoretical approach or pattern that we take for our project, the assumptions we make from the outset, and the way we position ourselves in relation to the subject matter and our Research Question.

positivism

relativism

constructivism

By far the bulk of traditional researchers, and some contemporary social science researchers, take a 'positivist' philosophical paradigm into their research, believing that any understanding about human behaviour and learning should be positive, tangible and demonstrable. As we have already suggested, most arts and humanities—and many science and social sciences—teachers and workers would take a more 'relativistic' view of human behaviour, seeing it as inescapably dynamic and shifting, unable to be positively pinned to a spot. Therefore, most take a 'constructivist' philosophical paradigm into the research, believing that humans construct their understanding of reality and scaffold their learning as they go along. Our research paradigm will be shaped from those deeper cultural or spiritual philosophical paradigms, as well as by the educational and cultural context in which we find ourselves researching.

The next level down, or rather inwards, in our hierarchy are the terms *topic*, *site* and *subjects*, though the order in which they appear will vary from project to project depending on where the researcher chooses to start.

topic

- *Topic* is easy. It is the subject matter of our research, whatever we have decided needs researching.

site

- *Site* is easy too. The site is the place and the people who will be the subjects of our research. It also incorporates all the other contextual factors, such as the particular timing of the research.

subjects

- The *subjects* of our research are the people whose behaviour we are studying (not to be confused with the 'subject matter' or topic!). The power implications of the word 'subject' make some contemporary researchers, including ourselves, uneasy about using this term, and we accordingly prefer the term 'participants'.

Research Question

Once the topic, site and subjects are decided, the purpose of the research needs to be framed as a *Research Question* (usually singular: we'll see why, later)—a question that will be central to the whole research and will drive the investigation, possibly with a number of sub-questions.

Normally, it is only really when the Research Question has been decided that it is appropriate to consider how the Question is going to be investigated or answered. Our research paradigm gives us a choice of methodologies from one of which we will choose our research method.

A *methodology* is a system that is based on a particular common methodical approach—sorry, that sounds like tautology, so we'll give an example.

▨ methodologies

> A key *methodology* used in educational research is action research, which starts by identifying a problem that needs fixing, or a vision that might be attained, and then sets out to achieve its goal by making experimental interventions.

To best investigate or answer our Research Question, we will organise these characteristic features, appropriately to the context, into our research *method*, which is just the sequence of procedures from the beginning to the end.

▨ method
▨ procedures

> In action research, the *method* usually consists of using a cycle or spiral of procedures where each cycle starts with planning, then goes on to action, then observation and documentation of the action, then reflection and evaluation of the data collected in the observation, and then replanning the next cycle based on what has been discovered.

Sometimes the method we have chosen does not work very well, or turns out to have gaps and limitations that could not have been anticipated, and we may even need to alter our Research Question. This is likely to entail adding new procedures and instruments, and possibly even incorporating features from another methodology. Then we can appropriately describe our *methods* (plural).

▨ instruments

> Kennedy, a researcher from an African country with civil disruption, set out to do some straightforward ethnography (his methodology) into the impact of the contemporary theatre forms used in Theatre for Development (TfD) and traditional performance activities on each other (Chinyowa 2005). It was to be based (his original method) on observations made during fieldwork in his own village region (where he had been brought up, but no longer lived). When he attempted to visit his 'home' village and apply these procedures he found that as an inhabitant of the capital, and an intellectual, he was now no longer *persona grata* in the rural area, and he was actively unsafe. After several uncomfortable brushes with local militia, he reshaped his fieldwork to involve case study analysis of groups elsewhere, combined with a short action research project with a group primarily created for this purpose. He reshaped his Research Question to allow it to be investigated, still within his basic research paradigm and topic but using safer procedures. These mixed methods eventually cohered into a valuable piece of research.

positioning

A crucial feature of the method is the researcher's *position* and this has two dimensions: our *personal positioning* and how we position ourselves as *observer* and/or *participant*. Nobody comes to research neutral, and it is necessary for us, as researchers, to identify where we stand in relation to the topic and subjects of the research (particularly necessary in research involving human behaviour). For the integrity of the research and for the reader's benefit, as honestly as we may, we must acknowledge our personal position. This means explaining why we are doing the research. It also means coming as clean as we can about our philosophical paradigm, including those personal beliefs, perspectives, ideologies and assumptions that form our own subjectivity.

> Jo has identified and categorised the various 'selves' she brings to her research (Raphael 2003):
>
> - *Research-based selves:* a fledgling researcher, an arts educator and lecturer, a person with a purpose and a goal to contribute something new and of value through research and to make a difference for the participants involved, a person who holds certain educational philosophies and beliefs.
> - *Brought selves:* a drama and theatre enthusiast, an occasional participant in drama, artist/performer and drama teacher, an academic, a parent, a person committed to issues of social justice, a person with a history of working with the arts in areas of disability and disadvantage, a person who holds certain philosophical and ideological views.
> - *Situationally created selves:* a teacher [of her theatre group—the research participants], a student researcher and learner, a director, a facilitator, a co-creator, a role model, a critic, mentor and friend, an audience, an advocate.

When we are choosing our method, we have a choice in where we want to stand in relation to our research subjects, and what role we ourselves will take in the research. This is known as *observer–participant positioning*, and is a methodological factor. Will we be participants, or just observe, or stand somewhere in between on a continuum as participant-observers?

literature

fieldwork

At some point in any research project, usually as early as possible after the topic and Question are selected, the *literature* must be consulted. In research jargon, 'literature' doesn't mean Shakespeare and poetry, but the sources of knowledge that already exist about the research topic—usually written scholarship in the form of books and journal articles. *Fieldwork* is the only word in the list that might not apply to every single piece of research, but in Education it applies to the overwhelming majority, because our research is so grounded in our practice. The fieldwork, self-evidently, is that portion of the investigation that is carried out at the research site, with the subjects of the research.

techniques

ethics procedures

The research procedures or *techniques* are, simply, those activities and sequences of activity that we carry out in order to make our investigation into the Research Question, from beginning to end. They include, for instance, the ethics procedures that we must carry out to gain permission to do the research, as well as the means of collecting data.

Literally 'what is given', *data* means any material that is collected during and as a part of the project. *Data sets* are just what they sound like, collected materials that have been grouped together, usually in the way they have been collected. *Data analysis* is the process of examining all the materials that have been collected, to make sense of them, and help to address the Research Question.

▦ data

▦ data analysis

The phrase *research instrument* simply means a kind of procedure, but the term is usually reserved for particular techniques that are designed and used to investigate a specific component of the research, to gather data or to analyse it. A questionnaire and a specially designed interview with a subject are two standard research instruments.

▦ instruments

This is where those words qualitative and quantitative start to become useful, if we think of them as applying to the instruments of our research.

- Is there anything that we can usefully measure in investigating our Research Question?
- Can we possibly make comparisons, or gather useful statistics, that is, numerical data?

▦ quantitative analysis

If so, then we need to turn to *quantitative* analysis—or 'metrics' as it is often known now. Of course, this includes the whole vast and complex field of statistics. That does not mean that we have to complete the whole of our research wrestling with the arcane symbols and terminology of statistics, which fill some non-scientists with apprehension. We may just use metrics for one or two instruments, where what we are examining is simple enough to yield statistics we can trust—figures that are not affected by factors that we have not taken account of, or that are beyond measurement themselves, known as variables. Some quantitative techniques are simple enough for beginners to manage themselves with no specialised training. There are examples in Chapters 7 and 8. Group questionnaires, for instance, can collect useful and easily interpreted numerical data, where respondents are asked to give simple answers from a limited range of possibilities such as 'Yes/No' or 'Strongly agree/Agree/Neutral/Disagree/Strongly disagree'. For the difficult statistical analysis, we can invariably get somebody to help. Both universities and commercial organisations offer services to crunch numbers for people who are not mathematically inclined.

▦ metrics

▦ statistics

▦ variables

- What is there in our Research Question that is not susceptible to measurement?

    If we are talking about any aspect or phenomenon of human behaviour, however small, there are many *variables* that defy statistical analysis.

For instance, in analysing the effectiveness of an integrated studies/experiential learning approach for teaching the history of the Industrial Revolution (a subject we used to teach using more traditional methods), we might first collect the nearest statistics, for example, by setting the same exam or assessment task and comparing the results with students' previous achievement in the exam. That would certainly give us a useful preliminary indication. But can we be sure that any difference is due to the difference in teaching technique, and even if so, have we really learnt much of use in the complex business of pedagogy? How can we identify what characteristics of the new pedagogy are responsible, and why? Have we taken into account the lesson content; the time of day and weather; the relationship of the teacher with the class as a whole and with each student (after all, they might just have had a poor and unpopular history teacher the first time, but a brilliant and popular teacher the second); the teacher's mood; the students' feelings towards each other and the subject content, including their relevant reading and what they know of the subject from television or their parents; their schooling, and their previous experiences in experiential and/or integrated learning; how many of them missed breakfast this morning; who stole whose boyfriend last week … let alone the macro variables such as socio-economic class, cultural orientations and gender! Can these be factored into the statistics?

■ qualitative analysis

To find out 'what characteristics of the new approach were responsible for the difference, and why?' (which is a more useful Research Question than just 'was there a difference?'), we need *qualitative* mechanisms that allow us to use our brains and experience to observe the behaviour, then interpret it in a meaningful way.

In the example above: listening to the students; talking with them; actually observing the lessons and writing notes of the details of the lessons; taking a video to analyse; comparing notes with other teachers of the same students; giving the students tasks like writing-in-role or the construction of period artefacts; employing outside observers and discussing with them what they observed … all of these can provide a quite different, and richer, order of *data* from which we can make far more complex *inferences* about the Research Question than we could from the exam results alone.

Most beginning research projects tend to focus on a particular question that arises in the context of one research site. However, with human behaviour, as with educational systems, organic change usually happens slowly. It can be very valuable in these circumstances to examine a question and gather data over a considerable length of time, by repeating at intervals some of the investigative procedures or tests. This can provide information on what, if any, changes are occurring, and more importantly, whether they are transient, permanent or transformative. This is known as a *longitudinal* approach.

■ longitudinal study

■ reliability

■ triangulation

The next consideration, when we have collected our data—quantitative or qualitative—is to ensure that it is *reliable*, that we can trust what we have been given. This process is traditionally known as triangulation, which has nothing to do with surveying, and isn't even as mathematical as it sounds. *Triangulation* means that data or inferences that have been corroborated from at least two other independent angles are logically three times as likely to be true as uncorroborated data.

Interviewing the students, for instance, about that 'integrated humanities/social science' class can be very useful but it can be unreliable. The students may give very insightful responses that show they have not only benefited from the new technique, but even perhaps reflected on it and can articulate their new understanding. That's good as far as it goes, but on the other hand, their responses can be coloured by a number of factors, for example:

- they enjoyed the new lesson, would like to repeat it, and have now got a stake in what is for them a more motivating technique
- they know (or suspect) the data is being collected to corroborate the teacher's faith in the new method, and being helpful young people, they unconsciously talk it up
- they really hated the previous teacher
- they have a crush on the new humanities teacher
- they are in a hurry to get lunch or the bus home, and think that agreeing with the questions is the quickest way out of the interview.

Accordingly, comparing (1) the students' interview responses with (2) their exam results, and (3) observations derived from an external observer sitting in on the classes, would provide information from three different sources and perspectives.

Many qualitative researchers now think even this term triangulation is too positivistic. Triangulation of perspectives demands fixed points, just as it does in surveying. Much of the data collected by qualitative research, especially into a field like Education, is shifting, ephemeral (only for today), dynamic, ambiguous or provisional. Other words must be found to verify or validate the data. 'Repeatability' certainly leads one to trust the data, at least in experimental research—we want those pills to work and the bridges to stand up every time, not just once. However, human behaviour is never identical to other human behaviour and contexts are never identical either. Moreover, some forms of qualitative enquiry, such as some case studies, explicitly look for what is unique. The adjective often associated with traditional forms of reliability checking, 'rigorous', which has descended through science from our old friend William of Occam, has recently become highly contested and even rejected by the same qualitative researchers. The only human body to demonstrate rigo(u)r is a dead one, and the same goes for human behaviour.

Accordingly, new key words have been adopted to ensure that there is as much reliability as possible within research: *plausibility*, *credibility*, *resonance* and *transferability*. The research should collect and analyse data so that an argument can be mounted that is *plausible* and not immediately able to be contradicted by contrary data. *Credibility* is a useful, if rough concept: are our findings able to be believed by reasonable people who have no stake in the project or its results? *Resonance* links the data together and outside the project by finding echoes of commonality and convergence with other data, and with other contexts beyond the project. Perhaps most importantly,

ephemerality

validity

repeatability

rigour

plausibility

credibility

resonance

■ transferability

■ crystallisation

■ contradictions
■ contestation

■ silent voices

■ data analysis

■ implications and inferences

■ synthesis

■ generalisation

■ documentation

■ thesis

■ dissertation

■ hypothesis

might the findings be *transferable* to other contexts beyond the project? (If not, what is our purpose for doing the project, other than solipsistic?) Even these now commonly used words are too definitive for some researchers, usually those involved in narrative or arts-based enquiry. Their data and what it reveals in analysis are so shifting and sometimes transient and ephemeral that they prefer the word *crystallisation*, coined by Laurel Richardson (2000, p. 934) to define the emerging reliability of their findings.

There is another very important consideration when addressing data: not only 'Is it reliable?' but 'Is it the whole story?' Might there be other data to be found that contests our hypothesis? Might there be other findings—either to give our data the lie, or throw doubt on it, or show that there are many alternatives, perhaps contradictory inferences that might be made? Good researchers actively look for this *contestatory* data, however much we are wedded to the primary data that so often seems to answer our Research Question the way we wish it to. To do that, we often have to find ways to listen to the *silent voices*, the testimony of those witnesses and respondents who avoid being interviewed, or who are overlooked, or who, for a thousand reasons, are not entirely frank and open in the responses they give. When data has been collected, the next stage is to make sense of it and then make meaning out of it. The first part of this is by data analysis, and we have a whole chapter (Chapter 8) that discusses the various ways in which data can be analysed; each research method has its own ways. When the data is starting to make sense, the researcher's intelligence, experience and imagination really come into play. What has been given and sorted has to be interpreted in some useful way, so that the phenomenon being investigated (the research topic and site) can be read as a comprehensible event or pattern, or coherent themes can be drawn from it. Here, we researchers have to get our grammar right—in knowing the difference between two words, often confused with each other: 'imply' and 'infer'. Our subjects and our data *imply* or have *implications* and we researchers *infer* and make *inferences*.

The inferences we make help us to *synthesise* the data into patterns of meaning. These in turn, we hope, will lead us first to a coherent picture of the phenomenon, then answer or at least address the Research Question. We may also often (but not always) hope that from this process of synthesis some *generalisable* conclusions and insights will emerge that can be useful and transferable to other contexts of understanding or practice in education.

The process of engaging in research invariably involves lots of *documentation*, and also invariably has to finish up with a culminating document that reveals and explains the research to others. This document usually needs to be given some form of official approval. In apprentice research, namely research study, this usually takes the form of a *thesis* or *dissertation*, and the stamp of approval is the degree it leads to, of course. The words are interchangeable, though in Australia a thesis usually refers to something longer than a dissertation (Honours dissertation, Doctoral thesis); the reverse is usually the case in the USA, however. In a nice irony of word derivation from its Greek roots, a thesis both starts and ends a research study: a 'thesis' is literally an argument or statement of a philosophical position … that must be tested for its truth. A hypo-thesis is something less than a thesis! See?

In professional research projects, the documentation may be in the form of a report, or a book. The major mode of dissemination of research throughout the sciences and social sciences is the *refereed journal* article. The stamp of approval for a book or journal is the approval of expert peers. A book is sent to expert readers before publication, and a refereed journal article must normally be reviewed blind (meaning that the identity of the writer is not known by the reviewers) by at least two referees who are specialists both in the field and in research methods.

▪ dissemination

And that's all there is to it really!

? REFLECTIVE QUESTIONS

1   Where do you locate yourself and your research along a spectrum with traditional positivism (an example of the 'object world') at one end, and interpretivist approaches at the other (examples of the 'subject world'), and why do you do so?

2   Is there room in your location for convergence, or mixed methods?

3   How would the six ethical principles we have gleaned from action research play out for your site(s) of research and/or practice?

WIDER READING

Creswell, J. 2012. *Educational Research: Planning, Conducting, and Evaluating Quantitative and Qualitative Research*. Pearson, Boston.

Grbich, C. 2004. *New Approaches in Social Research*. Sage, London.

Husen, T. 1999. 'Research Paradigms in Education', in J. Keeves and G. Lakomski (eds) *Issues in Educational Research*. Pergamon, Elsevier Science, Oxford.

RESEARCH AND THE PRACTITIONER

☑ CHAPTER OBJECTIVES

After reading this chapter, you should be able to:

- understand how practitioners' capacity for reflection is also a good basis for researching practice
- outline three main approaches to research design
- acknowledge the underpinning nature of experience as the basis for both research and practice.

 ## PRACTITIONERS AS RESEARCHERS

natural researchers

Good teachers, trainers, facilitators, evaluators and indeed most professional Education practitioners are automatically researchers. They are researchers in the sense of being those who examine what they do in order, for example, to improve teaching techniques, to understand and prepare for an age group or community group previously unknown to us, or at least to analyse and avoid a repeat of the day's disaster with the Year 9s. To do this, we evaluate and reflect on our practice, and we read books and articles and search websites to give ourselves new ideas. We also attend the professional development workshops that our education systems are constantly demanding; here we are invariably given an overview of the principles and theory behind whatever new literacy strategy or behaviour policy is being adopted, and we are sometimes invited to participate in modelled practical sessions. Informally, this could all be thought of as our research. Paolo Freire's term 'praxis' (1974) describes that highly developed educational practice that consciously articulates the theory on which it is based, and, in turn, generates new theory.

praxis

reflective practice

It is a short step to formalise that praxis as natural, good 'reflective practice' (we develop this in Chapter 4). Most of us, as practitioners, however, don't naturally think of ourselves as researchers. We don't have much time to engage in formal research—evaluating our practice and submitting our new ideas and classroom experiments to analysis and testing. Once we are out of pre-service training and in full-time teaching or facilitating mode, planning the next lesson or designing the next program is often as much as we have time for, let alone devising a strategy for investigating its impact, or documenting and analysing the last lesson. Sadly, too, the false dichotomy between 'practice' and 'research' that still influences our education systems and structures can discourage many of us from attempting to formalise praxis, as we claimed in the Introduction to this book. Sometimes, however, the need to research can be imposed on us 'for our own good'. Professional development or the need to upgrade our qualifications does force us to take stock, and prompts us to subject what we do to closer scrutiny. Nor do we need to abandon our practice when embarking on research. There is, in fact, very little research in education that is not tied to a particular practical context. Education is very much 'practical' (which is not to reduce it to the merely 'technical, or to the 'applied', although there are central elements of those in any 'practice'). For the vast majority of us, our professional educational context provides us with the Research Question, the research site and the target community. Most of the research methods explored in this book are based on fieldwork, either engaging in praxis, or observing and examining others' practices.

teaching versus research

◥ RESEARCHING PRACTICE

In research terms, Education is a 'social science', but also a highly distributed social and vocational practice: it crops up everywhere, not merely in schools. Education is messy and slippery. Moreover, it is hard to fence in. It is very difficult to hold a tight boundary around the variety of learning activities apparent in classrooms, training rooms and across many regular work sites, such as offices, factories, wards and community houses. We believe that this messiness is essential to good research. As the great twentieth-century philosopher Ludwig Wittgenstein put it:

researching practice

> We have got onto slippery ice where there is no friction and so in a certain sense the conditions are ideal, but also, just because of that, we are unable to walk. We want to walk so we need friction. Back to the rough ground! (1953, p. 107)

slippery research

Finding traction: back to the rough ground

Our practice is grounded in the settings where as educators we are responsible for the learning of other people (school students and adults). These are varied, complex and untidy—rough and messy—and so the ground of our research is both rough and messy. Educative practices and research both entail a process of enquiring into subject matter, of finding sources and starting points and an appropriate method, and of positioning the teacher/facilitator/author and a potential audience. Good practice entails perpetual reconsiderations and reconstructions in response to emerging evidence and experience and produces a tangible outcome to the enquiry. In short, good practitioners want to make a difference—and so do good researchers. Research can imbue every aspect of the actual experience of all creative educational practices: making, undergoing and responding to challenges. Even the most dyed-in-the-wool practitioners are usually

messy research
rough ground

challenges

quite happy to exhort the students or community and workplace groups to do their research thoroughly in all these functions. When we, as practitioners, engage in and take on a leadership role with regard to the participants' experiences, we enter the research process consciously, as well as conscientiously, with a moral intention to make a worthwhile difference to the quality of those experiences.

▦ research design

For the creative educator, once the topic or theme has been decided, there is a serious design task. Books must be consulted to find and learn enough background; experts may be brought in or contacted; members of specialised communities may be interviewed or observed. Program design and the learning activities (or 'pedagogy') available and selected for the subject or theme, are two intricately connected aspects of educative practices. But this is very like the tight fit between selecting 'what' and 'how' will make up a research design and its implementation. There is, in both educative practices and their research, an inherent messiness that needs to be acknowledged as a central feature of especially, but not exclusively, arts and humanities work: this should be 'designed in' to provide the Wittgensteinian 'rough ground' on which real traction is possible. Bland, smooth teaching, built on lock-step programs, with checklist outcomes, is not likely to generate the creativity we want in our learners—or in ourselves. Similarly, research, blandly designed to tell us what we already know, is unlikely to delve into the friction inherent in all human activities, and so little traction will be made beyond merely 'mapping' the way aspects of the world are taken to be. If Education is about discovering and mapping the worlds we perceive and construct—about new learning— then educators are, more than most, interested in unsettling the way the world, especially the 'object world', is taken to be. Hence educative practices and research practices, from those perspectives, should take the rough ground as their common bedrock.

▦ reading the topic

Educators, from whatever discipline, who work in this messy territory have first to research their topic carefully in order to find a coherent and authentic interpretation. Topics can be anything read as a 'text', that is, for meaning. Look, for example, at what we traditionally call a text: sacred texts like the Bible, works that are part of a literary canon such as Shakespeare, other 'classic' literature and the various holy books around the globe, to say nothing of science textbooks. But these books themselves— as well as performative, visual, aural and tangibly experienced events and all manner of artefacts, items on blogs and occurrences in the mass media—can and should be reread as 'texts' with a focus on meanings. The point is, some initial enquiry from within a frame of reference is essential, in both educational and research practices. This is the 'making' of something as the object of learning, or of enquiry. Undergoing and responding to that object of enquiry is itself a research process: after experiencing the lesson, activity or process, the learner is expected to analyse it and usually to evaluate its various components: did it meet the expectations of a genre, or particular educative purpose? How well did it do so? Can we generalise the major characteristics of this evaluation?

▦ common ground

One cautionary note: the research of the practitioner is not identical to that of the traditional academic researcher (see the search, not for 'rough ground' but for 'common ground', in the USA, as told by Stephen Davis [2008]). The purposes of our research are more explicitly subjective than those of 'standard' formal researchers: an historian investigating an historical event seeks knowledge and inferences that can be verified by some objective measures, while an educative practitioner, investigating the same event, will look for insights that are satisfying in their context, and, most important, professionally productive (how can I/we do this better next time?). Both types of researcher, of course, are equally subject to the lenses imposed by their own values systems, or ethics.

▦ divergence

◥ THREE APPROACHES TO RESEARCH

We are now in a position to identify three main 'ways of seeing' research, each of which will construct particular 'ways of knowing'. And as we do so, an important distinction is worth making. Chapter 1 is entitled '"Seeing" Research', Chapter 2 outlined the Western intellectual tradition, and now Chapter 3 has located practitioners and researchers alongside one another. In each of these chapters, we have been primarily dealing with *ontological* issues (i.e. what is the 'furniture' of the world?). *Ontos* means 'being', so each chapter takes up this abstraction by dealing with its bodily manifestation in humans as perceptual, or sensing, creatures (ways of 'seeing' and 'feeling' the world, which of course includes ourselves). The evolution of our thinking, in the West, about what the world contains—its furniture—feeds directly into *epistemological* issues: how is the world known? *Episteme* means 'knowledge' as it is experienced as growth in cognitive understanding (in contrast, say, to *sophia*, which is knowledge through contemplative wisdom). The ontological and epistemological are intimately intertwined in human experience, as we grapple with who 'we' are, and how we are said to be 'knowing' anything at all.

▦ ways of seeing

▦ ontology

▦ epistemology

So, at this point in the book, acknowledging that our thinking about research implies some fairly massive and historically hallowed assumptions about these two fundamental sets of issues, we plunge in to a structure that exemplifies aspects of both. It is likely that one of the following research paradigms—or approaches—will embed your particular research methodology. Each of these is a 'way of knowing'—an epistemological position. But equally, each brings assumptions about a 'way of seeing' humans in the world—an ontological claim.

▦ ways of knowing

The way in which our research leads us to see and to know will or should be directed by our basic purpose for doing it. So before we decide how to approach our research—what methodology or methodologies we will use, which we deal with in Chapter 4—we must first be clear about *why* we are doing it. There are two basic paradigms of purpose that are essentially distinct—and in some research must be kept rigidly so, and so have apparently quite discrete methodologies. Traditionally, these have been known as 'pure' and 'applied' research. However, to muddy the waters, there are also some common-ground purposes, where it is right and proper to juxtapose them, combine them, have them running parallel or even thoroughly mix them up … and where those discrete methodologies have be renegotiated, mixed and blended.

▦ purposes

This is certainly messy, but it isn't as bewildering as it seems, if we look at our research intentions as belonging in one of three paradigms of purpose:

- descriptive and interpretive (traditionally 'pure')
- change-oriented (traditionally 'applied')
- blended.

Descriptive and interpretive

An obvious purpose of research is to want to find out and describe how something works, why it happens or what makes some group of people tick. To do this, we want to disturb or interfere with it not at all, or as little as we possibly can; otherwise, what we are observing won't be what we wanted to observe before we came along! We certainly don't want to change it. Various methodologies have been established, traditionally in the sciences, to remain 'outside' the phenomenon we are observing. Among the most well-known of these is epidemiology in medicine, where, for example the population of an entire country can be surveyed to identify significant statistical variations in health. More recently the social sciences and arts have developed methodologies to observe human behaviour 'from the inside' but disturbing it as little as possible. The most common methodologies of this kind of research in our area are *ethnography* and *case study*. In our research, we can't actually remain totally 'outside' and 'objective', as we have mentioned in the Introduction. For this first purpose of research, of course, as soon as we start to try and describe anything at all, we are involved in selection and

■ interpretation

interpretation: we select what we want to describe, how we approach it, which bits we actually describe, which aspects we have to, or choose to, leave out. Even the traditional positivist *experimental* tradition, since Popper and Kuhn, and, yes, even since Einstein

■ provisional knowledge

(see Chapter 2), has acknowledged the provisional nature of knowledge. We take the line that all *description* is already perceptual: we experience the world in 'seeing it *as …*' something. Therefore we are also using the word *interpretive* rather than just *descriptive* to define this approach to research, because that word acknowledges the subjectivity of knowing anything. For the authors of this book, and most contemporary educators, 'reality' is not a universal given; we construct it socially. We are not using the term 'pure' for this kind of research, partly because there is no 'pure' reality out there, and also partly because this very research may not be at all disinterested—it's very likely that we want to apply what we find out in some way … but first we have to know it *as it is … what it means to us*!

Change-oriented

Our purpose in research may not be 'pure' at all. Does the research seek to find out what would happen if some change does take place, or some procedure different from the norm is instituted? If we think that something—a situation or context of human behaviour—could be improved, or is in a mess and needs changing radically, then,

■ change and impact

crucially, we want to know, as we make the improvements or changes, what impact, effects and outcomes the changes are having. If we bring into the classroom some new teaching technique to engage the slow learners, we not only need to know if it is working (whether it is speeding up their learning, or slowing them even further) but we also need to know the side effects—what impact it is having on the quick learners, and on the teacher!

The two most common methodologies for such research are *experimental research*, and the various forms of *action research*. In the first of these, the researcher is usually 'outside' the research, as far as possible; in the second, in educational settings, the researcher is usually the agent for change or improvement, or invariably implicated in the change, so instead of keeping outside the research, we are involved in or actively leading it.

▪ experimental research
▪ action research

Blended

Much educational research is designed with an open-ended structure, or one that is, to some extent, custom-built. This might be in order to further practical or intellectual ends: perhaps to try and identify some characteristic of practice that will improve our pedagogy, or our advocacy; or to get to the bottom of something that is very problematic, so that we may be in a position to fix it or look for an improvement by some kind of intervention in the future. Alternatively, some research is designed to examine a situation or context of human behaviour and at the same time seek to change or develop it. There are some methodologies that have been specially designed to combine the two paradigms of purpose, descriptive/interpretive *and* change-oriented. The research may blend the two paradigms together, or use them in sequence, or parallel, or align them in some other way. Often, today, researchers are turning to mixed methods, where the research design draws on components from the descriptive and interpretive methodologies, and from the change-oriented ones.

▪ problematic

▪ mixed methods

Each of these labels and their accompanying methodologies will be explained in more detail in Chapter 4, with examples. But before embarking on a piece of research under any of these labels, it is important to find out their common principles and perhaps their problems and limitations. What follows is our outline of how the *ontological* and the *epistemological* are intertwined in that which we all share, and that which is fundamental to all forms of learning, and, we argue, to all forms of Education: *human experience*.

▪ human experience

 # THE UNDERPINNING SIGNIFICANCE OF HUMAN EXPERIENCE

Most twentieth-century education research took its lead from science, and the scientific and quasi-scientific principles and assumptions embedded in movements in cognitive and social psychology such as behaviourism. Human actions and behaviour, like chemical compounds, motor vehicles and the human body, can be broken down

▪ behaviourism

to their constituent parts to be analysed and identified, the broken or inadequate bits fixed, new components attached and the whole reassembled. And that goes for the actions of the mind, too.

■ holistic research

Over the last few decades, there has been a significant shift in emphasis, with more and more education researchers tending to privilege the 'whole-person' focus on experience. This marks a recent change in what is regarded as worthwhile learning. In the Western world, for most of the past 2400 years, what was worthwhile was the mastery of ideas in, and by, the mind. The Cartesian assumption, from the Enlightenment, starting in the seventeenth century, actually goes right back to the Athenians, principally Plato. But as we noted in the Introduction, we live in an era of lifelong learning, and this is taken to indicate not merely the traditional understandings brought to us through the mind and its operations, but also the learning experienced by the 'whole person': the cognitive, the affective, the social and the psychomotor (sensory and kinaesthetic), to use the usual psychological distinctions, and all integrated in the human organism and human experience.

■ mind

■ whole person

■ children versus adults

Who has experience of this integrated holistic kind? For a while late in the twentieth century, if a single concept marked out the learning of adults from the learning of children, it was thought to be experience. The pursuit and accumulation of learning, and its refinement, best shown by adults, is usually underpinned by some assumptions about the integrity and persistence of experience. If an individual has lived longer (that is, has passed through childhood), they are regarded, initially, as more adept at identifying what they have learnt in the past and what they want to learn in the future. Moreover, adult individuals are also assumed to have insights into how they learnt best in the past, learn best now and expect to learn in the future. Experience, closely connected to the lifespan of individuals, is therefore a fruitful way to underpin research assumptions about useful approaches in educating individuals. But it is important to note that experience is actually not best regarded as the marker of individuality.

■ experience

■ social experience

As Phil Candy puts it, the assumption that experiences are only located in individuals is 'so deeply entrenched in the ethos of adult education as to be thought "obvious" or "self-evident" and to thus be beyond question' (1987, cited in Usher et al. 1997, p. 93). Candy and many other educators rightly remind us that humans are first and foremost social creatures, and that my sense of 'me' is derived from our sense of 'us' (not the other way around). Language acquisition, as Lev Vygotsky (1962) and Wittgenstein (1953) have each respectively argued, is a sociocultural achievement within which personal identities take hold and communication—the life-world or language game we cannot but be part of—shapes individuality. This is not to downgrade personal agency, or our sense of responsibility for our own actions. Far from it: it is only from a robust account of socioculturally located 'experience' that the mores and maxims of right action, such as keeping promises, can be even articulated.

How do children fare?

Is the experience of children different in kind from adults? Malcolm Knowles (1970) famously distinguished between children's and adults' learning. Knowles gave significant shape to the field of practice called 'adult education', at least in North America. His 'andragogy' theorised adults' learning through the explicit utilisation of experience. Adults learn best, according to Knowles, when they 'learn how to take responsibility for their own learning through self-directed inquiry, how to learn collaboratively with the help of colleagues rather than compete with them, and, especially, how to learn by analyzing one's own experience …[This] is the essence of the human relations laboratory' (1970, p. 45). By contrast, Knowles' 'pedagogy' marked out children's learning, in which instruction continued to be central, due to the limited and naive nature of youthful experience. Later, Knowles modified this crisp distinction in favour of more experientially inclusive learning for individuals of any age. Now, in the twenty-first century, we don't make this distinction. 'Experience' is a lifespan phenomenon: the longer you have lived, the more you can be assumed to have learnt. It is a matter of variability, of degree, not merely, as in the traditional Cartesian view of knowledge, a matter of 'degrees'—the formal acquisition of learning through mastery of mental understanding.

▓ andragogy

▓ lifespan learning

So if we take 'experience' as the point of entry to theorisations of adults' and children's learning, we can readily locate it within humanist scholarship more generally. Knowles quite explicitly drew upon the psychologists Carl Rogers and Abraham Maslow, but such an approach is also Deweyan (e.g. 1938), and educators in general were drawing on Dewey's vast publications well before 'andragogy' surfaced in the 1970s and 1980s. Dewey mainly had school-based education in his sights, but his advocacy of organic, holistic learning (and teaching) has attracted many educators of adults.

▓ humanism

As we move in to the details of these three research approaches, it will be apparent that in each of them experience, as outlined above, is being trawled quite finely. In fact, this is the place to make quite a strong assertion: we believe that learners *of any age* (not just children, or just adults) learn best when:

- we have a sense of our *self-direction*—or ownership—of the learning occurring through experience
- we can bring *all our experience* to that self-direction (obviously, younger people have less to draw upon)
- we have an *immediate need* to know something—our purposes are important, and can emerge in what we are doing as well as in what we are thinking—in 'intelligent action' (Beckett 2010a; 2012a).

What does this 'lifespan' interpretation of lifelong learning mean for approaches to research? All educators are, as we affirmed in the Introduction, concerned about interrogating—in critical detail, and with sensitivity and creativity—how experience presents itself to humans across the lifespan. But experience is rarely taken as a 'given'. The question then becomes: how do we access 'experience' for our research purposes? One important philosophical orientation that expresses this intensification of experience is *phenomenology*. There are few arts and humanities researchers who espouse other forms, and fewer researchers who stem from the *positivistic* philosophical tradition that most science has evolved into, especially

▓ phenomenology

▓ positivism

since the Industrial and French revolutions and the development of the Western economic system. Because of this diversity, it is important to explain it a little and show how this has arisen in Western scholarship. You will see that Cartesian thinking literally came from Descartes, but more widely is a powerful set of claims on what is worthwhile knowledge. Only now do we recognise that its main strength—that individuals can take responsibility for their own claims on knowledge by reasoning these out—also comes with some limitations.

As we mentioned in Chapter 2, Renaissance science emerged as a new way of understanding the world in its wonder by studying it as we experience it (rather than as the books and the scholars—the 'given wisdom'—tell us it is). In the seventeenth and eighteenth centuries, most scholars of science (*scientia* is the Latin word for 'knowledge', by the way) studied whatever phenomena interested them. Art and science were not separate worlds, only different paths towards the representation and understanding of experience—and sometimes not all that different. Sir Thomas Browne studied maths, horticulture and gardens, the nature of faith and superstition, archaeology and the anthropology of funerals, relished the excitement of finding dynamic relationships between them, and expressed his knowledge in exquisite prose. Isaac Newton studied alchemy as well as maths and physics. Leonardo da Vinci was a vegetarian engineer, architect and philosopher who invented things like a bicycle and a system of shorthand, and also painted a bit.

That engagement with knowledge has, in the last two hundred years, become more and more specialised and reified. The understanding of a global, finite world to be understood and exploited (hence globalised) did not start in our generation, but was articulated during and after the Renaissance, most famously by René Descartes, who came to distrust the existence of anything he could not directly test through experience; even the basic fact of existence could be proved to be true, since *cogito ergo sum* (I think, therefore I am). He further came to believe that mathematically based scientific knowledge of the whole material world is possible. The reification and commodification of this new knowledge and experience came with the need for its representation. What can be truly known can only be what stands still enough to be discovered, examined and declared to be true. With the gradual, intoxicating discovery that lots of experience apparently does do exactly that, those 'truths' became known and privileged as 'science', a 'tree of knowledge' with many branches. (See how a metaphor becomes entrenched as a philosophical 'given'?) Trees are reassuringly solid and unmoving, and of course they grow towards the skies and keep growing. Gradually medieval fatalism was replaced by a belief in 'progress', which was fervently held by the nineteenth and twentieth centuries. A new belief took hold that human society and 'civilisation' do move forward and can be improved by science.

Under modernism, the dominant philosophical stance of the twentieth century, human experience is sought only in behaviour, which is itself just another '-ology' to be nailed. New ways of accounting for human behaviour were devised and specialist disciplines arose that claimed to be material sciences, such as psychology and anthropology. Hence, as we have seen, *behaviourism* became the favourite way to explain human behaviour

(margin notes)
- scientific thinking
- integrated thinking
- I think, therefore I am
- commodification
- tree of knowledge
- progress

by dissecting human action, and particularly human cognition, into constituent parts and analysing those parts. Ironically, this completely ignores another of Descartes' gifts to understanding: the idea that mind and brain might be separate, and that, therefore, there could be (as later writers dubbed it) a 'ghost in the machine'. Descartes' idea of the duality of mind and brain then descended into a whole set of simple dualities: mind/spirit, art/science, intellectual/physical, which we in the postmodern world are still wrestling to overthrow. In learning, *Cartesian dualisms* have perniciously persisted, such as education versus training; high schools versus technical schools; profession versus trade; character versus skills; head versus hand—where the first-named term has the higher 'mentalistic' status, and the second term the lower status, ascribed to manual labour and those who do it (or, more judgmentally, should do it).

▨ Cartesian dualism

There is an ambiguous intellectual affinity between such dualisms and scholars who still subscribe to either a rationalistic or a positivistic vision, such as those with a *Marxist* philosophy—derived from the great economist and social theoretician Karl Marx, one of those visionary prophets of nineteenth-century progress. Even if you are not elitist, you could assume that 'if you are not part of the solution, you are part of the problem', as the old saying goes. In fields of education much broader than just drama, most of those who regard themselves as part of the solution have been very strongly influenced by playwright-educator Bertolt Brecht and his mentor Walter Benjamin. Their practices and theory are based on a deep ideology that society is driven by immutable material laws of the social control of production and supply. In this sense, Marxist *materialism* is positivistic. Yet for Marxists as much as for postmodernists, Education has an important material, even utilitarian, role in helping to reshape our understanding of how those laws of production and supply result in oppression and injustice, and therefore allow us to help change society for the better.

▨ Marxism

There are, then, *emancipatory* implications for those who challenge dualistic assumptions about worthwhile learning, and the policies and educative structures on which these are based. Marxism is one case of 'know the truth, and the truth will set you free', as we are told in another context (the Christian gospel). That we (that is, all humans) are often assumed to be freedom-loving truth-seekers indicates the intimately intertwined relationship—in much human experience, and particularly in education—of both the *ontological* and the *epistemological*, as we outlined above. The very natures of our being and of our knowing are, to use a neat technical term, 'mutually co-extensive and jointly exhaustive' (imagine a Venn diagram where the two circles map each other exactly, appearing as one). In this sense, *all education is emancipatory*: it strives to liberate (*educe* = to draw out) the potential in each of us. Our experience persists, but education can draw out its fruitfulness. So the 'whole person' as an ontological claim, in contrast to divisive dualisms, brings with it forceful epistemological implications. Simply, our 'ways of knowing' should be *holistic*.

▨ emancipatory education

▨ holism

For most of us, our interest in Education and in researching it is fired up by the expression and representation of 'whole person' experience as it is and as it might be articulated. For example, through Dewey's ideas but generalised beyond just children, or just adults, so that we can claim those three principles of 'better learning' for all humans. There are realities to be articulated, not a single reality (as a Given) to be presented. Few of us take a solely positivistic position on truth, at least in human behaviour. Objective description or analysis of human behaviour that will do for all time and remain true for all is neither possible nor realistic. (In Chapter 4, however, you will read of some hitherto unexplored possibilities for 'experimental' research in and through the arts and social sciences, as well as science.)

■ hermeneutics

You will probably come across the words *hermeneutics* and *hermeneutical* in your research reading; they are really just synonyms for 'interpretation' and 'interpretive'. We have reason to be grateful to Hans-Georg Gadamer, the originator of philosophical hermeneutics, which recognises that any interpretation is governed by our experience. Gadamer's pioneering 1960 work *Truth and Method* to a large extent opened up the field of research to notions of subjectivity and multiple interpretations—in fact to *phenomenology*. You will also certainly come across this word *phenomenology*

■ phenomenology

(and *phenomenological*), because it is really the dominant philosophical paradigm particularly for arts and humanities educators. It means, literally, 'study of the nature of a phenomenon', and it is further amplified below because it stems from a philosophical paradigm or perspective. As researchers, our descriptions and interpretations of any phenomenon depend on how that phenomenon forms part of the reality we have constructed for ourselves: a reality that is largely social and shared with all our community but, if we take a constructivist view of reality rather than a positivistic one, also has elements based in our own experience. The 'father of phenomenology' was the nineteenth-century German philosopher Edmund Husserl, and the term was really defined by Husserl's pupil, the existential philosopher Martin Heidegger—though how Heidegger reconciled what we describe below with his membership of the Nazi party is a mystery that has baffled historians and his biographers.

■ positioning

As we noted earlier, phenomenology is based in personal perceptions of experience and response. The language through which this is understood and communicated is a language drawn from a sensual base—it is 'felt', 'sensed', 'intuited', 'realised' and 'known'. In other words, it is acceptable for the researcher to speak personally—providing we acknowledge our positioning. The positioning and the language are manifested through questions such as, 'What does it feel like?' and 'How does it [that is, the phenomenon, such as 'pain'] present itself to you?' The knowledge is therefore understood through some sort of metaphor or culturally determined imagery. In recent years, metaphor, long banished by science as inexact, diverting and unknowable, has re-entered research as an important 'way of knowing'. Recent research into the biology and ecology of cognition—by scholars like biologist Maturana (Maturana and Favela 1987), anthropologist Gregory Bateson (1989) and systems theorist Fritjof Capra (1996)—validates the idea that we know through our body, our feelings or senses, and our social instincts, and not simply our intelligence,

and that we are not always fully conscious of this embodied knowing. Phrases like ▪ embodied knowing
'tacit knowledge' (Polanyi 1958) and 'flow' (Csikszentmihailyi 1990) are now part of our discourse in describing how we know and use that knowledge.

Further, this ontological focus implicates the epistemological: it suggests that our bodies do not simply respond to the world; rather they partly *constitute* the world, and in 'doing' so, literally generate understanding. This is now especially significant in arts and humanities education, and it should be equally the case in science and social science—because the body is something that carries experiences every waking moment. New work by neuroscientists such as Antonio Damasio—who writes books with titles like *The Feeling of What Happens: Body and Emotion in the Making of Consciousness* (1999) and *Self Comes to Mind: Constructing the Conscious Brain* (2010)—is providing exciting new insights into embodied, symbolic, artistic and holistic ways of knowing. ▪ embodied learning We need to know 'the skin we're in', or more academically, as the Sydney philosopher of education Marjorie O'Loughlin puts it in her *Embodiment and Education*:

> Dewey's understanding of human embodiment is clearly outlined in his account of the 'unity' of the human being. In this he provides a critique of the Cartesian subject, noting that the boundaries by which we have become accustomed to mark off the human being are very different from the energies and organisation of energies which make her a unified human being. Whereas we can grasp the boundaries—the skin—at a single moment, on the other hand we can grasp the unity only as something which occurs in a stretch of time. (2006, p. 15)

Research in Education is sustained, systematic enquiry, as we argued at the outset. Our human embodiment is the site of our (whole) experiences, which are themselves the raw material for such research, but it is the persistence of those experiences, and their sociocultural integrity—beyond any individual's 'skin' and the selfhood it encloses—that shapes educational activities, and, more substantially, our identities at and through our work (for example, as a professional practitioner: see Beckett 2010b; 2012b). Performances, exhibitions, writing and reading, indeed the conversations and challenges of life and work in and for themselves, all contribute as experiences to this lifelong, embodied learning, which is the researcher's best chance of constructing knowledge.

? REFLECTIVE QUESTIONS

1   Consider an example of friction ('rough ground') in your own practice context. How does reflection upon it generate a researchable issue?

2   Which approach, of the three outlined in this chapter, best moves your researchable issue forward?

3   Do arts-informed (or more specifically arts-based) experiences suggest ways you could design a research program around that issue?

WIDER READING

Beckett, D. and Hager, P. 2002. *Life, Work and Learning: Practice in Postmodernity.* Routledge, London. Chapters 1–3.

Davis, S.H. 2008. *Research and Practice in Education: The Search for Common Ground.* Rowman & Littlefield Education, Lanham, Maryland. Chapters 4 and 5.

Dodds, M. and Hart, S. (eds) 2001. *Doing Practitioner Research Differently.* Routledge, London.

Freebody, P. 2003. *Qualitative Research in Education: Interaction and Practice.* Sage, London. Chapters 1 and 2.

Singh, P. and McWilliam, E. (eds) 2001. *Designing Educational Research: Theories, Methods and Practices.* Post Pressed, Flaxton, Queensland.

METHODOLOGIES AND METHODS

4

☑ CHAPTER OBJECTIVES

After reading this chapter, you should be able to:

- distinguish between some main methodologies with clarity
- build on your preferred approach (from Chapter 3), with the selection of a robust methodology, containing some idea of the methods you could use to implement it
- develop confidence in your capacity to make research design judgments, so that your researchable issue (from Chapter 3) is rounded out.

This chapter provides a more detailed overview of some of the most frequently used methodologies in researching Education. We focus mainly but not exclusively on the qualitative, as there is greater diversity both of approach and the associated terminologies than in quantitative research—and rather fewer clear borders and precision. The methodologies have been arranged under the three main research paradigms that we described in Chapter 3: *descriptive and interpretive, change-oriented* and *blended* methodologies. There is much overlap, many confusing paths among the maze of methodologies, and even between these overarching paradigms. Researchers use various configurations and terminologies, and some are even fiercely territorial. This is no 'standard' map of the territory, just our ball of string to guide us through the labyrinth. Before we go further, we remind you of the need (expressed in Chapter 1) to become acquainted with the depth and range of all research methodologies. There are many well-regarded works of scholarship to guide you in this. We refer to some of these in Chapter 1, and in this chapter, but you will find many more in a comprehensive university library.

⬂ DESCRIPTIVE AND INTERPRETIVE RESEARCH

Ethnography

Ethnographic research has its origins in cultural anthropology; it derives from *ethno*, meaning 'people', and *graph*, 'a picture'. Ethnographers construct portraits of cultural life by studying an aspect of the social world 'intensively, intimately, and interactively' (Wolcott 1999, p. 288). Ethnographers describe, document and interpret human experiences *in situ* through fieldwork in a particular location, or within a community, for a prolonged period of time. Ethnographers collect and generate data through 'participant observation'—which means they look, listen, ask questions and interact with people within a social setting. The aim is to build an understanding over time of how a group of people construct and experience their world—to produce 'slice of life' accounts or, in Clifford Geertz's now standard term, 'thick descriptions' (1973).

▪ participant observation

▪ thick descriptions

Contemporary ethnographers view the world as socially constructed, with multiple, ever-changing realities. An ethnographic fieldworker is not a neutral, detached observer but an engaged co-participant who builds relationships with people within a social and political context. Collaboration, dialogue and negotiation characterise the interactions between an ethnographer and research participants. Educational ethnographers describe, interpret, analyse and represent the lived experiences of schools, classrooms and workplaces. When studying such settings an ethnographer tries to make a familiar context 'strange', that is, to see an activity or event in a fresh way and to respond to it with the heightened sense of a creative practitioner. In order to develop a holistic understanding of a setting like a classroom or a workplace, an ethnographer elicits and compares different types of data from a variety of sources. Researchers might explore participants' engagement in community workshops, or in school-based group projects, and describe and interpret the interconnected phases of planning, preparing, implementing, collaborating, socialising and reflecting.

▪ co-participant

▪ making the familiar strange

An understanding of a learning or community context emerges in a cumulative way throughout the interconnected phases of fieldwork, data collection and analysis, and writing. Data is generated from observations, interactions and open-ended interviews with students, teachers and other adults in the setting, as well as from videotaping, audio taping and photographing lessons and events. Ethnographic data includes observational field notes, descriptive narrative accounts and reflective and analytical notes, records and transcriptions of interviews, artefacts, documents, products of the project, students' writing, lesson plans and other texts. This data is analysed inductively, sometimes in collaboration with the participants, to elucidate the complex and multiple meanings and relationships that exist within communities like a classroom, a media production company or a local adult education group.

▪ fieldwork

▪ data collection

▪ inductive analysis

Ethnographer Kate wanted to investigate the artistic, educational and social impact of intercultural performance within a school setting (Donelan 2005). She studied the experiences of forty young people in a cross-cultural drama project led by an African artist-in-residence in a multicultural secondary school.

During her first phase of fieldwork, Kate collaborated with the African artist and a group of senior students who volunteered to be her 'co-researchers'. With their assistance she recorded and analysed the diverse experiences of middle and senior school students throughout the six-month performance project. The central performance text was a complex intercultural marriage: an African adaptation of the Greek Oedipus story, directed by an African teacher—artist, and performed by a multicultural Australian group of students. By making herself an assistant to the African teaching artist, Kate gained access to the varied responses of the participants as they interacted with each other and the text, resisted it at times, created, played with, shared, subverted, translated, embodied and performed these diverse intercultural performance elements. The ethnographic data also included interviews with young people, teachers and members of the broader school community; students' writing; photographs and longitudinal reflective data collected up to four years after the project. The ethnographic report was constructed into a narrative account of the difficulties, tensions, challenges and rewards of this ambitious intercultural drama and performance project within its school context. The researcher drew on a range of data to argue that kinaesthetic, playful, embodied and performative experiences are central to intercultural teaching and learning.

longitudinal data

In ethnography, the researcher is the chief research instrument. This role presents a number of challenges. An ethnographic interpretation of a workshop activity or a school or workplace event is inevitably selective, positioned and partial, framed by the educational, philosophical and ideological assumptions of the researcher. However, ethnographers try to balance their preconceptions by adopting an open-minded and critically reflexive approach throughout the study. Researchers need to remain aware of how they are constructing meaning during the phases of fieldwork, data analysis and writing, and to include a diversity of participants' words and viewpoints. An ethnographic account should demonstrate that interpretations have emerged as the study proceeds, that new questions have arisen and have been addressed, and that pre-existing understandings have been modified and challenged as data was collected and analysed. An ethnographic researcher attempts to construct a written text that is inclusive of the researcher's own analytical and emotional responses to the experiences, a report that engages readers in an unfolding narrative of educational and social events, and that suggests the characteristic qualities of the activity. Ethnographic texts are designed to illuminate and evoke the multiple perspectives of people within the social setting, to 'develop the story as it is experienced by participants' (Woods 1994, p. 311). Ethnographic texts should provide readers with a credible descriptive and interpretive account of the educational and cultural meanings emerging from the data, and the further questions generated by the study.

interpretations

multiple perspectives

Performance ethnography

■ embodied research

■ representation

A research approach that has become very popular recently among educational researchers in the arts, social science and health fields is *performance ethnography* (also called variously *performed ethnography*, *ethnographic performance* or simply *ethnodrama*). This was first mooted by anthropologists: looking for a way of keeping alive the very visceral and embodied experiences of human social behaviour that they investigate, they hit upon the idea of re-embodying it, re-creating and representing it through dramatic performance—turning the research report into theatre. This has been enthusiastically espoused by some ethnographers such as Norman Denzin (2003), and educators such as Johnny Saldaña (2005). Its special challenge is that we not only have to put up our artistry and research skills for scrutiny, but we have to marry them, without one harming the other. As ethnographers, we have a responsibility to report clearly and authentically what our witnesses or respondents have given us. In one way, re-creating them in performance helps this, because we can restore some of the real-life energy, visual and visceral impact of the original community. Interviews, dialogue and transcribed stories can spring back to life with the subtexts restored in full. On the other hand, from an audience point of view, it is not as simple as that. For a start, we need to identify our audience very clearly: insiders or outsiders? Is this a piece of reflexive documentation that we are offering back to the community of respondents (who know the background, and are looking for a new perspective, or reassurance and valuing of what they know)?

> A group of Norwegian researchers set out to find what makes their local soccer fan club tick. The researchers were all women, with no previous interest in football of any kind—not even in their famous local Rosenborg FC (Mette et al. 2002). They absorbed the culture, the stories, the atmosphere and the songs of the club sufficiently to perform their ethnodrama at a club evening, to an appreciative audience of insiders, who acknowledged the authenticity and celebrated their own identity.

Will there be outsiders to the situation (who need expositional background and an interesting story that they don't know, or to have their preconceptions addressed)?

> Another intrepid group, led by Linda and Barbara, set out to investigate internet sex and intimacy, which meant connecting in person as well as electronically with respondents, consumers and providers (Hassall and Hogan 2003). Their audiences, however, were fellow arts researchers, so they had to set the scene and establish connections between the audience and the subject. This was difficult as many audience members started out with very negative attitudes towards the subject (and subjects) of the study.

Obviously, the needs of insiders and outsiders are quite different, and we have an immediate structural and narrative problem when there is a mixture of both in the audience, as often happens.

Other tensions between the research and its performance are inevitable: all data collected in person and perhaps verbatim is not equally vivid or regarded as knowledge. The reporting that comes from systematic investigation is made by careful selection, editing and rearrangement of what is initially 'raw'. (This process of sifting by identifiable patterns into 'findings' is discussed later, especially in Chapter 8.) This poses an immediate threat to authenticity, and the 'truth' for the witnesses of such live or verbatim activities themselves. In addition, what if we are presented with the reverse case: some precious data absolutely essential for giving us insight into the participants or their community, but which they would prefer not to be aired in public? A research report can usually get round this by scrupulous attention to privacy and restricted circulation, but a public performance is quite a different matter. There are ways of circumventing some of these problems, and defusing the tensions, such as using the researchers' positioning as part of the performance, and using 'our story' as a narrative frame that is itself re-enacted. All these tensions and some of the ways of circumventing them are spelled out, with case study examples, in Ackroyd and O'Toole (2010).

tensions of performance research

authenticity

truth

researcher positioning

Case studies

As the use of this term in the preceding sentence indicates, case study is not, strictly speaking, a 'methodology', but rather a choice of what is to be studied: where we examine some phenomenon by identifying it, then observing and documenting a 'typical' or 'exemplary' instance of it. This means that the boundaries of the 'case' need very careful articulation. You could make a 'case' for an entire nation of people (Singaporeans), or a health population (smokers), or a school or a classroom, or even a single person, as we will see shortly. And you could systematically investigate any one of these as a 'case' of something interesting, and do it entirely by quantitative, that is to say, baldly experimental or positivist methods, and then analyse the data, looking for its special characteristics. Or you could do it entirely by qualitative methods, or by mixed methods. In the words of one of the doyens of case study, Robert Stake: 'case study is the study of the particularity of and complexity of a single case, coming to understand its activity within important circumstances' (1995, p. xi). There are a number of types of case study, but they all share these similarities of method. Yin (1989) put case studies on the methodological map, and since then, a diversity of ways to regard them has sprung up. Stake (2005, ch. 17) discusses three types: the *intrinsic* (the utterly ordinary, which we need to know more about); the *instrumental* (the possibly generalisable); and the *multiple*, or *collective* (more of a network of the instrumental, on several sites).

types of case study

This is where our cast-iron definitions start cracking. Even within these three types, a case study is a kind of 'shell' as it can be either a methodology or a method. It needs

■ case study variants   to be filled with content. So you can just declare your methodology as case study (and then fill it with methodical substance), or you can focus it as an *ethnographic case study*, or a *reflective practitioner case study*, and so on. These may be embedded in a *collective* type. It may also depend on whether the whole Research Question is to be investigated or answered by a case study, or just part of it.

■ teaching in Pakistan
> Wahid set out to provide a case study of teachers' professional evaluation and development in the Peshawar district, northern Pakistan, for his DEd thesis (Hussain 2008). On one hand, the 'bounds' of the case were geographical: the district is a government entity; on the other hand, the case was a careful selection of school staff who met culturally specific criteria: males, with extensive experience, in mainly secondary schools. Reflections—often candid—and ethnography sat adjacent in this research design, which aimed to get the 'stories' from diverse professional lives in a strife-torn part of the world.

Cases can be about specific individuals, about specific contexts or about a specific practice. A case study might even be utterly specific: of a single individual's practice—and even their professional identity.

■ multinational CEOs
> Jasmine didn't set out to do a case study, but her single-person fieldwork for her MEd thesis was based on a few extensive interviews with a CEO of a major multinational company (Cowen 2006). Through these narratives, she explored how the CEO's experiences contributed to his adult learning, and how such a 'tall poppy' was able to reach the heights from within his own resources. She contributed to mapping the reality behind many of the myths of 'lifelong learners'.

Or it could be multiple shorter cases that work together, such as:

■ food and hospitality
> Hilary explored how 'tacit' knowledge worked in food and hospitality industries in northern Victoria, revealing skill formation through observations and interviews with workers on assembly lines (Timma 2004). For this PhD, the limits of 'tick-and-flick' competency structures were shown in the richness of the accounts of decisions and flexibility shown by these workers in what are really three quite different industrial settings. Adult learning at work is articulated expressively through these productively diverse yet educationally convergent stories.

The purposes of case studies can be as varied as their context. Using a case study is appropriate in the case of sample individuals who the researcher believes are representative of wider categories. For example (all hypothetical):

■ representative case studies

- a nurse educator juggling the clinical, managerial and educational expectations her hospital context places upon her
- the corporate trainer stretched to meet performance indicators, but also committed to 'whole person' training
- first year teachers: balancing survival and growth.

This kind of *representative case study* is undertaken in the hope that it will naturalistically provide data and insights that might be generalisable across the whole category. A variant of this is the *bounded case*—something that is representative but also has boundaries:

■ bounded case studies

Just-in-time training, in many adults' workplaces, meets immediate learning needs, but should, if it is researched, be bounded by the explicit recognition that one context of immediacy will likely be very different from another context of immediacy. What's hot, here and now, will not be hot elsewhere!

Case studies can be *narrative*-based, where a story is told, as we noted with Jasmine's thesis on multinational CEOs (on page 52):

■ narrative case study

Getting the CEO's story down was intensive and also extensive. He responded to submitted semi-structured interviewing, and this was conducted both in London and also via email months later. As the depth of narrative reflection increased, Jasmine was able to assemble a conceptual construct to indicate how this 'case' varied from more ideological accounts of high-achieving 'lifelong learners'.

They can be *socially critical*, where the intention is to reveal or problematise some aspects of power relationships or constructions within society.

■ socially critical case studies

Gender relations in schools are often problematic, and teachers need to bear this in mind when planning classes. In this hypothetical example, Sandy explored, in one co-ed school 'case', whether boys' learning styles improved when they were engaged by visual materials (such as photographs), whereas girls were more comfortable with print-based texts. Small-group work and assessment task outcomes were drawn upon to make careful conclusions about the ways boys and girls relate to choices of teaching materials, in a shared school context. What does this mean for the way the school is run, and the way teaching is resourced and conducted?

■ case study
  limitation
■ non-generalisability
This catalogue of contexts may have made case study seem like a catch-all type of research, useful for any topic or site. But case study has one limitation—that you really cannot generalise from it, not from single or even multiple cases—which, if you recall, is sometimes one of the basic purposes of making research useful and transferable. In Joe Winston's words, 'a key tension at the heart of case study is the relationship between the uniqueness of its terms of reference and the generalisability of its results' (2006, p. 43).

The very limitation that you cannot generalise from a case study is actually a valuable asset in the study of many areas and subject disciplines in Education. As Leedy and Ormrod (2001, p. 149) point out, case studies are useful for 'learning more about a little known or poorly understood situation' and where 'the phenomenon under study is not readily distinguishable from its context' (Yin 2003, p. 4), which is very true of many community activities, and classroom ones for that matter. Literature, media and the arts actually provide potential research frameworks for investigating human behaviour. Fictional contexts can be very instructive: they offer safe creative spaces for exploring the nature of human experience, as we noted in Chapter 1, and will expand on later in this chapter. As John Carroll explains (1996), in dramatic role-based work we can see a framed context, and so in one sense, a *bounded case*, albeit a fictional one. Once 'the willing suspension of disbelief' is accomplished, the boundary-making devices of the arts—the screen, the stage, the frame, the binding of a book—allow the participants to respond with authenticity to the contrived world that has been established. Drama, dance and jazz music, for example, are by their very nature negotiated group art forms, and are, therefore, non-reproducible experiences. The participants create a unique set of social relationships. These become a single unit of experience capable of analysis and study. Because of the complexity of the interactions, the *whole* creative sequence needs to be studied.

■ arts-based case
  studies

Educational activities as case studies honour the agency of the participants and position them as experts rather than merely as a source of data for analysis. So case study data is useful when the researcher is interested in and deeply involved in the structures, processes and outcomes of a project. It is also useful when the researcher is able to interpret the nature of power structures and the interaction of the participants within them.

Historical research

An historical approach is quite a time-honoured form of research. The primary purpose of historical research can be descriptive or interpretive: a historical researcher can set out to record, to fill a gap in knowledge, to celebrate, to re-evaluate or to critique. Particular challenges may face those researchers who want to research history in education in current affairs, or in many areas of the arts and humanities. Organising play activities as part of flood relief, brainstorming creative ideas, parading in a street march, storytelling or singing in a choir can all be historically significant and collaborative community activities, which draw from many sources and appeal to our intellect, our sociability and our emotion. Their appeal lies in their sheer ephemerality—here today, gone tomorrow—a unique shared political, social and aesthetic experience among the makers, and sometimes shared with an audience. These qualities offer a challenge to the aspiring historian. How can we research and write history that captures the essence of these immediate experiences, or a cluster of experiences, and, indeed, why would we want to? By engaging our interests, however, those subject disciplines that deal in ephemera offer a responsive site for social and political change, and even activism. They are a cultural barometer. History, *presented* and, just as important, *re-presented* provides a broader understanding of cultural and educational contexts, offering the opportunity to understand how the myths and meanings that drive the culture or the educational system have developed.

- researching ephemera

- chronicling social change

- history as representation

The challenge is to find a way of constructing a history that offers not just factual information, but a sense of the unique social, personal and aesthetic experience. It may be helpful to see it as a jigsaw puzzle. Of course we can never fully reconstruct an ephemeral experience because we can never relive it, but we can try to construct a history by relying on multiple sources. This history might be communicated through interviews with participants, by recording and analysis, or even through the historical reconstruction of the actual event, happening or performance. The memory or the individual oral history record of the experience are as significant as the 'facts' relating to time, place, company and participants. That signals a note of caution: it is important to stress that history is always constructed, not absolute or unchallengeable. Histories are stories about the past, and reconstructing the past will involve elements of mythologising from the cultural, political and theoretical stances of both the historian and the informants.

- reconstructing the past

Usually, not all the jigsaw pieces are readily available. Information about past educational events often goes unrecorded, or is found in scraps from workshop notes, lesson plans or annotated assessments. Historians must become detectives, hunting out bits of information, selecting those that will assist in their construction of history and rejecting others. Once we have gathered the data we can turn to constructing our history through our interpretation of the material. Because education comprises such complex and responsive manifestations of human life, the investigation is complex and an interpretation may be always 'on hold'. This is particularly the case when dealing with the lives of the living, when the process of gathering material is never completed. Also, interpretation can be complicated by a smorgasbord of critical approaches and fashions, or even differences of ideology and culture among the researchers.

- interpreting sources

There are two kinds of information available to the historical researcher: secondary and primary source material. Secondary source material includes books written about the event or movement, including critical commentaries, biographies, histories and stories told about past activities and events by those who weren't there. Primary sources are those such as tapes and videos, and interviews with participants, which provide a first-hand insight into the experience being researched. Primary source material is rarely collected in a single archive. The researcher may need to tap many sources, public and private. A draft of a plan, a set of rough drawings, crudely annotated notes of a conversation or the like are essential primary sources for embryonic research, though

- secondary sources

- primary sources

not always reliable evidence. Consulting the marginal notes, interviews and scribbly journals of teachers or practitioners and their associates and intimates will certainly complicate the history, but may well round it out with reliability. A research subject's own original documentation can rarely be taken at face value, but must be read deeply and creatively; and sensitively and ethically, too—in the context of its own production.

In research in Education generally, it is sometimes difficult to differentiate between primary and secondary sources. Is the workplace and its policy context a site of primary sources? Well, clearly yes, as all sites are researchable, but it is easy to blur the primary/secondary distinction.

> For example, signs about English language skills courses on the walls of factories have to be 'read' as both primary sources (exemplifying equal opportunity policies, perhaps) along with the embedded question: how accessible are these signs to non-English-speaking workers? This latter question raises the notion of the secondary source: how do workers regard these signs (if at all)? And how can we tell?

The researcher has a responsibility to seek out and identify all the available sources of information, both primary and secondary, and also to cover the appropriate contextual background literature.

Philosophical and policy research

■ ideology

You may be familiar with Marx's frustration: 'Philosophers have only interpreted the world; the point is to change it!' He went on to do just that, as the history of the twentieth century shows. Yet in the world of research, there is a prominent place for sustained and systematic analysis and critique of concepts we often take for granted, and the ideologies that may underpin them. If you assume that the way we see the world is itself ideologically driven, you may take up policy studies as a form of research.

■ policy studies

The object of scrutiny would be various or particular plans and programs for legislative or governmental actions, which, in education, drive the provision and resourcing of, say, curricula or schooling or teaching. Critical policy studies apply a sceptical lens to policies, and researching these in that way may not require any empirical work—or, it may. Opinions and perceptions of policy initiatives and their enactments in organisations and practices would constitute empirical fieldwork, which, together with conceptual analyses, could generate comprehensive critique of, say, assessment policy in one school, or across a nation, or indeed the world. The current controversial status of 'high-stakes testing', such as NAPLAN, or the international PISA program, attracts many policy researchers because so much governmental, and therefore ideological, commitment to such testing provokes critique, which is the right atmosphere for vigorous research.

Closely related to policy research is philosophical research, which can also be undertaken completely conceptually (that is, without any fieldwork), or with some empirical component. Like policy research, the fieldwork would flesh out an analysis that was cogent and robust in its own right: in other words was logical, embedded in argument, and relied upon crucial earlier conceptual work to make some basic distinctions, and move beyond, or around them. For example, many criticisms of the distinction between schooling that provides for stratifications of students into 'technical' schools and 'high' schools (which was discussed in Chapter 3) start with arguing against the Cartesian duality of two substances (the Mind and the Body), upon which the privileging of high over technical schooling has been based. Currently, innovations such as the 'thoughtful classroom' (critical thinking in action) and 'mindfulness' (meta-reflection), and the new developmentalism called 'positive psychology', take a holistic approach to human learning, aligning well with the three 'lifespan experience' principles of better learning we set out in Chapter 3 (cf Beckett 2010a). Rather, philosophical critique of these could draw upon Aristotle, or Foucault, for example, to explore what practical virtues, professional communities or power relations were being implied or constructed in such educational innovations. For example, reconceptualising 'philosophy for children', which is a strongly established curriculum in several countries, can take research shape as a non-empirical thesis (Golding 2010), or as a blend of non-empirical and empirical research (Pietzner 2013). The philosophically oriented researcher is keen to advance critique that—through the force of argument alone (or with some empirical work)—establishes a better theorisation, or reasons for practices, than is taken for granted, or presently justified. Much the same outcome is the aim of policy research, although there the target would normally be a better prescription of policy in the area itself.

▦ philosophical
　studies

Other interpretive methodologies

A word that we come across more and more frequently in contemporary interpretive methodologies, including ethnography and case studies, is *rhizome* (noun) or *rhizomatic* (adjective), which refers to the kinds of findings or truths that the research is trying to investigate or uncover. For the horticulturally challenged, a rhizome is one of those plants (usually infuriating, like knot-grass; occasionally nice, like ginger) that does not have a single root, but survives, flourishes and spreads through a myriad of connecting underground rootlets or stems that throw up hundreds of apparently separate and distinct plants; when weeded and replanted, any of the bits can start off a whole new system. This has become a standard metaphor to describe the nature of cause and consequence in human group behaviour and motivation, or the kinds of teaching and learning models and strategies that form the subject of much educational research. The researcher recognises that the immediately identifiable characteristics of the topic under study are merely the visible bits of a vast series of connecting causes and consequences, which are feeding the behaviour or learning that can be seen. So the researcher, in phrasing the Research Question, usually (sensibly) realises that what the

▦ rhizome
▦ rhizomatic

research methodology trowel can uncover is not likely to be the be-all and end-all of the phenomenon, and recognises that any findings will be partial, subjectively experienced and in all probability as evanescent as the rootlets and shoots that germinate, flourish and wither within the rhizome.

The above are not the only methodologies that we come across within the interpretive paradigm, which by the end of this section can be seen to be something of a rhizome in itself! Ethnography, for instance, has a number of cousins—which may be a way of saying that there are a number of variants of phraseology, starting point and sometimes procedure. More recently, there have been a number of ethnographical approaches collectively known as *interpretive ethnographies* (Denzin 1997). Any of these can be easily accessed in the literature.

■ interpretive ethnographies

■ phenomenography

Another methodology still popular with educationalists is *phenomenography*. This word carries the added metaphor of delineating or mapping the phenomenon being researched—in practice, usually analysing learning techniques by asking the learners about them as the basis of the mapping. Among this methodology's adherents is the distinguished Swedish educator Ference Marton (1997). Phenomenography is not the same as *phenomenology*, which, as we mentioned in Chapter 3, is a construction of our own experiences, by each of us, within sociocultural contexts. Deep trawling through those experiences (such as the pain of childbirth) reveals how these are 'presented' to us. Holstein and Gubrium (2005) introduce interpretive practice and social action as research approaches by outlining their foundation in phenomenological innovation by Edmund Husserl (nineteenth-century philosophy) and Alfred Schutz (twentieth-century sociology): 'the scientific observer [*sic*] deals with how the social world is made meaningful. Her focus is on how members of the social world apprehend and act upon the objects of their experience as if they were things separate and distinct from themselves' (Holstein and Gubrium 2005, p. 485).

■ phenomenology

Some research methodologies, in this mapping and presentation exercise, use techniques of visual representation—photographs, sketches etc., and even sculpture and clay modelling—done by the researcher or participants, as key forms of data collection and analysis. These are frequently used in research that targets political action (Finley 2005). They are now becoming very popular in Australia in social science and humanities research (e.g. Moss 2008). One widely used method in education studies centred on visual arts data collection, particularly but not exclusively in arts subject areas, is *a/r/tography*. This acknowledges the threefold positioning within the research study of the artist (a), the researcher (r) and the teacher (t).

■ a/r/tography

■ ethnomethodology

Perhaps the most assertively phenomenological of all of them, *ethnomethodology*, is still widely used. Coined in the 1960s by the social researcher Harold Garfinkel (1967), ethnomethodology sets out to explore social interactions for their own sake and in their own unique context. It does not look at, for example, a school lesson or community theatre event as a manifestation of the sociological, cultural or psychological forces or the institutional background that those participants bring to it. As Peter Freebody (2003) and Kelly Freebody (2006) describe it, ethnomethodology differs from other sociological perspectives in that an ethnomethodologist considers social contexts and institutional relationships to be haphazard effects of grassroots interactions, as constructed by their members through their everyday experiences. Usually by concentrating on the talk, and studying how people mutually construct their talk, the researcher sets out to identify the unique structures and rules that shape the whole interaction. Because talk of one kind or another—often called 'discourse'—is a major feature of most learning situations, this methodology is often applied to classrooms.

One technique that has been used in ethnomethodology, which makes it quite attractive in the arts and the humanities in general, is for the researcher deliberately to set up some kind of surprise or abnormal intervention in the 'everyday interaction', in order to see how departure from the norm changes it, thus more effectively highlighting what *is* normal. That makes this research method similar to our second 'interventionist' paradigm, though the purpose of the ethnomethodologist's intervention is to establish and identify the norm, rather than to challenge or change it. Referring back to our discussion on power in Chapter 2, this disruptive intervention may also present a dilemma or even an ethical problem to the researchers. In order for the disruption to the norm to work as a catalyst, the research participants usually have to be unaware of it. This shifts the research intervention towards the confidence trick, and reduces the power, agency and control that the participants have in the situation—they are more genuinely 'subjects' of (and to) the research.

The research procedures that are commonly used in ethnomethodology to analyse the interactions, such as *member categorisation analysis* and *conversational analysis*, derive from older forms of linguistic and classroom analysis, and follow strict guidelines for the gathering, transcribing and analysis of talk, often focusing on the minute details. That, of course, presents both opportunities and challenges for education, since talk is usually only one of many layers of text happening in places like schools and classrooms, and may be much less articulate or readily understood than the paralanguage—the non-verbal signals and eye-contact. All discourse carries *meanings*!

At this point we need to warn readers that in the research world, the word 'discourse' means much more than just talk, and there is a whole research methodology, or series of linked methodologies, known collectively as *discourse analysis*. Carol Grbich (2004, p. 40) puts it well when she states that '[d]iscourses are the spoken or written practices or visual representations which characterise a topic, an era or a cultural practice. They dictate meaning and upon analysis may indicate the individuals or groups whose views have dominated at a particular point in time'.

This notion comes from Foucault (1972) and has been very influential in all sorts of research. Maggie Walter (2006, ch. 6) correctly draws its influence from the philosophical work of Ludwig Wittgenstein, who 'stressed the active component of language use, suggesting that the meaning of a word is inseparable from its practice … meaning is derived by reference to the wider social context and interaction' (p. 137). You analyse discourse by scrutinising language, which means anything that is textual and carries meanings: the most obvious linguistic forms are what is in print, or is heard or is spoken. It is worth noting that Foucault's famous example of discourse analysis is a plan for a building, Jeremy Bentham's circular prison, the Panopticon—of which

Margin notes:
- establishing the norm
- power in research
- member categorisation analysis
- conversational analysis
- discourse
- discourse analysis
- meaning in usage

the most famous local example is the convict prison at Port Arthur. In its central surveillance and wedge-shaped cells, it 'constructed' prisoners as acting as if they were under surveillance, even if it was not clear (to them) whether they were. They were thus complicit in their own behaviour modification.

> Julia, who we first met in Chapter 2, investigated a range of retail franchise operations, to show that immersion in training programs before and just after the shop is 'open for business' is better conceptualised through Foucault's 'knowledge-power' nexus (especially the Panopticon metaphor) (Camm 2012). This approach enables stronger self-directed learning for new franchisees which can be designed in to the training provided by franchisors.

■ reflexivity

Power and knowledge are *reflexive*; they work together to change how people see each other. It follows, according to Foucault, that all language is critical, in that, either explicitly or implicitly, it locates speakers and hearers each to the other. Over centuries, experiences like madness, or poverty, or success can be analysed discursively to show who is doing the defining of whom, in even talking or writing about such experiences. In recent times, social policy debates about being unemployed, or gay, or a woman in the corporate world have all been discursively deconstructed to reveal pejorative assumptions throughout. The demeaning police slang of a 'domestic' incident is now reconstructed as 'criminal assault' against, typically, women. Thus a Foucauldian discourse analysis will 'reveal the power relationships within any text … establish[ing] regimes of truth … that determine the acceptable formulations of problems and their solutions' (Walter 2006, p. 143).

Research as a whole does this, but doing it from within a critical discourse analysis heightens the reflexive nature of research. Literally 'power-full' questions include: Where is the researcher located, with what assumptions about herself and her ideology, and to what extent is she aware of this in her research design? How does this awareness change the way the research has been undertaken? Does it, ultimately, show how power is exercised through textual and linguistic forms and practices?

> In this hypothetical and fairly common example, Belinda wanted to show how senior school curriculum choices were shaped by the 'high-status' subjects leading to university entrance, and she did this by analysing the timetable construction: which subjects were grouped where, and what clashes were overcome or created, even before letters were sent home to parents and middle school students. In this way, teacher 'talk' about careers and study pathways was already located in preferential ways, and students' choices circumscribed by what was already preferred (by the school) because of the ways it was made available, first, in the very structure of timetabling.

There are, of course, other approaches to recording and analysing data that can and have been used in educational research, which are beyond the scope of this book to describe in detail. Moreover, particularly with holistic research methodologies, where they are mentioned in this book becomes somewhat arbitrary. Many people would classify *grounded theory* as a methodology. It has certainly been influential in the development of some of the methodologies we are describing. Grounded theory, first outlined by Glaser and Strauss (1967), is a qualitative research method that acknowledges that human reality is socially and symbolically constructed, constantly changing in relation to other facts of social life. It is guided by the assumption that people have patterns of experience, and when they share common circumstances they also share patterns of meaning and behaviour (Hutchinson 1988). Like many methodologies, or methods (and grounded theory can be both), it lends itself to social justice enquiry, because what is 'grounded' is 'a set of flexible analytical guidelines that enable researchers to focus their data collection and to build inductive middle-range theories' (Charmaz 2005, p. 507). In this way, ideals and values actually held by participants can be built into the data as it is aggregated and shaped. A little more on this method is found in Part B.

▦ grounded theory

It should be noted that most of the forms already described in detail (and the *blended* forms described in the section below) are *holistic*, that is, they are attempting to understand and encompass social behaviour and/or experience naturalistically. So we reaffirm the significance of whole-person, lifelong and experiential integrity in research, as we stated in Chapter 1. Underpinning all this is an assumption that humans are agents; we make decisions based on what we regard as within our power to enact, or outside our power to do so. The enacting is the manifestation of our agency, or autonomy. Lifelong learning assumes a robust sense of agency!

▦ human agency

Some researchers have attempted to use forms of analysis of either the wholeness of these human experiences or aspects of them. Two of these are notable and perhaps worth trying. *Semiotic analysis* attempts to codify *actions* into a system of *signs*, each of which denotes a particular and classifiable meaning. For thirty years, this has been a common form of analysis of written texts (e.g. Gottdiener et al. 2003), and it has been applied to the visual arts too (M. O'Toole 2011); there have even been efforts to categorise that most evanescent form of public communication, theatre, into a semiotic system, most famously by Keir Elam (1980) and Martin Esslin (1987).

▦ semiotic analysis

The problem in all this is that human experience is a complex text. It doesn't stand still to be examined, and the meanings are so many-layered and connotative as well as denotative that a static analysis system is hard put to delineate more than the outline. Hence, the increasing depiction of research projects as rhizomatic.

Another method well-hallowed in classroom research is *interaction analysis*, which looks at the spoken text of human interaction, such as a classroom, and breaks it up into brief segments for close analysis. This was popular in the 1970s (e.g. Flanders 1970), in a fairly simple form that, for instance, identified every three seconds who was speaking (very revealing—'progressive' teachers discovered with some shock that it was still nearly always themselves). More recently, it has been rediscovered by educational linguists, in

▦ interaction analysis

more sophisticated forms of interpretive analysis that can be applied to analysing at least the verbal or 'talk' components of most workplaces and classrooms. In the ongoing blurring of genres, some of these interpretive forms of analysis, such as 'conversation analysis' have become, as we have seen, the key instruments of ethnomethodology (Austin 2003).

⬂ CHANGE-ORIENTED METHODOLOGIES

Action research

■ change

■ problem solving

Action research is not about describing or interpreting what happens; it is about change and about using research to solve real problems. Carr and Kemmis (1986) are among the leading names here. In an update, McTaggart and Kemmis (2005, p. 559) remind the reader that action research covers participatory, classroom action, action learning, action science, soft systems and industrial action research. Action research has become very common in educational research and there are many useful readers applying the methodology to educational contexts. In *Research for Educators* (Kervin et al. 2006) action research occupies the last chapter since it 'captures the important elements of a systematic research process in the context of the everyday work of teachers … [these elements being] immediacy, utility and practicality' (p. 193). We agree! Action research, in one form or another, is becoming one of the most popular methodologies for arts and humanities education research, perhaps because such research does not just mirror reality but refracts it, to show us how reality might be if things were different; such research 're-presents' realities, rather than simply 'presenting' them. If you add to that the idealism of many educators, in both schools and community settings, there's a strong impetus to try to improve things by making them different.

■ participant research

■ real problems

■ cycles and spirals

Action research, almost by definition, is nearly always participant research—the researcher or research team is the one attempting to make the change. The origin of the methodology is usually ascribed to the psychologist Kurt Lewin in the 1940s, who insisted that research into human behaviour must take into account environmental factors, the situation and context. Moreover, he believed research should not just take place in the laboratory, but should deal with real problems in their settings. Lewin applied his research to the battlefield, the factory and the community—he sought practical answers in changing human behaviour to fix real problems (Lewin 1952). Human behaviour in social settings, whether in a factory or school, is always complex and not responsive to quick-fix solutions, so action research developed as a careful system of trial and error. These were initially conceptualised as a series of four-phase cycles but are now more three-dimensionally characterised as spirals incrementally progressing towards the goal. The research plan is based on first steps, not on aiming to fix the whole problem at one go. This can take account of the failure of any of the steps without throwing out a whole preconceived plan.

Action research is about change and intervention. Initially, the Research Question is usually conceptualised as a *problem to be solved*, or a *vision to be achieved*. The success of the action research is likely to be dependent on the thoroughness of the *pre-planning*, which must take into account all the relevant factors that can be identified. First, the problem or vision must be clearly delineated. Then the *context*—and that includes the researcher's position and role in it—needs to be described as fully as possible. All the *stakeholders* must be identified: those people who stand to benefit by the successful solution or achievement. The *negative stakeholders* must also be named—those who might feel they have something to lose, or who might feel threatened and try to spoil the research. At this point, it is quite a good idea to use that old standard of business practice, the SWOT analysis, trying to see all the *Strengths, Weaknesses, Opportunities* and *Threats* that the research will bring. Then a careful assessment must be made of the *resources* that can be brought to the project, and the *limitations* that will provide its boundaries, including the timelines. Finally, it is helpful to step back and try to get an overview of the *checks and balances* that need to be in place.

It is really at this point that the first spiral or cycle starts, with the *planning* phase, first with a detailed re-examination of the whole context, this time to determine where we might make a start in solving the problem or achieving the vision. That results in a first *action* phase, some single intervention to change the status quo that one may expect to be achievable (that's essential—not a grand and hopeful wish). This phase must be *observed* (and documented) and then as the next phase it must be *evaluated* and *reflected upon*. This naturally leads to a phase of *replanning* according to how the first step was evaluated, and a new cycle starts, devising the next intervening step … until the problem is solved, or the vision achieved—or time runs out!

Often the vision is not achieved, the problem not solved … at least, not as originally conceived at the start of the research. However, action research is never wasted. At the very least, some unproductive interventions have been ruled out. What invariably also happens is that by carrying out the cycle of interventions, new factors are revealed that change the way the Question was being looked at, and perhaps suggest a whole new Question, or a lateral approach to the problem itself.

Experimental research

As we noted in Chapter 2, empirical experimental research is the time-honoured, spectacularly successful traditional approach of science and medicine, of William of Occam (the fourteenth-century Franciscan who we introduced in Chapter 2, who wrote 'never multiply your entities unnecessarily'—which is the literal translation of the Latin phrase we quoted there, and in slang, 'K.I.S.S.') and his predecessors and successors. It assumes the 'facts' will determine the truths sought in research. Most weeks, on our television, we see the latest medical research news from laboratories addressing in this way fundamental health and science problems, with advances from which we will probably, and eventually, benefit. Such an approach to education is pilloried in the first chapter of Charles Dickens' *Hard Times*, where the schoolmaster Thomas Gradgrind beats the 'facts' into his charges.

Margin notes:
- problem
- vision
- pre-planning
- stakeholders
- SWOT analysis
- resources and limitations
- planning
- observation
- evaluation
- replanning
- positive outcomes
- empiricism

While no one wants children beaten (at all! ever!), this research approach is probably not used nearly enough in contemporary Australian educational research. There are a number of reasons for this. For the most part, experiments can only test limited (that is to say, isolatable) concepts, whereas education researchers are frequently attracted to the holistic, the live and the ambiguous. They are also fearful of the metrics and maths that experimentation usually entails, and the positivism (that is, the assumption of objective truth) it may seem to imply.

■ positivistic
approaches

Moreover, those education workers in the arts, humanities and social sciences rarely find themselves in an ethos or culture steeped in experimental research, as scientists, and also science teachers, who work in laboratories, invariably do. Education occurs in diverse and messy 'naturalistic' settings, not the contrived control-group. However, there are very good reasons for using experimental research, if not always as a methodology for its own sake, then as a method that may be linked with action research or case study. Experimental research provides different and important insights—especially when they translate into statistics that can be defended and used in improving our work or developing our advocacy.

■ measurement of
change

Basically, experimenters are looking to measure some sort of change in something or somebody, whether it be a state of health, an attitude, behaviour or a chemical composition. In education, we may want to be the cause of change in learner behaviour, change in the level of knowledge and change in understanding of issues. Corporate training, for example, comes from within a time-hallowed behaviourist approach to learning: if training is to make a difference, then outcomes must be measurable, and the kind of productivity that trained and retrained workers need to show must contribute to the 'bottom line' of the organisation. In such contexts, human resource professionals and other adult learning experts are, not surprisingly, centrally concerned with measuring how learning, through training, makes that sort of difference, not just to individuals at work, but also to their employer's viability in the market.

Shane was in charge of a 600-strong industrial workforce for a major car manufacturer (Johnston 2007). He researched how training on the factory floor was best designed so that multiskilled teams could maintain a productive 'just-in-time' manufacturing environment while handling, within their teams, the various quality issues that inevitably arise in complex manufacturing. Some of these were what to do when a machine broke down, if workers couldn't speak sufficient English to read safety and maintenance manuals, and if staff turnover (possibly due to job dissatisfaction) generated downtime spent on induction of new staff. He came up with a training design that focused on workers' interpersonal satisfactions as the core of a workforce training plan based on 'whole-person' learning experiences at work, not merely 'hands-on' behavioural competencies.

The holistic methods of research we described in the previous section help us to understand our contexts in all their complexity: how others think or view the world. They may also help us to develop materials and approaches to improve our professional effectiveness. However, there does come a time when we want to be able to measure some particular aspect of the effectiveness of an approach or method in a way that goes beyond the subjective and negotiable. For instance, we might want to try to garner further evidence to back up what seems, from our qualitative and anecdotal data, to be happening, but minus some of the *variables* that make it hard to prove. Alternatively, ▓ removing variables we might want to know whether something that seemed to work in our own classroom could also work throughout a state system. Once large numbers are involved then statistics and experimental designs are very useful tools.

In an experiment we start with just such a *hypothesis*, which we then test. A hypothesis ▓ hypothesis must be tested not just for success, but against failure, otherwise it will remain just a statement of faith. For instance:

> Hypothesis: I believe that Year 7 students who have had a year of integrated curriculum will achieve higher scores on a standardised literacy test than students who have not.

This hypothesis is the kind of claim that has been made for years as to why certain curricular changes are desirable. The hypothesis might (this example is hypothetical) have emerged out of our own observations as acute and reflective teachers; or it could have emerged from a case study or qualitative action research project, and have some anecdotal evidence to back it up. We may even have some preliminary statistics to corroborate it.

> 'My' Year 7s for the first time this year had five hours of 'integrated curriculum' each week, and I see that they have done exceptionally well on the standardised literacy test held at the end of semester. When they were interviewed, a large number of the students ascribed their improvement to the pleasure they got from these classes, and the way it increased their motivation for writing, such as fiction (historical 'diaries') and protest letters to fictional councils. Let's demand that the Principal gives all the Year 7 classes five hours of 'integrated studies' of this kind every week—and in fact every school in the state should follow suit.

So far so good and up to a point, convincing, but the Principal and the state curriculum body, quite properly, would still question this hypothesis, particularly as it would make massive resource demands and squeezes on other people. What they would certainly question is the *variables* that 'I' had not definitively excluded. In any ▓ variables experiment there are two kinds of information that must be identified and taken

■ uncontrollable
    variables

■ controllable
    variables

into account. One set, the *uncontrollable* or *independent variables*, is usually what the researcher is looking to measure. The other set, the *controllable* or *dependent variables*, are already there and/or in the hands of the researcher—the researcher must seek to have control over them, either by excluding them (making sure they don't apply in this experimental situation), or by taking account of them some other way.

Let's continue the hypothetical case.

> Perhaps the class is a more literate class than usual, for some demographic reason such as a shift in the school admissions or a higher socio-economic influx from a new housing estate built in the area. Perhaps it's a class that has had exceptional teachers in the years before me. Perhaps I am the exceptional teacher, and the students are just responding to me. Perhaps the results are better merely because the 'integrated study' itself has given them much more practice in writing and in a range of written genres. Perhaps it's that mysterious element known as the class chemistry—or collective sense of communal success or failure—that teachers know so well. Perhaps too, in the interviews, they want to tell me what I want to hear, since we all enjoy our work ...

Can we possibly negate some of these variables, so that we can reinforce and support some of our qualitative inferences about exactly what it is in the curriculum work that has made this surprising difference?

■ control groups

Experimental research would be the logical next step, and the most obvious kind is the controlled experiment, rather like in medicine, where in testing a new drug an *experimental group* of patients is given the drug, and an equal *control group* given a placebo, and the results compared.

> When we compare the literacy test results of students who do 'integrated' humanities/social science classes with those who don't, we need to build in controls that get rid of some of those variables. Next year, let's give my Year 7s to another teacher, who is also prepared to use this timetabled block for five hours a week, and compare the literacy results with those of a colleague who shuns it. (Not necessarily a recipe for staffroom popularity, especially if results support our hypothesis, but a useful measure that takes the personal element out of the equation and establishes some comparability.) Better still, we can pick a sample of students in each class with similar literacy levels and cultural and socio-economic profiles, and compare their literacy results after the experiment.

■ statistics

In one sense, the larger the numbers the better, as they make the statistics more versatile when identifying the key variables, because they identify more obviously the 'outlier' and the central factors impacting on the phenomenon under scrutiny. We will give a very brief 'methods' explanation of this use of statistics in Chapter 7.

> For instance, we might choose a number of classes from a diverse range of socio-economic and geographical environments to do the 'integrated' work, and compare them with an equal number of *control group* classes from the same locations who do not do that work. Moreover, we need to make sure the *experimental* classes and the *control* classes both get a similar range of teachers in terms of experience, successful results, teaching techniques and so on. We must also monitor the work carefully to ensure that the 'integrated' classes do get their five hours every week, and the control classes do *not* get any, but that otherwise they get virtually identical teaching (quite hard to police, given the complexities of school timetables and staffing, and the flexibility teachers have to make their own pedagogy and lesson plans).

We might also remove the personal factor almost completely by *double blind* testing. In medicine, tests are routinely double blinded, so neither the researchers nor the patients know which is which (the researchers so that they cannot consciously or unconsciously bias the findings or drop leading hints to the patients, the patients so that psychosomatic improvement or self-delusory reporting cannot affect their symptoms).

▥ double blind

> Therefore, it would help reliability of the test if neither the teachers nor the students knew there was any special scrutiny of the work, so that neither could be unconsciously influenced to make a 'special effort'. However, that would entail covert observation, which is ethically questionable and would be hard to persuade ethics committees to permit.

By this time, alarm bells may be ringing for many readers, especially about the practicability of such a grand experiment. So, large numbers do not necessarily guarantee better results.

▥ size and practicability

> Are there so many Year 7 teachers around who are able and permitted to use so much 'integrated' work when their colleagues don't? Can we guarantee that all, or a significant proportion, of the paired classes will not have teacher changes, or that the experimental classes will have a year's uninterrupted teaching of weekly 'integrated studies', and the control classes will not have this (e.g. from a student teacher or an enterprising relieving teacher)?

Experimental research, large or small, therefore brings no guarantee of foolproof results, and no absolutes. It is up to the researcher to decide whether to persevere with this major experiment (whose results are likely to carry considerable weight, but where controlling the variables is harder), or drop back down to the level of the five classes per week (in 'my' own school we do not have control over so many variables, but those

■ results

■ judgment

we can control are easier to control). Whichever we choose, we have—as with any form of research—to interpret the results, and use our professional knowledge and experience and our shrewdness of perception. In the case of experimental research, we bring our judgment to assess what variables have been effectively excluded, and our perception to identify the variables that we might not have taken into account in the original design, and those new ones that have arisen during the experiment. We can still end up with some useful results and new insights.

Design experiments

■ holistic experiments

■ refining theory and practice

Design experiment, the term coined by Allan Collins in 1992, or *design-based research*, is a newish methodology that is gaining contemporary currency in educational research. It derives from the experimental processes used in the engineering sciences and has developed as a way to carry out research that aims to test and refine educational designs based on principles derived from prior research. Though called an 'experiment', this is a closer cousin of action research than of traditional experimental research—for one thing, it is naturalistic and holistic. Perhaps it is really just another way of categorising and defining action research, but its antecedents in practical science help to give it a clarity that can be useful to the educational researcher. The research tests hypotheses and generates frameworks, and so aims to result in the production of models of practice, teaching artefacts, and theories of learning and teaching. The research thus has the dual goals of refining both theory and practice.

The stages of a design experiment involve:

- scanning the field, including both the specific context as well as documentation of similar studies
- setting a key conceptual goal
- designing an intervention, mapping the conceptual journey for researchers, teachers and students
- implementing the intervention, 'perturbing' the field
- assessing, refining, iterating, considering the learning trajectories; identifying indicators, honing tasks
- developing products and generating reports.

■ context significance

■ contingency

Design experiments are generally large-scale, long-term and take place in naturalistic settings, focusing on understanding the messiness of real-world practice. The *context* is central to the study, rather than being regarded as an unavoidable variable: drawing on ethnographic methods, the context is richly delineated. In many workplaces, such as schools, the researchers and staff collaborate as co-researchers, often with 'expert' input by a leading academic or practitioner in the field. Therefore, the studies remain open to the behaviours and the complexity of the current context—in other words, the raw material in design research is inescapably contingent: one action begets the next, and so on, often in unpredictable (and perhaps unrepeatable) ways (Kelly 2004, p. 135). Participant actions and input require frequent and ongoing discussion about how to proceed. Formative and progressive assessment and intervention strategies focus on instructional methods and student artefacts to create and refine theory. Thus the 'end-users' contribute to the research. Moreover, not only is the designed artefact (teaching materials, model of practice, etc.) shared, but rich descriptions of the specific context explicate the guiding and emerging theory. The research can generate evidence-based claims about learning that may be transferable to similar contexts and have the potential to produce products, programs and theory that become validated through their use and refinement during the research process.

↘ BLENDED METHODOLOGIES—FOR DESCRIPTION, INTERPRETATION AND ONGOING CHANGE

Reflective practitioner case study

Reflective practitioner case study is one of those methods where what we do merges seamlessly into how we research. In one sense a logical and rich extension of Kurt Lewin's ideas, Donald Schön's (1983) phrase 'the reflective practitioner' has become a commonly agreed ideal of practice in many professional contexts including contemporary education. We have drawn attention to this throughout Chapter 2. Briefly, Schön also articulated and formalised reflective practice as a research methodology (re-badged 'reflective practitioner case study'), centred on the personal, contextualised case study of the researcher/practitioner, without the need for the external 'expert' intervening. The method rejects the traditional social sciences' outside-in approach to researching professional contexts—which Schön dubbed 'technical rationality'—in favour of a scrutiny of practice that involves the practitioner's own construction of meaning, purpose and significance in his or her practice, often through narratives and critical journals.

    In education, for instance (as it happens, not among the professions that Schön principally chose to scrutinise), it means starting with 'me', the teacher. I observe myself to refine my own perceptions of what is happening in my classroom, how I am dealing with it, and what the problems are that I perceive may need addressing—rather than looking at the problems of a teacher or a classroom from outside, with a view to solving them. For this, as Philip Taylor (1996, pp. 29–30), drawing on Schön's famous terminology, makes clear the teacher needs not just reflection on action, as might be used by the action researcher, but reflection in action in 'my' understanding of my own context (both explicit and tacit), and how I can use this to reshape my own and then others' behaviour. Schön observes that when he does turn his attention to education, 'this process of reflection-in-action … not only applies knowledge but generates knowledge' (1995); he also noted acerbically how much of schooling tends to actively inhibit reflection-in-action, for both teachers and students.

■ reflective practice

■ scrutiny of practice

■ reflection on action

■ reflection-in-action

Reflective practitioner research is already, and should be, a popular approach by educators across all disciplines, both in school and non-school settings, such as in the corporate world. Taylor, an advocate of the method, urges: 'for … educators to ignore reflective practitioner design is to remain ignorant to [*sic*] the kind of artistic processes that are the lifeblood of our work' (1996, p. 27). This stresses a fact that many of us take for granted through the nature of our work—and others among us equally blithely overlook—that, as well as teaching skills and processes, we are also constantly engaged in artistic processes and decisions. Schön emphasises the 'artistry of practice', by which he means the expertise that seems to make itself invisible, so effortless does it appear. Sports players, mathematicians and musicians can seem to show this: interrupting them in what Csikszentmihailyi (1990) calls 'flow' would destroy the very expertise we applaud. To analyse this phenomenon, as researchers, is therefore very difficult, as the unit of analysis is the 'performance' of the game, the play, the surgery, the lesson, the closing legal argument and so on. To fragment this professional artistry-on-display, as researchers, is to lose it! Yet real, powerful expertise is apparent. Knowledge claims are made as a result of this artistry. Professional expertise is often built around this practice ('I just knew what to do next …').

This 'artistry' in *performance* perhaps gives the claims of those educators who privilege pedagogy (that is, performance) an edge over those colleagues whose grasp of *content* is the primary focus of their practice. But that is itself an assertion that would need to be tested by research such as reflective practitioner research. Moreover, because the pedagogy of professionals' performance, in this new era of lifelong learning, is itself still new (and therefore looks 'low status', or a bit flaky …)—and the physical and spatial demands alone entail considerable variation from the educational and curricular models that teachers and trainers learnt from and still use—many new professionals have learnt, as a matter of survival, to be constantly reflective about their practice. After all, the obverse of expert practice is 'malpractice', and who needs that?

Most Significant Change and Activity Theory

There is a cluster of related methodologies that take the basic principle of the reflective practitioner case study one step further. *Most Significant Change* (MSC), an increasingly popular methodology, sounds as if it belongs in the previous section, and like its close relative, *Activity Theory*, the expectation of change is central. MSC is a system of evaluation and monitoring of interventions for change and improvement in education and similar fields, involving the participants in dialogue and narrative. It was devised and named by Rick Davies in the 1990s to define his own work in rural development in Bangladesh: as a dialogical story-based technique to facilitate program improvement (Davies and Dart 2005). It is used in education and training contexts, as a form of corporate group analysis and professional development, as much as an individual research methodology that involves collecting and analysing participants' stories and their own commentaries on them. At the time of writing, the South Australian Education Department was

Margin notes:
- flow
- artistry in performance
- evaluation of change
- corporate group analysis

using MSC for its corporate training program (South Australian DECD 2012). However, MSC is also finding favour with researchers intending to implement some change or improvement, and looking for a participant-centred method of finding out whether it is working or not.

> Richard applied MSC in a media education project in a male high-security prison, where a high proportion of the inmates had severe literacy problems (Jones 2006). He introduced cameras to the prisoners—giving them instruction manuals but no training—and invited the prisoners to document either their stories or aspects of their lives. The prisoners quickly mastered advanced techniques of art photography—firstly having to master the manuals—and then produced artistic photographs and the contextual narratives to explain and support them. Their literacy levels were monitored, and in an unexpected spin-off, their artworks were exhibited.

Activity Theory emerged from the work of revolutionary Soviet applied psychologists of the 1920s and 1930s who recognised that human behaviour is dynamic and does not stop still to be examined. In short, Activity Theory is a way of observing and categorising personal and social activity as it happened. Its contemporary refinement, Cultural Historical Activity Theory (CHAT), is used in social sciences, and is increasingly attractive to researchers in education, as it derives from the work of the educational theorist Lev Vygotsky (e.g. 1978). CHAT starts from the premise that learning is socially constructed, and that knowledge, learning and activity are inseparable. CHAT also uses other educational favourites from Vygotsky, such as the notion of scaffolding learning and the Zone of Proximal Development (e.g. Engestrom 2003). It provides a more formal model (than MSC) of analysis of human behaviour and response to changes. It looks to identify the successful collective transformation of a community through mapping the social, cultural and historical aspects of its activities—including specifically designed interventions and initiatives—such as curriculum reform or pedagogical innovations.

categorising social activity

analysing response to change

> Sue and Angelina are embarking on a project using CHAT to research the effectiveness of a new pedagogical framework for sustainability education (Davis and Ambrosetti 2012). To help young people care about the impact of their actions on human and environmental eco-systems, they are trialling a pedagogy that brings together Vygotsky's dimensions of learning, activity and knowledge, through utilising arts-based environmental education strategies and digital technology. They are using CHAT to research both the learning outcomes for the students, and the impact, if any, of that learning.

Narrative enquiry

The reader may have noted that the word *narrative* and the idea of *stories* and their analysis occurs in the blended methodologies section. However, it may be helpful to consider narrative as a discrete methodology, as it can really embody the whole research process from start to finish. In the last thirty years, there has been a burst of scholarly interest in narrative, from a wide range of fields of scholarship. In a comprehensive update, Susan Chase (2005, p. 651) notes that 'narrative inquiry in the social science is flourishing … [as] an amalgam of interdisciplinary analytic lens, diverse disciplinary approaches, and both traditional and innovative methods—all revolving around an interest in biographical particulars as narrated by the one who lives them'.

▓ narratology

▓ virtual narrative

There are the literary studies that have led to 'narratology', for instance. There is a current rash of scholarship on the internet on virtual narrative (when we Googled the two words 'narrative + research', we got over 60 000 000 hits, of which several of the first ones listed were related to education). Narrative has also impacted on fields as diverse as social psychology and philosophy ('storying ourselves', how humans construct our personal identity and our social reality as a series of narratives), eloquently articulated by the philosopher Alasdair Macintyre:

> If the narrative of our individual lives is to continue intelligibly—and either type
> of narrative can fall into unintelligibility—it is always the case both that there
> are constraints on how the story can continue *and* that within those constraints
> there are indefinitely many ways in which it can continue. (1982, pp. 200–1)

That interest has flowed into studies of education and of language, with some distinguished educational and linguistic scholars, such as Harold Rosen. The conceptualisation of teaching as narrative then flows into research as another natural sequel to reflective practitioner research, which perhaps adds an extra dimension. Certainly narrative enquiry is becoming very popular. However, for educational practitioners who deal in narrative as *reflective practitioners* or *MSC* researchers, or using *arts-informed enquiry* (see later this chapter), in all of which narrative can be part of their core business, the distinctions between these research forms as discrete methodologies can become a little blurred—there are so many synergies between them; the rhizome factor again. It's all about the stories—and their conscious construction.

The form has, however, been delineated with a number of distinguishing characteristics and controls, most notably through the work of Jean Clandinin and Michael Connelly (2000), who note that the form of narrative enquiry embodies both the phenomenon under study and the research method. This is because the narrative that the researcher constructs as both method and report also comprises recounting the full historical and social context of the research, and also the researcher's own position.

▓ voice

▓ multiple selves

▓ researcher positioning

For this they use the metaphor of 'voice' and the concept of 'multiple "I"s', demanding that researchers identify and distinguish the various relevant roles we are playing—in the case of school-based and also in community-based research, perhaps—researcher, teacher, parent, critic, etc. This forces researchers to be honest about our own positioning in relation to the research site, ideologically, for instance.

Clandinin and Connelly also identified that in research into personal experience the narrative is bound to be simultaneously focused in a number of directions, which they condensed, logically, into the notion of a three-dimensional enquiry space. These dimensions are *inward* into the *internal conditions*—feelings, hopes, moral dispositions, etc.; *outward* to the *existential conditions*, paying attention to the wider environment and social context; *backward and forward* to acknowledge the *temporality of experience*, the historical conditions and the intentions of the researcher and researched.

▨ three-dimensional enquiry

> Gillian's primary school students were all doing classroom music. Many students had come from overseas (Howell 2009) and had suffered war experiences in the Horn of Africa. Initially, the students found the freedom of classroom composition very threatening. But as they were allowed to assume different identities, with the aid of photographs of others, and through various instrumental forms (e.g. percussion, wind), they took delight in simple performances and eventually 'owned' a classroom production celebrating peace and growth.

Arts-informed enquiry

This is where we invite the scientists and social scientists among our readers to take a deep breath and dive into waters that you may have previously regarded as alien. You too can learn to swim and achieve satisfaction and achievement here at the opposite end of the methodology spectrum from conventional scientific research. Just as scientific and statistical methods can provide valuable knowledge about the nature of learning in music or the effect of an arts-rich curriculum and pedagogy, so *arts-informed enquiry* can use as its raw material the science lesson, the geography hypothesis, the second language learning practice, just as naturally. It's all a matter of how you conceptualise and then represent what you do, by adopting forms that have been designed to investigate and depict human behaviour: the metaphorical and representational forms we call 'the arts'. This is, one way or another, the project of all artists as well as all of us educational researchers. How can we keep afloat in these waters? There are two ways of using arts-informed enquiry: as a complete methodology, or as a method within another form. For example, within ethnography or action research, either where the researcher is a central part of the research or the research participants can be persuaded to use art-making for their own purposes—as has been alluded to earlier in a/r/tography. Further development of this, as a method, can be found in Finley (2005).

▨ art-making in research

The use of the arts in educational enquiry is a relatively new phenomenon in Australia. While in the last ten years it has had a significant impact, this has not been without some controversy. As with other advances in new research methodologies in education, there have been struggles with research conservatives who have narrow views about what constitutes 'real' educational research. In recent years the use of the arts has had considerable support from arts-sympathetic education philosophers such

■ subjectivity

■ metaphor

■ poetry

as Laurel Richardson (1997) and Tom Barone (2001). Arts-informed enquiry not only acknowledges, but actively privileges, the subjective dimension in the research. This allows the researcher to contemplate an aspect of the research context aesthetically as well as analytically, constructively as well as reductively. The researcher can scrutinise it through the lens of metaphor as well as literally. Arts-informed-enquiry can fulfil much the same function as poetry—in the words of that old arts-informed researcher William Wordsworth: as 'emotion recollected in tranquillity'. The data-gathering may itself take the form of poetry:

> Tracey was investigating gender-specific behaviour in schools through an ethnographic study of an all-boys class and their female teacher. In her own words:
>
> Honouring the voices of participants in any case study research is paramount. While field notes serve a necessary task of providing the researcher with reflective insight into the everyday 'happenings' in the classroom, it is the data provided by the participants themselves, vital dialogue that serves to illuminate their 'stance' and 'voice', that gives the researcher substantial clarity and understanding for analysis and synthesis. It was the poetry that participants wrote for me during my research time in the classrooms that proved most enlightening, such as a long poetic reflection from Year 12 boys. It was written collectively and was one of the important pieces of data I collected about attitudes to being in an all-boy classroom. (Sanders 2003)

■ aesthetic refraction

Another of the simple forms of arts-informed enquiry is an extension of narrative enquiry, where the stories of the research participants are given an aesthetic dimension that acts as a kind of refractive mirror alongside standard data analysis, to provide different kinds of insight into the subjectivities of the situation.

> In the case of Chris, the aesthetic component was a fictionalised vignette based on her own responses to what she was observing in the research site, and in fact to distance herself, as she was the participant researcher and reflective practitioner. In her own words:
>
> I chose to write about the fieldwork (a community arts project based in a school) in the form of a novella. The novella reflected the chronology of the project, encapsulated key events and suggested multiple perspectives on these events, as participants were transformed into characters in the narrative. The engagement with a literary text offered the opportunity to explore the place, the people, the absences, silences and contradictions of the field from a distance. By deliberately constructing Pip, a third-person identity for the community artist/researcher, I was better able to see and understand my place within the constellation of events that surrounded the making of the arts project. I could explore possible interpretations of the impact of the community artist on the school and the school on the community artist.

Pip: lunchtime

Lunchtime at Belbrook Primary School. The children run from classrooms, lunch downed in record time while sitting at their desks with teachers looking on. Lotte is on playground duty in the quadrangle. Andrea is heading for the slope, a preppie on each hand. … There are games to be played, holes to be dug, buckets to be filled, and so little time. … Pip's passage through the playground is noted. The Grade 6 boys fly down from the other end of the basketball court to bombard her with questions about their play. Can they use their skateboards and their bikes? Phillip leaps down from the basketball court to the walkway in a single bound, almost collecting Pip and her bag with him. She laughs and Phillip bounds away with Jonas in pursuit. As she moves on, Evie, the new girl in Prep, rushes over for a hug, followed by Peter, the Grade Two boy who wants to be the Principal in their play. With a quick word to each of them, Pip extricates herself and continues on her way.

'Hi Pip. Have we got drama today, Pip?'

'Where are you going, Pip?'

'Look what we found down the slope, Pip. Cicada shells.'

'Hey Pip, can I have a good part in the play? When is it going to be ready?'

'Are you Max's mum? How come you haven't got the same name?'

'Are we going to play that blindfold game again, Pip? That was good.'

'See ya Pip. See ya tomorrow.' (Sinclair 2005)

As Robyn Ewing and David Smith (2004) observe, research has now extended to using poetry, painting, sculpture, readers' theatre (really, yet another form of ethnographic performance), even quilting and collage to theorise researchers' personal and professional lives, to interpret educational experiences, to better understand selves and improve professional practice in education. In Diamond and Mullen's words, this has enabled the location of 'new epiphanies within texts and people's lives' (1999, p. 22) because it has created different dimensions to traditional understandings. Arts-informed enquiry as a research strategy can provide a balance between rigour and creativity, imagery and ▦ rigour and creativity accuracy, the individual and the collective. Two examples provided by Robyn Ewing, involving the creation of literature and painting, illustrate some of the possibilities:

> To explore how one child with specific learning difficulties and his mother, a classroom teacher and special needs teacher, experienced the dilemmas raised by his being different, the researcher Anne wrote narratives derived from in-depth interviews with each participant and then constructed a fictitious meeting of all four, deliberately bringing the voices of the different participants together (O'Donoghue 1999). She pointed out that the voices of the parent, child and classroom teacher are rarely heard in the special education debate.

A current research project is a self-study addressing identity, belonging and isolation, as a second-generation Hungarian immigrant growing up in New South Wales, Australia (Cutcher 2004). Alexandra created a portfolio of representations based on the data she collected through extensive interviews with her parents, analysis of her own memorabilia and a visit to Hungary, diary monologues enhanced with visual artefacts from the lives of the participants, block prints and portraits of the participants, a series of paintings that deal with the various themes that have emerged, poetry concerned with the themes and a memoir novel.

Ewing writes:

> These art forms express for me profound emotional truths. If we are to embrace our humanity and validate the lived historical experiences of individuals then we must embrace this subjectivity as knowledge, as emotional, intuitive intelligences in the understanding and meaning making of our lives. There will never be an absolutely true representation of a life or an experience. Thus the authenticity of meaning is what I strive for, that I have the essence of what has been shared and captured. (2006)

Arts-based enquiry

■ artwork

A more ambitious approach is to use *arts-based enquiry*, where all the research takes the form of a custom-made artwork. We have already mentioned performance ethnography, which is probably the most widely used form of arts-based enquiry. Another brave approach for the researcher confident in their command of the aesthetic is to create a

■ exegesis

free-standing artwork, and an accompanying critical exegesis. This might chronicle how the process was achieved, the way the content and form developed and their relationship, or the particular structural or contextual problems that the artist-researcher faced.

Tony came to arts-based enquiry quite apprehensively, from his extensive background of quantitative research. He describes the interplay of creative and academic processes in what turned out to be an appropriate balance for him in his PhD thesis:

I decided to write an autobiographical monodrama. I felt that the artwork itself was the contribution to knowledge, and the exegesis the supporting evidence. The first year was spent collecting data from both reading and primary sources. The second year saw the bulk of the play written, where my supervisor took on more the role of a dramaturge. I struggled with the concept of an exegesis until my supervisor suggested that we could have a three-part exegesis. In the Generic Exegesis I outlined the background literature that informed my choices as a playwright. The Process Exegesis detailed the process that I went through in the writing, directing and performing of the play. The Critical Exegesis considered the responses to the work of art as it was written and then after it was performed. It included reports of interviews, and the results of an audience survey. In the end, it was accepted by my examiners that the new knowledge came both from the work of art, which was unique, and from the findings in the exegeses. (Millett 2002)

If you are attracted by art's charms, be careful. There are a number of issues regarding arts-based enquiry that continue to be debated. These include:

issues for arts-based research

- What are the canons of arts-based enquiry and by what criteria do we judge an effective example?
  Directly related to this question:

- Who should be the judges? Who should develop the criteria to assess the artwork?
- If we use Eisner's famous notion of *connoisseurship within an aesthetic curriculum* (1979), who are or should be the connoisseurs for arts-based enquiry in education?

connoisseurship

- What should be the balance or emphasis on 'creativity' and on 'enquiry'?
- How does the process and product(s) of an arts-based enquiry differ from the production of a creative or artistic work?
- Is this kind of research really just a sophisticated form of navel gazing—or mass media? Is research based on 'navel gazing' legitimate and appropriate in education?
- What are the limits of diaries or blogs as research tools, rather than as 'therapy' or journalism or simply as pushing celebrity?
- Should those who employ the arts in enquiries in education be permitted to have the same access to funding, resources and academic power bases as those undertaking research using more traditional quantitative and qualitative approaches?

Moreover, would-be creator-teacher-researchers need to remember the caveat mentioned in Chapter 2: that using an educational or a collaborative artwork or creative product can be very problematic and involve issues of ethics and of intellectual property, and even, where assessment of students or researchers is concerned, probity.

ethics

- Who owns the blog? Those who can access it? Or add to it?
- Who is named in it?

This is an ethical minefield even where there is clearly a binary relationship in our research between the 'researcher' and the 'creator/creators'. How much of the intellectual property of the creative product made by the researchers actually belongs to those respondents? This becomes even more complicated and potentially compromised by the addition of the third dimension of the 'teacher', or trainer, or human resource professional, especially in workplace environments where organisational claims on knowledge management and ownership have real legal clout.

intellectual property

MIXED METHODOLOGIES

By this time, the reader will have understood the rhizome factor of research methodologies and methods, and realised that there is quite a lot of overlap between these research methodologies and their methods, both philosophically and practically. Reading the manuals and handbooks of qualitative research will confirm this. What that implies is *not* that 'anything goes' but that no one method

■ commonalities and distinctions

is sacrosanct or 'pure'. Embarking on any of the methodologies, we come across virtually all those key terms whose definitions formed the second part of Chapter 2, in roughly the order we have spelt out. Each term has a distinct purpose, character and emphasis. We have to be sufficiently familiar with these to give ourselves a choice of how we head off from the starting point, and there are three dimensions to this starting point:

- the Research Question: what we want to investigate or find out
- the underlying philosophical and ideological paradigm
- the context: what can be practically attempted from where we are situated.

■ mixed methodologies by stages

When these three dimensions are articulated and acknowledged clearly, *then* is the time for selecting the methodology. Especially where the answer to the first and third dot points is 'a lot', because the research question is very complex and involves a lot of people, and the context is rich and many-faceted, mixed methodologies may be essential. The simplest way of implementing this is to break up the research into discrete stages, each with its own distinct methodology.

> In a hypothetical example, researchers may be brought into a long-time poorly functioning school with the express purpose of helping its authorities to improve the school through restructuring it.
>
> Stage 1 will sensibly be a descriptive/interpretive diagnosis, to get to understand the dynamics of the school in detail, and identify all the factors that might help or hinder any intervention aimed at 'improvement'. For this, it will be important to get as accurate a picture, in whole and in detail, of the school as it is, running normally. This could include both an *ethnography*, with the researchers embedded within the context for a sustained period; some *quantitative analysis* such as surveys and questionnaires; a retrospective or historical and *contextual investigation* of the school's recent history; and the gathering and analysis of as much of the school's *statistical data* as possible.
>
> Stage 2 will be based on what kinds of evidence are revealed: Are there problems (and opportunities) administratively? How do they impinge on the curriculum and pedagogy? What are the problems (and opportunities) among the human relationships, and how are these related to the administration and the curriculum? Stage 2 might move into *action research*, trialling a preliminary intervention, with the researchers taking an active participant role in driving it through its sequence of cycles, and building in a component of sustainability, so that they can eventually withdraw from participation without harming the project.
>
> In Stage 3 the researchers re-assume observer status, and set up a number of long-term *evaluation and reflection* strategies, once more being careful not to disturb the normal flow of the school and thus corrupt the evaluation. Also in Stage 3 the researchers might turn to *narrative enquiry*, to throw a new kind of illumination over the whole project, and interrogate what they and others charged with changing the culture of schools can learn more broadly from the successes, exigencies and failures of the project.

Two real and nicely complementary examples can show how this kind of mixing of methodologies can be practical on a small scale. These current PhD projects are both to do with development in China (now there's a rich and many-faceted research context!), working at opposite ends of the socio-economic scale.

> Rebecca's PhD (Song 2013, in progress) investigates East–West business communication in the corporate workplace, with fieldwork conducted in Chinese and English in three cities (Sydney, Beijing and Shanghai). *Ethnographic* and *narrative enquiry* each shapes the design of this project, which inevitably deals with substantial cultural complexities. She grapples with shifting identities—nationally, locally—and interpersonally.
>
> Yi-Man's PhD (Au 2013, in progress) investigates capacity-building in non-government organisation (NGO) trainers. These trainers are charged with helping communities to change and adapt to contemporary life, but are poorly educated themselves in dialogic, critical or reflective pedagogy. She developed an *action research* training project based on an innovative dialogical approach, with herself as the trainers' trainer modelling the method with her participants. Midway through, she realised that while there were some significant changes happening, and also some significant blocks and resistances emerging, she was unable to distinguish in her data how much of that was due to the new pedagogy, and how much to her own qualities as a teacher. Accordingly, she modified her methodology to include a strand of *reflective practitioner* research, and developed a model of analysis to help her sort out the pedagogy wheat from the personal response chaff.

Changing horses mid-stream

Yi-Man's experience is not unusual. Neither our Research Question nor our choice of methodology is final or irrevocable. Though the researcher's philosophical/ideological paradigm is unlikely to shift, our context, research site and subjects certainly can and often do; the Research Question too may need to change or be modified, as it is investigated. That in turn may suggest a shift into another methodology, or methods and instruments drawn from another, as this 'case from contingency' shows:

▪ contingency

> Having intended to survey several hundred Victorian nurses about their professional development decisions, Therese and her PhD changed direction, when it was obvious that nurses' complex lives were not going to be captured in this way alone (Anderson 2001). She sifted data to identify—by purposive sampling—a couple of dozen individuals, who agreed to interviews centred on the way they juggled shifts, families, partners, leisure and hospital politics, in addition to their continued learning. Thus, to see more of the contingent 'mosaic', Therese mixed and matched methods.

Research often has to take into account physical changes in the research site or subjects. There are many case study researchers concentrating on a single child, or a very small sample, who have found their subject snatched away in the middle of the study, by parents, illness or other contingencies that had not been sufficiently anticipated.

> Those working in volatile or logistically problematic locations may face major disruptions, such as two recent projects in different parts of Africa where the researchers, both knowing the unpredictabilities of their situations, dealt with the problems calmly and resourcefully. Kennedy, who we met in Chapter 2, had to reorganise his whole research to take account of the fact that his Zimbabwean fieldwork site was now forbidden or at least physically dangerous territory (Chinyowa 2005). He found himself changing from straightforward ethnography to a very effective patchwork of action research and case study. Patrick faced extremely unpredictable and under-resourced bureaucracies, and similarly volatile village conditions, in his action research study of gender equity initiatives in Uganda (Mangeni 2006). He too reshaped his fieldwork to make the best use of opportunities much more limited than he had anticipated, and came away with plenty of rich data.

The crucial thing for all research is that we must clearly understand, map and be able to defend any changes we make.

META-RESEARCH

■ researching research

With all these possibilities of research methodologies and methods—their complexity, interrelatedness, flexibility and even the tensions between them—it is tempting for the bold education researcher to become sidetracked into making their major task the chronicling and mapping of the research process, researching the research—meta-research, in other words.

> One of us was commissioned to research the learning of managers at work (Beckett 1998). Because this was little understood at the time, grassroots research was thought to be of limited use: there was no grasp of a typical case, or purposive sample. So, a survey of previous research in Australia, with overseas links, was made. Allowing for the particularities of work contexts was difficult, but eventually a meta-analysis of the main ways research into managers' learning at work could be generically shaped was completed and published.

In fact, virtually all research that takes an individual approach to a methodology, or uses mix and match methods, must, at the very least, be carefully documented and justified, particularly in terms of changes to the researcher's positioning and the exigencies of fieldwork. Examiners of theses and assessors of research funding applications always scrutinise the methodology very carefully, to ensure it is rigorous (or plausible!), practicable and well justified. For beginning researchers, this can be a daunting thought, as they are struggling to get to grips with rationales, new procedures and sequences of procedures. However, unless we are going seriously into meta-research, the focus on methodology needs to be kept in proportion—along with the anxiety level. There are plenty of handbooks and papers available for all the methodologies in this chapter—in fact, there's already quite an industry of meta-research for arts and educational research.

? REFLECTIVE QUESTIONS

1 Choose an approach that contains a methodology that you think will work for the issue that you want to research. What role is implied in this methodology, for you, as the (main) researcher? Can you link this role with your current educational and managerial practices: the workplace, with its responsibilities and expectations of you, and those you may have of it?

2 What ethical challenges for fieldwork or data collection does this chosen approach generate for you? How do you intend to meet these challenges, and maintain the integrity of the research?

3 Think eclectically! Across the three approaches here, and the various methodologies within them, is it better for your topic to 'mix and match'? If so, what might that look like, in the design of the fieldwork, or data collection?

WIDER READING

Carr, W. and Kemmis, S. 1986. *Becoming Critical: Education, Knowledge and Action Research*. Falmer, London.

Creswell, J. 2012. *Educational Research: Planning, Conducting, and Evaluating Quantitative and Qualitative Research*. Pearson, Boston.

Denzin, N. and Lincoln, Y. (eds) 2005. *The Sage Handbook of Qualitative Research* (3rd edn). Sage, Thousand Oaks, California.

Yin, R.K. 1989. *Case Study Research: Design and Methods* (2nd edn). Sage, Newberry Park, California.

POSTSCRIPT TO PART A: A WARNING

On reading a draft of the chapter in the book on which this one is based (see the Acknowledgments), one of the editorial committee noted sharply that there needed to be 'more on critical theory stance as a dimension of all research. What you have written is too bland'. She was right then, and right now; we are not doing research to reassure ourselves, and whatever research paradigm and methodology we use, we need to take a critical stance, and take nothing at face value.

■ critical theory

■ blurred genres

■ hermeneutics

Her comment highlights this, ironically, since 'critical theory' is itself often called a methodology, but one that we have purposely not used, since the phrase is one of the most contested in qualitative research. It is used by two sets of researchers historically coming from deeply opposing philosophical paradigms. On one side were the Frankfurt School's social and cultural theorists, inspired by Marx, such as Walter Benjamin (1973) who both influenced and was influenced by Bertolt Brecht. They saw critical theory as providing an alternative understanding of society as a foundation and a prerequisite for social action and change. On the other side were the literary critics epitomised by F.R. Leavis (1975) who were looking for the aesthetic elements and the writer's true meaning in mainly written literature. They were deeply concerned with human morality, but not with radical politics. In recent times, in that 'blurring of genres' referred to in the Introduction, the two versions have been edging towards each other, and indeed, blurring. This process was in fact started by a later member of the Frankfurt School, Jürgen Habermas (1987), who advanced critical theory as an alternative to the hermeneutics of Gadamer …

Whoa, whoa! Are you, readers, beginning to get nervous as we start to throw at you these scholarly-sounding assertions with alien labels such as 'Frankfurt School' and old writers you have never heard of? We should warn you:

1   The self-important-sounding paragraph above is, in fact, a rather condensed and very oversimplified précis of an academic discourse that will mean little until you have read the books, and which most researchers in Education will not need to bother with.

2   Incidentally, the authors' dates quoted above are very misleading, since all three of the writers actually wrote the books cited long before the publication dates of the editions we use—Benjamin had been dead for over thirty years!

■ change of address

3   Oh, and by the way, have you noticed yet the change of address in this very paragraph, from 'we' to 'you', altering our power relationship now and for the rest of the book?

Those three little traps are why you need a critical stance, and to have your wits about you at all times—so as not to get caught out, but to work out what might be important, and follow it!

EPILOGUE TO PART A

The Agony Column
Part 1—Getting started

Dr Sophie answers your questions about research degrees. This month: *Getting started*

NB: In Dr Sophie's column, all stories are based on the experiences of the authors with real people, but names, addresses and several genders have been changed to protect the innocent and deter the litigious. No correspondence will be entered into.

Q   A PhD sounds like fun and I reckon I'm up for it, but my colleagues at school tell me it's a waste of time. Are they right, or what should I tell them? *Feisty Freethinker, Freycinet*

A   That depends on you.

There's a bit more to a PhD than a fun run, and the thrill of the chase quickly gives way to the realisation that you are sharing half a decade of your life or even more—and your nearest-and-dearests' lives, too—with a very demanding companion. This column isn't called 'The Agony Column' for nothing. Doing a PhD is, or should be, a life-changing event. As for your colleagues, you don't have to take notice of them, but make up your own mind. Perhaps they don't want that kind of change, or don't yet need it in their jobs, but in case you and they haven't noticed, the paperchase for increased qualifications with increased remuneration and better job prospects is certainly a strong motivator if you are as ambitious as you are feisty. On the other hand, you might just relish the intellectual challenge, and like reading a lot of thick books with no pictures. I can't tell from your email, but if either of the above fits you, then go for it. Oh, and do hang on to your idea of 'fun'—because you have to be (or become) passionately *engaged* in your quest, which is part of 'fun', and you also will need at times to be playful, sceptical and ironic, which is the other part of 'fun'. You can do a PhD without having a sense of humour, but it's a long and dreary road for you and your supervisor.

Q   For over ten years I've seen the amazing effects of the arts on kids' learning and their lives. I've got my own schools' touring music and theatre company, which the kids always adore. I have decided to use its visits to schools in some research that will show the principals and teachers how the arts increases literacy and learning skills, self-esteem and self-confidence in public, and social skills, especially for kids at risk and with special needs. Where shall I start? *Johnny@theartsrock, Darlinghurst*

A   Don't. Go back to your company and stay doing what you are doing, and get better at it, and more critically reflective, then come back and apply again. Johnny, what you are trying to do isn't research at all, but advocacy, and it's wildly overambitious anyway, as well as hopelessly impractical. You actually sound very much like me, several decades ago.

If you are still reading this after that start, don't despair, but get patient and get clever. Those of us who have experienced the life-changing power of the arts (or the behaviour-changing potential of sport, or the magic of science, come to that) know what you mean, already, instinctually. That's why so many of us continue to turn up every weekend to ill-kept playing fields with ill-mannered parents, peer through the twilight on freezing science field trips looking for fauna that saw us coming a mile off and decamped, or tune instruments and change costumes in staff toilets like you … and worst of all endure the casual put-downs of our less passionate colleagues, especially the ones who have all the power and status and wonder why we do it. But those latter folks have also heard our grandiose claims and stories for nearly half a century, and generally don't believe them—and they are usually too busy with the tasks of orthodox wisdom, of running day-to-day classrooms, to take time out to see and feel the power of sport, scientific discovery or the arts for themselves. But just occasionally they do, and you could make yourself useful by focusing your company's work on just one thing at a time, making sure it speaks not just to the students but their teachers and parents as well, and encouraging them to spare the time to experience it and talk with you about it. Then you might have a convert or two on your hands, especially if you are honest enough to see with their eyes the things that might still be wrong or inadequate about your work, or at least the trade-offs you have had to make; that's not weakness. It'll be a lot more convincing to acknowledge the deficits and gaps and failures, as well as the triumphs. That, you see, is a vital part of any real research—what we call looking for the negative data.

Before you do any formal research study, you can and should make a start with that. First off, look at your company program evaluations, which I'm sure you're expected to distribute: How genuinely even-handed are the questions? Do you invite that negative data? How carefully gathered is the data, or do you just dish out the form to those busy teachers or the principal, and then collect it at the end, or even let them send it back days later, when some of them will just have taken the line of least resistance and ticked the No 2 box—'satisfied'—all the way down (because they actually didn't see much of your show but don't want to miss out next year)? Have you found a way to get genuine and thoughtful responses from the students themselves? When you've achieved a way of evaluating your company's work that does all of that, then you will be ready for your PhD.

Q I have a very good friend, an experienced science teacher who has been pressured by her school and system to do a Masters, but it's nearly thirty years since she's done any studying, and she's afraid she is not clever enough at fifty. Her nephew got his PhD in biochemistry at twenty-five. She is doing some preliminary coursework with some honours students, and says the kids in the class are all far quicker and sharper than she is. *Kirsty, Ballarat*

A I'd say that fifty is a very good age to start a PhD. At her age I was in the middle of my own PhD, which I had not even thought about until a couple of years before. I suspect that 'your friend' is actually you. You can tell 'her' that in the thirty years since she last studied, we have developed lots of people-friendly methods of research, which honour and utilise the wisdom that thirty years of professional experience have given you ('her').

And as for those smartass kids in your coursework group, you should know that they most of them are actually in awe of you, though they won't tell you that. They know they may be quicker on the draw, but they also know enough to recognise real depth of lived wisdom that the mature students like you bring to the work.

You can also discount that young biochemist; this is one area where education and pure science are very different indeed. There is some evidence to suggest that scientists are at their intellectual peak in their early twenties; a PhD using orthodox scientific research methods needs a sharp and recently trained mind, and the candidate is usually supported by a research team of much more experienced researchers who can provide the background and tools to ensure certainty and accuracy of data analysis. 'Your friend' has something that her nephew does not; it's called life experience and can get in the way of pure science, but is absolutely essential in nearly all studies in human nature and social behaviour. Those of course include education.

The youngest student I have supervised insisted, against friendly advice, on going straight from his glittering honours achievement into a PhD, looking at classroom practices, before ever teaching full-time in a classroom, himself. He was a voracious reader, and figured that he could make up the deficit through book learning and his own very sharp intelligence—much like your friend's nephew. To some extent this was true, and in the end he achieved a worthy and competent PhD, but he gave himself (and his supervisors) a very hard time, especially at the end, and mainly because of all those books. He had read everything in sight, but didn't have any idea of what to accept and what to leave out, especially when what he read did not match up comfortably with what he was observing in his fieldwork. He didn't have the filters of experience to know what was worthy of believing, nor the confidence to cut out what was suspect or irrelevant. His first draft was three hundred thousand words, and he was incapable of bringing it below a hundred and fifty thousand without some very savage surgery by his supervisors. And good though the thesis was, I have always thought how much better it would have been if that brilliant young mind had been more patient, and prepared itself for the task with a few years doing what 'your friend' has been doing—getting out there, teaching.

Q Everyone knows that my topic (Drosophilae: education and the post-colonial implications) is the next big thing in interdisciplinary studies. But the only supervisor the university can find for me says he can't see where I am coming from, and I don't think he'll be able to take me where this topic will undoubtedly go. He is my problem. The university owes me a better deal. Can you advise me how to get it? *Herman, regional one-university city (withheld on request)*

A No, Herman, you're your own biggest problem at the moment. Neither you nor your topic has any automatic entitlement to anything. I'm not surprised the university had difficulty finding you a supervisor, as not too many education academics are versed in both fruit-flies and post-colonialism. Be grateful, a bit more humble and more patient—give him a chance. You may see the possibilities, but like him, I can't, and like him, I would need a calm explanation, properly argued, of 'where you are coming from' and why you think this subject is even worth studying, let alone it being a 'big thing'.

Q A close friend and sparring partner over many years wants me to be her PhD supervisor, though the two supervisions I've been involved in have been with students I did not know prior to the study (though we all ended up good friends). Is this wise? Oh, and she lives in Sydney. *Chen, Melbourne*

A From your friend's point of view, to know your supervisor in advance is a priceless asset, as many PhD students in education apply to a university, perhaps because it has a highly reputable faculty, or is local, and they have to take pot luck with whoever they get. For a student, forging a strong personal relationship with the supervisor is always a crucial aspect of the study and—as you have already found—in the end gratifying to you both, as educational to the supervisor as the candidate, and often very long-lasting.

Starting at the opposite end, with a personal and professional relationship already forged, has obvious advantages … but also an important potential drawback, I have found, which you would be wise to acknowledge in advance. If there is a) an element of competitiveness in your relationship—she's your 'sparring partner' you say?—it can create really awkward issues for you both; equally, b) if either or both of you deep down doubts the other's ability; or c) again if you have a radically different philosophy or belief system. In any of these cases, you shouldn't touch each other with a bargepole. I had a close friend, of long standing, with all three of those issues in our relationship—which neither of us acknowledged. He very sensibly (probably instinctively) chose one of my other colleagues as his supervisor, and had great success initially, at Masters' level. Unfortunately, when that supervisor left suddenly, effectively abandoning him, my friend was forced, reluctantly, to accept me … and for two years we had a really awkward time, during which for whatever reasons his enthusiasm and commitment waned; my colder, more logical approach dampened his more spiritual vision and ardour; he didn't enjoy giving me his very roughly written drafts to read, and I enjoyed reading them even less. Then by the time I too left, as far as I knew he had just given up and defaulted. Later, I heard that he was picked up by another more simpatico colleague, who somehow helped him through to completion. He did not respond to my email congratulating him, and I have barely seen him since.

If you are sure that's not the case, both of you should take the opportunity with both hands. A robust professional friendship is a gift from the gods for supervisor and student alike. I've supervised two colleagues based next door, and had many warm and wonderful discussions, and quite a few intellectual battles, in the doorway between our offices with them both, separately and together. These were as revelatory to me as to them, but more importantly, they came away better focused—and both of them deservedly won international awards for their theses. [Memo to any supervisor … see if you can attract highly talented and experienced students: the opportunities for reflected glory are endless!] There are lots of other advantages, both before and after enrolment. In your case, your friend has the opportunity to discuss the whole project with you before embarking on it, so you don't have to start where newly appointed supervisors often do, trying to pull a stranger's rough and vague idealistic outline into some sort of shape, simultaneously trying to read between the lines to gauge what the student's underlying experience, philosophy and prior reading might have been.

Started on your research and still got problems—or a whole bunch of new ones? Write in to us, as Dr Sophie's agony column will appear next month, entitled:
Getting it done!

PART B

DOING RESEARCH

MAKING A START

5

☑ CHAPTER OBJECTIVES

After reading this chapter, you should be able to:

- frame a Research Question properly
- locate yourself as a researcher within an approach that will actually answer the Research Question
- shape a research proposal.

↘ STARTING POINTS

This is where the book turns into a practical handbook, and so we are changing the form of address, as we move from discussion to giving you advice. Where and how you start your research will obviously vary, and depend on several factors. First, your motivation may spring from your *personal* context, your *social* context or your *educational* and/or *vocational* context … or, of course, the interplay of more than one of these.

▇ multiple contexts

One Australian researcher, Fida, has completed a PhD centred on the *educational context* of health and sexual health in the curriculum for young Muslims (Sanjakdar 2006). Her *social context* is the Australian Islamic school and its community and she locates her research within a paradox: 'these schools claim to present a holistic and balanced Islamic education; however, studies in health and sexual health education are omitted from the curriculum' (Abstract). Her *personal context* is as a professional in this curriculum area, and as a Muslim educator intent on exploring the potential for 'curriculum conversations', by examining teachings from the Holy Koran and Hadith, as well as through extensive fieldwork. These three factors combined strongly to provide a topic, a site and a Research Question.

Motivation is a very important factor. The true picture of the researcher is never the traditional stereotype of the solitary, dispassionate scholar, detached from emotion, cool and objectively methodical. Research is always driven by passion: to know, to challenge,

▇ motivation

■ intuition

to prove, to disprove, to improve. Often, a research topic begins as a hunch, an intuition, a suspicion or a doubt, that when 'worried at' develops into an intellectually rigorous hypothesis or Question.

■ research and practice

Similarly, the one-time dichotomy between 'research' and 'practice' is dissolving, even if for some purposes it needs to be maintained (such as commissioned research that is intended to inform government policy). We discussed this in Chapter 3 and developed the idea in Chapter 4, when we surveyed some of the popular methodologies now in use. Whatever your current practice and/or your educational concerns, you can take advantage of some aspect of the dichotony for formalised reflection and investigation. As David Wright observes (in a contribution to the original drama research book) perhaps it is more than that:

> I think this relates to recognition of the pervasive nature of the research enquiry process and the way(s) in which research expands into ongoing practical reality … (and the researcher's tendency towards obsession). In this sense it is 'living research'. When an enquiry of substance is undertaken it is almost inevitable that it influences personal philosophy (as a citizen) and personal practice (as an educator). Hence, a good researcher needs to be aware of this and to take it into consideration in the imagining and construction of research. (Wright, in O'Toole 2006, p. 71)

Focusing the research topic

Once you have made the decision to embark on research, and identified a theme, topic or area of investigation, one of the hardest tasks of the whole enterprise has to be undertaken: to focus the topic so that it can be usefully studied. Almost invariably this focusing involves shrinking your initial impulses, not only to clarify them but to fit in with the logistics of your context. Thinking of the literal meaning behind the metaphor of 'focusing' may be helpful. As we often claimed in Part A, we start with seeing the world 'as' something—as falling under a 'way of seeing'. We perceive in concepts—not with totally naive and innocent eyes, but with eyes that can recognise in a new image a familiar shape. Focusing the lenses of a pair of binoculars means making the image sharper, replacing the blurred outlines with a distinct shape. And through the lens, we can't look at everything that the naked eye can make out; the peripheral vision is excluded, so we can only look at what is in the centre of the image.

■ lenses

There are two aspects to the focusing, which must be considered together. The first part is identifying exactly what your Research Question is, and the second is examining whether, how, and how much you can investigate this Question with the personal and contextual resources you have at your disposal. These resources include an enthusiasm for learning what others have established before you: there are traditions of systematic investigation, and you will be well served to acquaint yourself with these traditions so they, too, become 'familiar' ways of seeing, from which you can depart, or which you can embellish.

■ resources

The Research Question

Crucial to any research is a good Research Question: one that turns the topic you have chosen into a source of investigation. And that usually means, grammatically, a single sentence that ends in a question mark. The question mark is very important, even if you know that you will not have provided a complete answer at the end of the study, and particularly if you are starting with a hunch. As a basic discipline, it always helps to ensure that you are phrasing the study interrogatively—starting with, for example, 'What …?', 'How …?', 'Why …?' or 'Whether and if so, how much …?' Not only will that help to clarify what you are doing, and to decide whether you can in fact begin to address that Question, but it will keep you on the straight and narrow during the study—make sure you do not stray off into interesting territory that does not actually address your Question.

> questioning
> central Question

Particularly in early research, you should aim to work towards a single central Question. This will ensure a clear line through your study, and make sure that overlapping but distinct lines of enquiry do not get tangled. Do not be afraid of the 'shades of grey' in research. Your single Question can quite usefully begin with 'To what extent …?' because this will invite a subtle reading of the answers you provide. Rarely is a black-and-white answer possible, or even desirable, in Education research. As Part A showed, much of our systematic research enquiry is probabilistic, emergent and therefore indicative (rather than decisive) of key aspects of human experience.

> shades of grey

Nevertheless, we must not be content with vagueness, or take refuge in the banal. Questions should have bite! Furthermore, a single central Question may end up with a number of sub-questions, which is fine as long as you sort these into a hierarchy of priorities. (It is possible to have more than one Research Question, but that is usually better left to complex, advanced research projects.) It's equally important that the priorities and relationship between the questions are kept clear and distinct.

> sub-questions

Inevitably, the formulation of the Research Question will have a lot to do with the site and subjects of the research. To use a fictional example that we will return to:

- Can the use of workshop/darkroom/performance/studio techniques improve literacy?

  In formulating a central Research Question, this is a good *pre*-question — identifying the *topic*. However, it is rather sweeping and vague, so your next step inevitably is to ask yourself how you could investigate this Question, which might lead you straight to the *site* and *subjects* of the research.

  - Is the use of (particular) techniques with my current Year 6 class improving their literacy and confidence in the use of books … and to what extent?

  This is a better Question because it is not so sweeping: you actually have a chance of answering it with subtlety by the end of the research, either in ways that can be measured (quantitatively) or otherwise identified (qualitatively)—or gaining useful insights anyway.

What are features of good Research Questions? They should invite answers that are *generative*—by which we mean they invite a new claim on a 'way of knowing' (cf Chapter 1). Accordingly, they should avoid staying with 'What ...' 'When ...' 'Can ...' 'Is ...' questions (even if you start out with these), and instead should favour a more nuanced format: 'To what extent ...' is generative, as we saw earlier. 'How can/ could ...' is also generative. But so is any Question in a form that suggests a link worth exploring between three entities or phenomena. Consider:

> • How may food safety training be best delivered to small business owners in a market-driven/deregulated commercial environment?

generative questions

Here, food safety, small business ownership and market forces are linked from the most specific concept to the most general. Generative questions often 'blow out' (like a trumpet shape) towards the most controversial or elusive concept, inviting exploration of A (local) to B (slightly further) in light of C (big idea). Some more examples:

> • To what extent can classroom music teaching with ICT develop Taiwanese music curriculum policy?
> • Under what circumstances should a nursing education curriculum reflect the experiences of undergraduates in clinical situations of grief and dying?
> • How does leadership of an arts program for adults with disabilities build the genre of 'outsider art'?
> • How can a surgical education program better draw upon professionals' workplace learning to improve the competencies of Australian surgeons?

problematising

Good Research Questions, we argue, generate a problematic relationship between three entities or phenomena, such that they invite more than mere 'mapping' in being answered. An A in relation to *only* a B can be usefully explored (causally, or interpretively, or in some mixed modality), but if that is all there is, how is the world *critically* or *creatively* researched? How is the world problematised by such a simple framing of the Research Question? There should be a C—a wider, innovative frame of reference that sets the edginess of the Research Question well.

Overall, we advocate short Research Questions (maximum thirty words) that imply relationships between three entities or phenomena, such that, in answering these questions, something critical or problematic or innovative can be feasibly claimed. This claim can be as much by strong (non-empirical) argument as by robust (empirical) fieldwork, or combinations of both. But if the Research Question does not *invite* this critical or problematic or innovative response, it may be just another mapping of some aspects of the world (like a street directory)—and who needs more of that?

The researcher's context

The researcher's own context must be considered well before this point, which is where the thinking and planning begin to be formalised. First, you need a *base of support*, commonly a university, if you are doing a research degree program or applying for a research grant. Even if, by chance, you are doing independent research and may have picked up this book to try to find out how, you will still need both personal and logistical support.

university support

Personal support can come in the form of a *supervisor* or *mentor*. For a research student, the personal comes in the form of a supervisor (in PhD supervision, two co-supervisors are becoming standard practice). For somebody applying for a grant to do a research project, an experienced mentor who's previously been through the same process is very valuable. In addition to their own experiences of research, supervisors or mentors may have had additional training in thesis supervision or in grant-writing techniques.

supervisor
mentor

The supervisor or mentor should be able to give advice on the next stage, the preparation of the first formal piece of documentation: in the case of a degree, the research proposal; if you are doing a piece of independent research, the submission for funding or other support. That's why it is important to find a congenial supervisor or mentor—one who you like and can trust professionally, and even more important, one whose *philosophical paradigm*, or *research approach* (as we discussed in Chapter 4) is compatible with yours, so that the research isn't bedevilled from the start with conflicting ideas or misunderstandings. If you are engaged in degree research, it is useful at the start to determine with your supervisor the frequency of supervision meetings: how often you want them and how often you need them. A good supervisor will be aware not only of the academic demands of your research and how much intellectual guidance it will need, but also the psychological demands, which relate to your confidence and experience … so here's something to try to be honest about. Some people are more dependent learners than others—especially if you have not done research before, or studied recently, and may be apprehensive about your ability. If so, how much ongoing reassurance and guidance do you actually need, and how much would be really self-indulgent? Supervisors are busy people—and so, usually, are you. On the other hand, confident self-starters and autonomous learners can trouble the supervisor less initially, but can also be headstrong or reluctant to ask for help. They may not quite realise what this research stuff entails, and charge on into a tangle that later will need lots of time and morale-boosting to sort out.

compatibility

level of dependence

The supervisor will be as keen as you are to develop the research plan to the level of a proposal or submission, as soon as the Research Question has been clearly articulated. That entails selecting a methodology, working out the logistics and timeline, and writing a rationale for the project.

proposal

Positioning the researcher and choosing the method

Even before selecting a methodology, however, don't forget to work out your own *theoretical* or *philosophical position* specifically in relation to the Research Question, as we urged you to do in Chapters 3 and 4. If you remember, that means identifying and articulating through what ideological, intellectual and emotional lenses ('ways of seeing') you are looking at the research—how you perceive the phenomenon under investigation. You must acknowledge (as best you can at this early stage) your biases and the preconceptions you will bring to the project; your expectations of it. That in turn means scrutinising your personal and egotistical investment—as the primary stakeholder in the research, what exactly is your stake, and how might your motives create tensions within the research? As one beginning researcher put it:

▓ positioning

> I am passionate about a technique known as a 'community of enquiry' and its power to address literacy; I want the research to give me ammunition to strengthen my case for expanding [the use of] philosophy [teaching techniques] in my school; I don't however want to be landed with rewriting the school's whole literacy program, but I do want to be personally involved in the research; and I want to get a higher degree credential as soon as possible.

It is worth taking the time at this point to do that personal stock-take, because it may influence your choice of methodology. As Daniel Lapsley puts it, when discussing the formulation and framing of meaningful research problems in Education:

> The starting point of critical enquiry is biography … The problem of situating must be pursued intentionally. One must seek out colleagues, engage new ideas, attend colloquia, form study groups, and work collaboratively in both formal and informal settings … Similarly one must master the literatures of one's discipline. (2006, p. 300)

This is sound advice. No one can come to their research area without an understanding of both the personal and the scholastic context in which the research will be located. In Chapter 6, we detail how the scholarship needs to be mastered in a literature review. But even before that, you should come to terms with the context of your Research Question by being open to the various other ways it may have been perceived. A Research Question never speaks for itself: it speaks 'into' (and even 'out from') a tradition of scholarship that you need to unearth. Lapsley reminds us of both the 'review' and 'context' purposes of literature when he continues:

▓ contextualisation

> There is no shortcut to expertise, but then there is no surer way to situate one's stance than to understand the history of intellectual problems that repose in the classic literature of one's discipline. But one should also study philosophy and be conversant with meta-theory because these will provide the conceptual tools for framing one's enquiry and for addressing foundational questions. (2006, p. 300)

▓ Western traditions

Chapters 2 and 3 are our 'ways of seeing' meta-theory in this book: we provide an account of the main Western traditions of systematic enquiry that Education researchers (as social scientists) need to understand. As your research gets under way, and you locate your Question in one of our three 'approaches' (see Chapters 3 and 4), your methodology will be underpinned by its own literature review, as will your substantive

Research Question. Re-examining the Research Question, you need to ask (maybe with your mentor's assistance) these further questions:

- Which methodologies (keep the plural at this stage, but think of them one at a time) could be used to throw light on this Question, and which would seem to offer the most potential?
- Which methodologies are you philosophically and temperamentally suited for and attracted to?
- Which methodologies would be logistically possible, and which would be quite impractical, given your research context and site?

Now, while choosing the methodology, you should examine the other aspect of *situating*, or *positioning*: the *observer–participant continuum*. What distance from your research subjects do you want, what distance is appropriate to the Research Question, what distance can you manage or is logistically available? Obviously, this will have an enormous bearing on your choice of methodology. As a *reflective practitioner* you are normally the centre of your research study; as an *action researcher* you are sometimes the centre; as an *experimenter*, you normally aim to be distant from the subjects. You may even incorporate in your research structure ways of detaching yourself, such as using external observers and interviewers, anonymous surveys or double blind tests.

■ distancing

Before you finally make a choice of methodology, or at least before you start the research proper, you should do one more round of preliminary analysis of your context. Who are the other stakeholders in your investigation? There are two parts to this question:

a Who are the positive stakeholders—who stands to benefit from you investigating or answering the Research Question?

■ positive stakeholders

Consider the literacy example above. Positive stakeholders might include at the micro level: the research subjects, their parents, your colleagues; at the macro level: the philosophy of education community, the educational system, the school community.

b Who are or might be the negative stakeholders? Who might not benefit, or might see the research as threatening?

■ negative stakeholders

Negative stakeholders might include those of your colleagues who believe in other literacy strategies and systems, and those who distrust and fear philosophy; the school principal who does not want to face the resource implications of expanding philosophy, because of the professional development outlays in up-skilling the teachers, and the provision of better facilities; even some of your students or their parents, who see philosophy as a waste of time that would be better spent on more direct literacy pedagogy like phonics or drills.

Considering the list of negative stakeholders at an early stage will probably not only clarify the project and the methodology quite helpfully, but will also save a great deal of time and heartache caused by stumbling over them once the research is under way.

↘ DEVELOPING THE PROPOSAL OR SUBMISSION

▨ proposal

▨ submission

Having now given a good deal of thought to your positioning, and to the theoretical or philosophical rationale it has (the 'meta-theory'), you will be asked to prepare the first formal document of your research: the proposal (for a degree) or the funding submission (for a grant application). If, by any chance, you are undertaking the research neither for accreditation nor with external funding, then you should do this task anyway—it's good discipline and will give the research an anchor from which you can't drift too far.

▨ clarity

The whole proposal should be written in plain, clear English. Some application pro-formas actually specify this, as the project may well be assessed by a scholar or expert from another discipline. The format of these forms can vary a little, according to the university or funding agency. However, the following elements are common to most (they have been adapted for this book from the invaluable advice to her students given by Angela O'Brien—another of our original drama research informants, in O'Toole 2006, p. 76):

▨ title

The title should be clear and if possible compelling but not tricksy. This should be followed by a brief description of the project. It should set down the purpose, the content, the significance of the research, and where appropriate, the relevant background leading to the research—though this may be asked for elsewhere.

▨ Research Question

The next section should set down the key Research Question or questions with any subsidiary questions. It should be very brief—perhaps a clear statement followed by the Question or set of questions.

The third section should—again, as succinctly as possible—outline the approach you intend to take. You might discuss your approach to:

- your theoretical positioning (rationale or 'meta-theory')
- the literature or literatures you intend to consult, and have already consulted
- the methodology you intend to employ, or if you intend to mix and match, how and why
- whether you intend to use fieldwork, creative art-making or other empirical techniques and if so, what and where
- how you will collect data
- how you will analyse the data approach.

At this early stage, it may be difficult to give a detailed timeline. However, an outline of the whole project should be worked out approximately, including any fieldwork, the dates of which should be locked in as early as possible, and any expected breaks from the project. This should incorporate timelines for the initial literature review, data collection, empirical or experimental work, data analysis, and writing up and reporting. Particularly if the timeline is still shadowy, it is valuable to try and work out some key milestones. If the research is funded, that may well be demanded anyway.

▦ timeline

If you are doing funded research, the format of the reporting will probably be set for you, and need not be addressed in the submission. However, you may well be asked to indicate what outcomes you are expecting: books or scholarly papers, product development, changes in practice, patents, policy recommendations and so on.

▦ outcomes

Some idea of the necessary finance and resources you need will be automatically demanded as part of a grant application, together with a justification of the budget. A budget is not usually a formal part of a degree research proposal, but it can still be very useful to calculate one in advance. Research will inevitably take time resources, and often material and financial costs, direct or indirect—not only from yourself but from your subjects and research site. Our anonymous beginner muses again:

▦ budget

> Is my school willing to dedicate the in-kind costs to my 'community of enquiry' research—my time and that of my colleagues? Are my colleagues willing? Will there be travelling costs entailed for me in visiting the research site(s)? How will my interview and questionnaire data be transcribed and collated? And so forth.

You must not forget to fully reference any texts, documents, statistics or other sources you have used in the proposal. However, the referencing should not be too extensive. This would clutter up that clear exposition of the research proposal you are aiming for. Besides, a proposal is not the place for a parade of prior knowledge; you need to show just enough to demonstrate that you do know what you are proposing.

▦ references

If you are doing degree research, some supervisors will expect an indication of the shape of the thesis in the proposal: a list of chapters, perhaps, even with a descriptive sentence or two about each and a specimen literature review. At the risk of seeming subversive and offending some of our colleagues, we would advise you to actively resist all of this at such an early stage! And resist it as long as possible, even though the security of shaping your study to preordained structures is very tempting. Once your thesis takes shape in your head, or in your notes, you will inevitably work towards that and that only, and close the door on many wonderful opportunities for other inclusions or more flexible shapes that are part and parcel of many of the methodologies we have already canvassed in Chapter 4. There are standard components of all theses that must come in somewhere, and standard methods of formatting them. However, researchers should live in the present and not anticipate the future too fixedly. Beginning researchers, too, should not try to run too far with anticipating the complexities of academic discourse before they can walk.

▦ flexibility

◥ ETHICS APPROVAL

All researchers wrestle with issues of ethics because they are so connected to the authenticity and validity of the research project. Most educational research projects need formal ethics approval, since we are dealing with human subjects, often minors. Ethical principles are central to our work, and in Part A (on page 22) we listed several that should guide us. As we have seen from the discussion of power and ownership in Chapter 2, the researcher has a responsibility to protect the participants in the research— it's a basic and necessary part of the researcher's role in collecting authentic and valid data. In order to encourage people to 'open up', the researcher must promote and maintain a culture of trust, transparency and confidentiality over the course of the research project. These values have been codified in many places around the world, but we refer you to the Nuremberg Code (which arose in 1949 from the Nuremberg War Crimes Trials after the Second World War) in which voluntary consent, avoiding harm, fruitful results (a social good) and continuing risk assessments are the key points (Walter 2006, pp. 57–8).

human ethics

trust

So there are a few ethical procedures that researchers need to *prepare* before they enter the research site, *maintain* while they are gathering data, and *reflect upon* when writing the findings and making the final analyses. Our colleague Lyn Yates states that good research is about 'something that mattered' (Yates 2004, p. 17). You will pin down what matters partly through ethical scrutiny.

ethical clearance

If your research involves interviewing or working with other people, particularly minors, no matter how 'non-risky' it might seem, you need to gain *ethical clearance*. Researchers usually have to start with the very time-consuming but unavoidable task of filling in an ethics request form—and maybe even two, one from your institution and one from your subjects. For example, state education departments have their own ethics procedures for working in a school. You may even be faced with a particularly frustrating catch-22, where each institution gives its approval dependent on seeing the written approval of the other! It's natural to be impatient at this kind of constraint, but it's unavoidable, and if you aren't filling in the given forms, you should be doing your own ethics checks anyway. You can usually make things easy for yourself, and help the ethics committee that will review your application, by not flagging too pretentiously your research's expected effect on your clients. In fact, many universities and research institutions have 'expedited' ethics application procedures for what they call 'low-risk' research involving human subjects—into which category most of your research will fall.

expedited ethics

When in school settings, it is always worth stressing that you are observing/working with/interviewing the students as part of their normal curricular activities (if this is the case). Grand and hopeful claims about giving the students changed self-esteem, new expressive powers or changed emotional and social attitudes can sometimes incur the suspicion of ethics committee members who may be cognitive psychologists or sociologists, some of whom still tend to think that much innovative pedagogy in contemporary education, especially techniques involving behaviour change, is a rather uncontrolled and disreputable form of psychological or social engineering.

If you are an outsider to your research site, it is essential to gain inside information. Sometimes this raises 'commercial-in-confidence' worries, and in many corporate settings is a legitimate source of ethical and legal concern. Written approval on letterhead from those best placed to have thought this through (apart from you!) is essential, and will be sought by a university ethics process. That means identifying the gatekeepers (those people who hold the power of access, and can support your research or make it difficult or impossible) and finding at least one sympathetic insider. The insiders will be able to guide your data-gathering at their school or industry site, both in terms of what you can collect and what is worth collecting. They will also alert the researcher to the protocols that need to be observed, and help you to allay any inside fears about the research. Though much of what passes between researcher and insiders will be 'off the record' and even confidential, it is advisable to keep confidential notes in a personal journal to maintain validity. Don't forget to let the insiders know you are doing this.

In the early stages of gaining access, there is invariably a question of *risk assessment*. You must gain informed consent from all participants and all other indirect stakeholders—some of whom might have negative feelings or agendas towards your research. Letters of consent are important documents that are legally essential wherever minors are concerned, signed by parent or guardian, and they should be stored carefully for easy retrieval. What these letters do is outline the how, what, why, who and when of your research in plain language; your responsibilities, such as how the knowledge gathered from the site might be used and stored; your expectations of the participants, and their rights as 'volunteers' in the project. Below we offer you a standard template for a parent's or carer's letter of consent, filled in for a specimen project. Each research institution has its own rules about this. It may need to be on institution letterhead. When working with minors, we recommend that you should also, wherever possible, give the participants one to sign to give their consent for themselves, though this is not usually demanded. It can make students feel important and like they have a sense of ownership of the project, rather than feeling like guinea-pigs. It's a good idea to prepare three copies of each for signing: one for the researcher's file, and one each for the parent and participant.

(Name of carer, personalised if possible)

Dear Mr & Ms Woolf,

(Name of researcher and university/institution, under the guidance of supervisor, with a brief explanation of research and the time-frame of the project)

My name is Russell Bertrand—as you know I am your daughter *Virginia's* class teacher. I am conducting a PhD research study in the Education Faculty, Bloomsbury University, under the supervision of Professor Daisy Dewey, entitled '*Words, Words, Words: Telling a Hawk from a Handsaw*'.

$\rightarrow$

Margin notes: gatekeepers · insiders · protocols · risk assessment · letters of consent

The study investigates whether using philosophy teaching techniques measurably improves children's literacy. My fieldwork will entail two English lessons per week for nine weeks, where literacy concepts and skills will be taught through a 'community of enquiry' approach.

I request your approval to, for example:

- *(access documentation — state what)* allow me to access your child's literacy reports from this and any previous schools
- *(conduct field observation or special activity — state number and frequency)* conduct observations in the eighteen bi-weekly research classes and include an external observer (Professor Dewey) in the first two and last two of these
- *(interviews — state number and frequency of interviews)* audiotape two fifteen-minute interviews with your child, one before and one following the research classes. These audiotapes will be kept by me for three years after this project, and then destroyed. Data gathered in these interviews will be solely on the teaching techniques and associated group work, will remain confidential and will only be used for the research
- *(video, photographs etc. — state how these will be used and whether they will be destroyed or returned)* video your child during some or all class sessions; the videos will only be used for the purposes of the research; they will remain confidential, and be destroyed following the research.

(This next section is always compulsory)

Your child's participation in this study is voluntary. If you or your child choose not to participate or to withdraw from the study at any time, there will be no penalty and it will not affect your child's participation or assessment in the subject. If s/he chooses to withdraw from this study, your child may take any previously gathered data. The results of the research may be published, but your child's name will not be used.

(State fields of knowledge to be developed and how the data will be used)

Your child's participation will help to advance the field of literacy teaching. I also expect there to be a direct benefit to your child, and I am confident that there will be no adverse effects.

(State where the data will be stored)

The interview and video data will be stored in a locked cellar in the Bloomsbury Circle Writers' Club.

(State contact numbers and/or email)

If you have any questions concerning the research study, please contact me on principia@mathematica.com, or telephone me at school: Summerhill 6666

(State research contact numbers)

You may also contact my supervisor (d.dewey@uniblooms.edu.au) or the secretary of the Ethics Committee at the university (e.forster@uniblooms.edu.au).

Yours sincerely,

Russell Bertrand, BEd, MA

****

I give my consent for _____ to participate in the above study.

Signature _____ Date _____

Strict ethical behaviour needs to be upheld during the entire project, of course, not just at the beginning. Participants in your research are entitled to see how you are operating and what you are collecting, and occasionally they may ask to review your notes. Participants should be free to see what you have collected or gathered from the site as part of their 'story' and their intellectual property. This often helps to allay their fears, and rarely will they ask to see this material again. However, you do not have to reveal everything; you can keep confidential analytical notes, hunches and inferences to yourself, as this is the intellectual property of the researcher and still a 'work in progress'.

■ sharing

Sometimes it is imperative to the validity of the study that the researcher does not discuss the evolving data with anyone other than the research team (supervisor, etc.). That means—in spite of the paragraph above—not discussing it with the participants, more than absolutely necessary. Discussions at the site can dilute the aims of the project, and, more detrimentally, affect how participants respond to questions or behave in the research environment. Most participants want to help the researcher, especially if a good rapport has been established and maintained, but good intentions can taint the data so that you see and hear a contrived image of the site—that is, one that the participants are constructing for you. This is another reason for sharing only information actually taken from the field notes and interviews, and not any of the analytical data.

■ confidentiality

On the other hand, a good researcher needs to be responsive. Indeed, some forms of research and research relationships demand constant dialogue. If you are endowing your participants as 'co-researchers', you will need to discuss aspects of the research thoroughly with them. Even if there is more distance between the researcher and participants, the participants may wish to bring their own data to the project, or share the ongoing discussion, or contribute their own insights. All this can be immensely valuable. It is a very delicate balance, and a matter of common sense and the shrewdness

■ dialogue

of your own judgment. You need, above all, to be aware of where your research stands on this tightrope. If you feel that some aspect of the research may have been affected by an inappropriate exchange of information, or a relationship that has led to some tainted data, then it is important to declare this.

▨ anonymity

Anonymity of the research site and the participants is absolutely necessary as you process the data. However, depending on the type of research, you should consult with your ethics committee if you feel the need to keep names and places intact before the research gathering begins, or if full anonymity in the final report is impossible (for example, if the site is immediately recognisable by its unique character or description). There are several ways to use anonymity, and most researchers tend to create pseudonyms for participants as this gives the research a human and authentic quality. However, if the researcher is dealing with many participants, using numerical or alphabetical ordering may help to manage the volume of people. Participants may choose for their real names to be revealed in the final report, and providing that is unanimous and formally documented, this is usually acceptable.

You should keep your ethical agreements under review. It may be necessary to revise the consent letter to address new issues that bubble up out of the data, or to accommodate new lenses that may affect how you analyse the data.

> In a typical example of this, in one research project, a participant at the research site informed the researcher that he was gay but not yet 'out'. As the research data began to take shape, his disclosure became more relevant to the findings. The researcher had to ask him for permission to discuss this personal information because it seemed truly organic to the processes she was observing.

▨ data storage

You must, at all times, keep track of where your data is stored, and it should all be stored in the same place for the time designated in the letter of consent. So you should think in advance about a storage location where it will not be accidentally destroyed, or possibly accessed by persons not associated with the research team. A lockable filing cabinet is probably the best place for storing and coding the data. Most universities and research institutions also have specific requirements for the storage of e-information, including password protection.

While waiting for the ethics clearance, there is nothing to stop the background work proceeding on the research: mastering the literature and refining the methodology. The happy day will arrive when your ethics committee finally gives clearance, and your research project is under full sail!

? REFLECTIVE QUESTIONS

1   What risks and possibilities are raised by my choice of a research site, especially if I am in some sense a practitioner there? Who are 'my' stakeholders?

2   'To what extent' [note!] does my Research Question generate critique or creativity in order for it to be well investigated or answered?

3   How does my research proposal carry forward a systematic investigation of my Research Question?

WIDER READING

Conrad, C. and Serlin, R. (eds) 2006. *The Sage Handbook for Research in Education.* Sage, Thousand Oaks, California.

Creswell, J. 2012, *Educational Research: Planning, Conducting, and Evaluating Quantitative and Qualitative Research.* Pearson, Boston.

Foreman-Peck, L. and Winch, C. 2010. *Using Educational Research to Inform Practice: A Practical Guide to Practitioner Research in Universities and Colleges.* Routledge, London.

Habibis, D. 2006. 'Ethics and Social Research', in M. Walters (ed.) *Social Science Research Methods: An Australian Perspective.* Oxford University Press, Melbourne.

Johnson, B. and Christensen, L. 2012. *Educational Research: Quantitative, Qualitative, and Mixed Approaches.* Sage, Thousand Oaks, California.

Kervin, L., Vialle, W., Herrington, J. and Okely, T. 2006. *Research for Educators.* Thomson Social Science Press, Melbourne. Chapters 1–4.

THE LITERATURE

 CHAPTER OBJECTIVES

After reading this chapter, you should be able to:

- feel confident in seeking relevant bodies of literature for your research topic, and in 'unpacking' your Research Question
- read these works critically—with an eye for the main claims you can make about them
- write a review that is partly descriptive of the literature, but which also weaves a 'silver thread' of argument towards a set of claims that are the conceptual springboard into the fieldwork.

ACCESSING THE LITERATURE

Simply put, at the outset of any research project you need to have some idea of what is already known on the topic. This is collectively referred to as the 'literature'—and most of it usually resides in books. There are, however, many other sources of information covered by that term 'literature': previous research reports and theses, statements of policy or procedures from the research site, archives, film and video, and, increasingly important, e-literature (the vast and indiscriminate pool of information, and misinformation, on the internet). One very rigorous tradition, derived from science, demands that before even embarking on a project, a complete review of all available literature must have been carried out, encompassing virtually all that is known about the topic. This is necessary to ensure probity, and to avoid repetition, even unwittingly, of other people's research. Some supervisors and research departments make this a requirement of the research process, demanding a completed literature review of this nature before proceeding any further.

■ diverse sources

Such finiteness (alas or fortunately, depending on your viewpoint) rarely exists in Education, which is a social science. We deal, as we have indicated in Part A, in provisional knowledge, in shifting dynamics and human behaviour that is context-specific, and all contexts have unique attributes. Moreover, as educators, we are often working in a multidisciplinary mode across a number of research disciplines, and that means 'literatures', plural. A single project—it could be a program evaluation in a school or a corporate workplace—might need some understanding of philosophy, history, sociology, educational psychology, statistics, post-colonial theory and cultural studies. To try and encompass all of any one of these, especially before you start the project,

■ literatures

would daunt anybody. Not only that, the literature constantly changes and expands as you progress through the research. So we urge you to be aware of the limitations of regarding literature as a pre-packageable, descriptive stage of your research.

Literature is, however, still crucial to your starting point, and throughout the study. It may be more helpful to think of the literature as part of the landscape, the scenery along the road of your research journey. You need to know what surface you are stepping on, and equally you need a sense of the texture of the landscape and the climate. Some of this must be done before you set out, at least a bit of mapping and a careful look around in the form of a preliminary review—a first cut of what is around, which should emerge from the bare bones of your proposal, as we discussed in Chapter 5.

■ mapping

So, having 'scanned' the various bodies of literature relevant to your topic, what next? Let us change metaphor. After all, in Chapter 5, we made some strong comments on how the better Research Questions move beyond 'mapping', or a street directory view of the topic, and so it is with reviewing the literature. Journeying along, in the mind, is actually best regarded as weaving a silver thread. That silver thread is not so much a descriptive review of literature as a *critical review*—finding and following the valuable silver among the tangle of the weave. But what does 'critical' mean? We believe a good review will partly describe what others have claimed in various bodies of scholarship, but will also weigh up where these claims stand in relation to your particular interest. Here you would need to be mindful of the type of research you are engaged in. All reading, reviewing and writing should be critical. In asking what knowledge various users of research want, Robert E. Floden states:

■ critical review: the silver thread

> Authors of research reports should be conscious of the rhetoric they employ, making their choices explicit rather than leaving them implicit. If the intent of the argument is to persuade policy-makers to adopt a particular course of action, the rhetoric must use arguments that will lead the reader in that direction. In so doing, the author must abandon the image of cool impartiality. (2006, p. 33)

Now, we are not advising you use such advocacy from the first page of your literature review! What we are suggesting is that a worthwhile review (and, overall, a worthwhile thesis or report) will argue for claims that are defensible, and not merely survey, descriptively, what others have stated. You must argue towards a clear position that you take on others' scholarship. And in reviewing others' claims, be aware that this rhetoric is already in the text. Take a quizzical, even sceptical, stance to the authors you come across from that first reading, as they should, were they to read your work.

Any research report of a finalised study, such as a thesis, must establish its credentials by indicating how intelligently and thoroughly the study has canvassed what is known about the topic. In a total of, say, 80 000 words (the usual length of a PhD thesis in Australia), you should allocate up to 20 000 words to a review. By contrast, reports of experienced researchers, presented in the form of a refereed article or book, or a commissioned report for a government department, may prefer to embed the literature within the substance of the report. If you are simply writing a journal article, of, say,

■ review length

7000 words, you do not really have space for a thorough and separate review. Whatever your boundaries, it is particularly important for apprentice researchers to demonstrate how thoroughly you know the relevant literature. This usually means separable literature reviewing as part of the final thesis, and we would suggest this should be about 25 per cent of the overall length, even if it is distributed in smaller chapters. There are exceptions to this, but it is usually wise to plan for it at the outset, and as the final literature review serves many useful functions, it is worth identifying in advance what you will be aiming for. These various functions are:

contextualising

- Your literature review will first and foremost contextualise your research within the broader field of study. You can expect that some of your readers (and certainly examiners) will be familiar with the literature and want to know what the project's main influences are.

defining terms

- You can use the review to define your terminology and explain your key terms. Some specialised terminology has a generally agreed meaning, for example 'behaviourism', to which you can sometimes refer as a shortcut. Other terms, such as 'critical', have a range of meanings particular to different traditions of research or practice, or different countries—'critical enquiry/critical thinking/critical theory', for instance (we have already come across that unhelpful tangle in the Postscript to Part A on page 82)—and it is crucial for the reader to understand which of these traditions is being invoked.

primary literature

- The review will demonstrate that you have read the key theoretical works that you are using for the basis of your research, known as the *primary literature*.

secondary literature

- It will also demonstrate that you have sufficiently researched the field, and delved enough into those other fields necessary to the enquiry (e.g. educational psychology, cultural studies), known as the *secondary literature*.

main arguments

- It will briefly outline the relevant arguments of the authors who you refer to, using succinct quotations.

critical traditions

- It will, where necessary, place the authors cited in their academic and even biographical context, to help the reader to understand which critical tradition those scholars come from.

evaluation

- Further to this, it will critically evaluate these arguments and reveal your own stance in relation to them, as a basis for developing your own argument, or what is new about your research.

To make this critical stance explicit, we suggest that the conclusion to such a review is a short, direct set of claims (rather than a summary) that lists the points of support and agreement with others. You can also raise your own questions about this literature, such as the points on which others have been silent ('gaps'), where there are important disagreements ('tensions') between others' views, and where there are new circumstances or contexts requiring new approaches (which, not surprisingly, you can rectify in what you plan to do).

⬂ MAKING A START

So, let's dive in! While you will find the most thorough and detailed treatment of academic issues in books, just as important are the scholarly journals. For scientists especially, they are actually more so, because new discoveries and advances are usually published first in journals. 'Education' in general, and the areas covered broadly by the arts, humanities and social sciences within Education, now have a number of well-established and significant international research journals, some of which are in print, some online, and some both. Browse recent issues of some of these, just for their contents pages, and you will find a point of entry to your topic. Now that all library holdings are online, you can do this by Boolean searching (keywords, authors, titles and so on), as we explain shortly.

▪ scholarly journals

What are the main types of Education journals? There are comprehensive Education research journals, such as the *Australian Journal of Education*, the *Oxford Review of Education*, the *Review of Educational Research* and the *Harvard Educational Review*. There are discipline-specific journals, such as the *Australian Journal of Music Education*; *English in Australia*; *Educational Philosophy and Theory*; *Reading Research Quarterly*; *Theory and Research in Social Education*; the *Journal of Aesthetic Education* and the *Journal of Science Education and Technology*.

▪ discipline journals

You may have a methodological or more localised interest. Examples of these are the *International Journal of Qualitative Studies in Education*, *Educational Action Research*, the *Creativity Research Journal* and the *Asia Pacific Journal of Education*. Or you may want to take a 'middle rung' perspective, such as through the *Journal of Curriculum Studies*, *Teaching and Teacher Education*, *TESOL Quarterly* and the *Teachers' College Record*.

Non-school contexts are covered, for example, by the *International Journal of Lifelong Education*, *Studies in Continuing Education*, the *Adult Education Quarterly*, *Studies in the Education of Adults* and the *Journal of Vocational Education and Training*. We could also have listed some prominent journals in early childhood and in higher education as these are, also, 'non-school' contexts.

▪ adult education journals

As you cast your net into the other literatures you need, you will find thousands of potentially useful papers in hundreds of journals. If this is starting to make your heart sink in apprehension rather than rise in excitement, turn to your mentor, supervisor, or a good friend who knows more about the field than you do, and remember that you do not have to know everything that has ever been written. Besides, many journal articles, if they are any good and relevant in our field, are frequently cited by our colleagues, and you can always start with those.

Knowing where to start is sometimes the hardest part. This is partly a matter of careful preliminary analysis of your research topic, driven by curiosity, and partly by instinct and gut feeling, as this reflection by Penny Bundy, an experienced researcher and meticulous reader, demonstrates.

■ advice   Bundy also offers some wise advice:

> What do I read? How do I read? How do I find the literature? How I answer
> these questions varies from project to project as we engage in different types
> of research projects and each requires a different initial approach. From my own
> experience I can identify at least three:
>
> - when I am intrigued by a question that emerges for us from our earlier or
>   current practice or experience (but we don't have an informed theoretical
>   understanding of it)
> - when I am passionate about a research topic because it grows from our
>   earlier or current theoretical contemplations/reading
> - when a research topic is totally new to me—maybe because I become
>   involved in someone else's research project/topic and have not earlier
>   contemplated or studied in this particular area, or maybe because I have
>   an externally driven need to find a research topic, this seems an interesting
>   place to start … but … I hadn't ever really thought about this much before.
>
> I think my own work most often fits the first category. So where do I start?
> I begin with a brainstorm. As I do this I contemplate: What seems to be at the
> guts of this phenomenon that I'm interested in? This gives me a number of
> different areas to begin my reading. From the ideas of one author grows a feast
> of literature.
>
> - I draw on my knowledge of a range of authors who work in these fields.
> - I do key word searches in the library, browsing through journals, browsing the
>   bookshelves.
> - As I read (and I read the whole article, the whole book etc.—not just
>   snippets and quotes) I take copious notes and reflect on the ideas being
>   expressed—testing them out against my understanding of practice and
>   contemplating them in relation to other ideas of other authors.
> - I make particular note of interesting authors being cited in the work. I turn to
>   their work, read them and do the same thing again.
> - As well as using these as starting points, I pick the brains of colleagues and
>   supervisors: Who have you read? What have you read?
>
> The second category is easy to deal with, as my previous interest ensures I
> already have a starting point in the literature, or know where to look for one.
>
> My advice to anyone starting a project that falls into the third category above
> would be to use their colleague or supervisor to get a 'basic' reading list to form
> a starting point—then follow some of the ideas above. (Bundy, in O'Toole 2006,
> pp. 85–6)

HOW TO READ

It is worth reading the above vignette carefully to see how a truly meticulous researcher works with the literature. However, Bundy's idea that one must on every occasion 'read the whole article, the whole book' perhaps needs modifying. As you browse shelves or indices, or do keyword searches, you are bound to come across a great deal of literature that is really irrelevant, or so tangential as to constitute a digression from the focus of your research. So we recommend that before getting an armful off the shelf, and settling down to 'read the whole book and take copious notes', you can bring both what you know and your intuition into play and save yourself a lot of time. Changing or at least expanding our metaphor once again, we recommend the stance of the 'educated magpie', who goes out with a sharp and inquisitive eye looking for glittering pieces of silver, and when she finds them, is clever enough to know how to thread them into her nest.

'magpie' collecting

First, before you go far you can usually find out a bit about the key authors in the field, with whom you must become familiar. Ask colleagues and mentors, or go to a source that you have already heard of. When you have started to read, comparing the bibliographies of the books you are already finding helpful is a useful trick, too—to see which writers are cited multiple times. The title and subtitle of the book can often give you a hint of its usefulness; then as you open it at the contents page, you will almost certainly get more basic clues. This is where the back brain, or intuition, is handy: if a chapter or article title jumps out at you, you can try turning to that page, and giving it a preliminary scan, speed-reading through to see what other words and sentences jump out as relevant, or alternatively reveal that it is outside your quest. Conversely, you shouldn't be intimidated by the fact that the book may be by a famous author, tempting you to plod dutifully through, when your instinct and your consciousness both tell you this is off target for your needs. On the other hand, neither should you be deterred just because a book is difficult. Sometimes the same book will need to be revisited a number of times over the course of the research. Concepts that appear difficult to grasp at first reading can be startlingly clear and relevant once you've spent time in the field.

key authors

bibliographies

intuition

persistence

re-reading

The main thing is to keep your wits about you—stay fresh enough to recognise the 'silver thread' of any argument you could establish, and stay critical enough to read the subtexts. As you read, you should be realising that each author has been through much the same process as we have described in this book so far, and so you can interrogate what you read: you can try to figure out the philosophical paradigm within which the author is writing, what particular ideological or methodical approach s/he is taking, what inspired or drove the author to write this particular book or undertake this research. And that may entail revisiting some authors' works during your research project, to see if your understanding of what they are saying has changed and deepened as your own understanding of the topic has deepened. Equally important is to look for what they are not telling you, to listen for the silences and omitted voices. As Bundy sagely continues:

critical reading

A couple of things I've noted with this approach though—you need to read very critically. Just because it's written doesn't mean it's true! I find I need to return to some of the key authors I've identified and re-read their work several times during a research project. As my awareness and understanding grow, I find I can start to read the same author and the same work with quite a different understanding at different reads. I also find it important to be open to the

> theoretical frameworks (often unstated) influencing any particular author. What
> is the author's bias? Where are the gaps? What aren't they seeing? Is there
> another school of thought that might look at this from another angle? Is there
> another field I could explore that would extend my understanding of this area?
> (Bundy, in O'Toole 2006, p. 87)

⬂ DOCUMENTING THE LITERATURE

retrieval

Reading thoroughly, selectively and critically is vital … but so is remembering what is relevant, and remembering where it comes from so that you are able to retrieve it at will. Nothing is so frustrating in the whole of research—and it happens to all of us—as half-remembering a gem of previous reading that would crystallise or clinch an argument … and not being able to find it. So, although you may be impatient to dive in and devour the literature, you must be methodical from the beginning, and this entails a number of processes:

cataloguing
summarising
sorting, coding
mapping

- cataloguing what you have read
- making summary critical notes, including pointers
- sorting and coding your reading (and perhaps re-sorting periodically)
- undertaking preliminary mapping of linkages.

software

There are some very handy electronic software that can help you, if you are technologically literate. For cataloguing, using EndNote or a similar program is a good way of making sure your bibliography is properly recorded and available whenever you need it. There are also a number of programs such as NVivo and ATLAS.ti (which we shall discuss in Chapter 8) that can help you to sort and code qualitative data, which, of course, includes the literature.

bibliographical details

Once you have selected a book or paper that you think might be useful, you should record its full bibliographical details, even before you read it. You may cast it aside quickly as irrelevant, but in two years' time you may need to revisit this area, and you will probably have forgotten what you did not use. Checking the bibliography saves you retracing old ground. What you must record are the author's name(s) in full, the title and subtitle, the date, place of publication and publishers, or journal volume and number—and if the work appears in an edited volume, the editor's name(s) and the title of the anthology. Once you have done this, you should have no difficulty tracing your reading either by the author or the title. There are a few standard referencing systems that most books and journals follow, and so should you. Ideally, you should choose a referencing system at the start, and record all the key details in this format for every book and paper you read. This is not so important when using software like EndNote: all the details that you list are recorded, but the format can be decided later and changed at whim without compromising any of the records.

With that initial bibliographical reference, you should include a brief note about its apparent content and focus, and if you are rejecting it without reading it, why.

Then, as you read, you should always do so with pen and notepad (or electronic ▪ notepad
equivalents) right at hand, because research reading is not just passive intake of words
from a page, but quite an energetic occupation. There are several kinds of notes to be
taken, all with page or section references:

- any particularly relevant ideas, paragraphs and sections—and briefly, why they seem
  relevant
- your own notes linking these to ideas from other books or your own research data
- particularly apt quotations (and don't forget the page number!)—if they are long, say
  several paragraphs, just make a general note: at this point you don't have to choose
  the exact quote you might use later
- internal citations from other books and papers that sound important, and might
  become part of your own literature review (turn to the author's bibliography and
  note the full details straight away).

This may seem a very laboured way of reading, especially if you are trying to do it
in bed or on the beach. It will actually save you endless hours of frustrating and futile
're-searching' for what could easily be at hand.

Janet Macdonald, another of our sources from the field of drama research, shares this
checklist and example of her own practice with her students (Macdonald, in O'Toole
2006, pp. 88–9):

Documenting and retrieving literature: I use the following pro-forma as a way of
cataloguing, storing, but also doing early analysis and linkages … this also comes in
handy for coding the data later.

For the purposes of your research, you should include the following detail:

- your name
- the date the article was retrieved/read
- the citation *and* call number of the article—using correct citations
- a descriptive paragraph giving a summary of the information contained
  in the article
- a list of page numbers from the article where possible quotes or important
  information can be found
- cross-references to other articles you have read or ideas you have conceived.

See example below:

Joe Bloggs

2 March 2001

Bailey, Lucy 1996. 'The Feminisation of a School? Women Teachers in a Boys' School.'
Gender and Education 8 (2), pp. 171–84.

PN 97831.321

I found this article riveting as it deals mostly with how female teachers' status is tied to how they dress and 'perform' their role as 'teacher' for the boys. It also mentions notions of how boys might sexualise their female teachers and how they 'categorise' them. DOES NOT discuss DRAMA, but does acknowledge the number of women in the boys' school teaching 'soft' or 'arts' subjects.

172: quote on 'power' and gender — use

174: the notion of deviancy and pedagogy — follow this up in Foucault

180: discusses gendered curricula — find example in field notes

183: gives a brilliant description of an arts classroom with a female teacher

Cross-refs:

Foucault

Judith Butler and the Performance of Gender

See article by Maclean and Gilbert on boy-culture with male teachers

Think about the 'roles' women play in all-male environments: How much is expected and how much do they buy into it? How do I gather evidence to support this?

THE INTERNET AND OTHER SOURCES

▦ internet

The internet is the world's biggest library and also the least discriminating. However, Google or another good search engine, lots of patience and a nerve tonic are all you need. If in doubt, ask the children—they usually know more than your IT service, and can get you where you want, quicker. *Caveat emptor* every time you go in, of course, but there is a lot of excellent material in the public domain that is available to

▦ journal websites

beginning researchers. Academic journals, however, may be best accessed once they are subscribed to, but they do usually provide lists of contents and abstracts of the papers on their open website, and, indeed, the main publishers of journals have lists of their own 'stable'. By browsing under the main categories—such as discipline areas, by title—you can find the more helpful sources. If you are associated with a university or college, it is quite likely that the institution already subscribes to the online version, and may also have hard copies on its shelves. Another advantage of being connected to

▦ libraries

an educational establishment library is that they always have good search engines for journals and other online copy, which will do a lot of your preliminary browsing for you quite painlessly. You might need to approach searching laterally, especially internet searching. Just because you find nothing on your key words doesn't mean there is no useful research on your topic. If you look at Macdonald's example on pages 113–14, the book she found useful was not on her discipline subject of drama at all, but it still illuminated her topic.

There are a number of useful quick reference sources that are entirely free, such as the invaluable Wikipedia and its accompanying Wiktionary. These are full of silver threads of scholarship generously shared—but here's where *caveat emptor* must be exercised vigorously and everything double-checked, as Wikipedia proudly announces on its home page that it is 'the free encyclopedia that anyone can edit' and so it's also full of fool's gold. Many university departments generously put a lot of their commonly used reference and background study material online for anybody to use. Many individual academics are equally generous (or egocentric, or both) and provide material such as their latest papers on their web page, or on a public domain site that you can often reach via common web links or by Googling. Whole academic arguments and battles rage on subject websites and conference websites. There is a new breed of e-academics who rarely, if ever, publish in hard copy.

When accessing the web, the usual reading rules apply: make sure that the site is fully referenced and that the date you retrieved the material is logged. It may well be necessary to copy out some of the quotations in full or download the article if permissible, since web-based material has a habit of disappearing and being replaced, often without warning.

Wikipedia

universities

Research site resources

If your research is connected in any way with a particular research site, such as a school or a workplace, it may be worthwhile looking into the archival material available there. You may unearth some background material that affects your quest, or the way you approach your fieldwork: perhaps policy statements, or previous research reports. It can also be valuable to investigate comparable locations and institutions to see whether they have any useful archival material of a similar kind for comparison.

archives

All of this takes time, but should not hamper your research. There are no set guidelines to tell you when you have read enough to be able to move on to the next stage of your research, which is your own new data-gathering. It depends on how literate you were in the area before you started and how deeply you need to be steeped in the literature and its paradigms before you start your data-gathering (especially since immersion will help with a genuinely 'critical' conclusion to your review, which serves as a conceptual springboard into the fieldwork). It also depends on whether there are cultural or other sensitivities that you must take account of before you finalise your data-collection instruments, your interview questions and so on.

Sometimes an immediate start on data-gathering is necessary, so you have to read the literature concurrently. Be reassured that almost everyone has to 'backfill' their literature review, even as the thesis or project is nearing its end: there are often emphases and underpinnings that must be provided early on in the final document, but the need to do so was not apparent until the main achievements have been identified. This is normal!

backfilling

Overall, the three best guidelines for a robust handling of the literature are your own intelligent (i.e. critical) reading of your scholarly context; your intuition and instinct about your readiness to dive in to the fieldwork; and taking advice from those more experienced than you are, on issues of relevance, balance, intellectual modesty and innovative rhetoric!

? REFLECTIVE QUESTIONS

1 Have I relied upon both primary and secondary sources, and bodies of scholarship, which I can show are explicitly connected to my Research Question?

2 Is there a clear set of claims I can make about the gaps, tensions and research potential of the literature I have reviewed, which supports the design of my fieldwork?

3 What additional refinement of the review do I anticipate after the fieldwork is completed, and as I write up my project or thesis?

WIDER READING

Creswell, J. 2012. *Educational Research: Planning, Conducting, and Evaluating Quantitative and Qualitative Research*. Pearson, Boston.

Eisner, E. 2008. 'Persistent Tensions in Arts-based Research', in M. Cahnmann-Taylor and R. Siegesmund (eds) *Arts-based Research in Education: Foundations for Practice*. Routledge, New York. See also Chapter 1, 'Arts-based Research: Histories and New Directions'.

Ezzy, D. 2006. 'The Research Process', in M. Walter (ed.) *Social Research Methods: An Australian Perspective*. Oxford University Press, Melbourne.

Johnson, B. and Christensen, L. 2012. *Educational Research: Quantitative, Qualitative, and Mixed Approaches*. Sage, Thousand Oaks, California.

Kervin, L., Vialle, W., Herrington, J. and Okely, T. 2006. *Research for Educators*. Thomson Social Science Press, Melbourne. Chapter 4.

DEALING WITH DATA

☑ CHAPTER OBJECTIVES

After reading this chapter, you should be able to:

- design data collection and generation, being aware that the ways people participate in these will shape the quality and quantity of the data
- settle on sufficient and relevant documentation of this collecting, generating and participating
- stretch your understanding of data to include what is not immediately obvious, such as silent, negative and background 'voices'.

⬂ COLLECTING AND GENERATING DATA

Here's a contradiction for you: though, as we've remarked, the word 'data' just means 'what is given', in fact it's not given at all—you have to go looking for it! And by the way, the word 'data' is technically plural, though it's commonly used as a singular noun, so you can say 'the data shows …' or the 'data show …'—your choice, but you must be consistent about it.

Here's an overview of this fairly long chapter. First, we outline collecting and generating data: hunting and gathering. These are the fundamental aspects of all fieldwork. But because this book is serious about the diversity of approaches now available to Education researchers, and the authors locate themselves in the arts and humanities, we are keen to give prominence to negative, silent and background 'voices'—the hidden quarry. This is consistent with the experientially holistic and humanistic values we espoused in Part A, especially in Chapters 2 and 3. Then, we build on those values by developing 'participant data' in its many forms—farming your data yourself—including the experimental, where statistics are introduced as important sources of fieldwork, especially in 'mixed mode'. Finally, we set out the documentation of data, in light of the diversity of data collection and generation apparent throughout this chapter.

hunting and gathering

By now, whether you are following the book sequentially, or turning straight to this chapter, you will probably have decided on your basic approach, as we set out in Chapter 4. A lot of research that is 'interpretive' will mainly involve *collecting* data. Often, in fact, you will strive *just* to collect, not to generate new data that changes the research site by your presence and thus creates new variables. (This is not always true of some contemporary forms of ethnography, but it often is of simpler ethnography and certainly of case studies

collecting data

■ generating data

where you are an outsider.) If your research is 'change oriented' one of your primary tasks will be *generating* new data that you then collect, usually as you go along. If the research uses one of the 'blended' methodologies, then the generation and collection of data will be an ongoing, cyclic process, with the data you collect and the research site informing and augmenting each other. For instance:

> Here are some hypothetical examples of when it is appropriate to collect and when to generate data:
>
> In a *case study*, observing another teacher's Year 8 humanities class with an endemically high proportion of special needs students, your aim will be to *collect* material that corresponds as closely as possible to the norm of that classroom. Generating change is the last thing you want to do.
>
> As an *action researcher* with a high proportion of special needs students in your Year 8 humanities class and limited resources, you want to address their complex requirements. Following your pre-planning, you will start the first cycle with a particular strategy designed to address the problem of lack of diverse resources. That strategy *generates* new data specific to this context, and the data you *collect* will be focused on the impact that this strategy is (or is not) having on your agenda.
>
> As a *reflective practitioner* with that Year 8 class, you will begin by *collecting* data on how you normally operate in this particular context, as honestly as you can. As you process and analyse the data, it will suggest improvements that you might make in your practice. As you put these into effect, you will be *generating* a new and modified context, on which you will *collect* data to feed into your research that will *generate* further changes or modifications.

■ research approaches

Whatever your choice of research approach and methodology, there are well-tried methods of both generating and recording the data, and introductory research textbooks to help you, so it is important that you read the appropriate methodological literature in the Wider Reading lists at the end of each chapter. This chapter gives only a general guide to some of the more important principles.

■ data surfeit

The main problem you are likely to encounter is not shortage of data, but a surfeit of it. Because human behaviour and learning are so complex, whether we are generating or collecting data, there is always a wealth to pick from … therefore, most of this chapter will be about how to pick and choose. Even more than with the literature, you will be tempted to be conscientiously comprehensive, and cover all aspects of your research topic, site and subjects' behaviour. You must try to preserve your sanity by remembering that your research is not in the business of absolute truth, and what you do will be both partial and provisional. Every bit of data you generate will be there to be recorded, and subsequently analysed. Judicious selection of the data you want to hunt, from before you even start, is the way to prevent your prey turning round to bite you.

Collecting data

Whatever your research topic and context, you must believe that you will find something new, or at the very least, confirm or disprove for the first time something that was hypothesised but unproved. Research never just means 're … searching' over old ground. Even if you are composing a purely philosophical and non-empirical, conceptual piece of research, where you read, ponder, argue and then write the results of the analysis, you are looking for new insights from old literature, or new arguments on traditional topics, albeit of contemporary interest. In that kind of thesis, the literature—both classical and contemporary—becomes all of your primary data, and no ethics clearance is needed.

<aside>new knowledge</aside>

Most of us start research with a more empirical research context, however. You need to do 'field' work, literally: out in the field (wherever that is). If you are working within an interpretive paradigm, such as ethnography, interpretive case study or historical research, your research site, once chosen, is a 'given'. Your task is to collect data from it in as 'natural' a condition as possible. While this is actually an impossibility, it is one you should strive towards. If you are doing historical research, you have the advantage that the primary documentary sources stand still to be searched for useful data (usually, anyway).

<aside>fieldwork</aside>
<aside>site data</aside>

Your research is never purely descriptive, or neutral. When you begin to research you must acknowledge your philosophical, ideological and attitudinal positions. But you also need to be wary of what Foucault (1970, pp. 323–6) called an 'unconscious archive'—those assumptions we make that are so much part of our contemporary context and the way we think that we cannot readily be aware of them. Those may indeed emerge to bite you as you research the documents. That's why descriptive research is always also interpretive.

<aside>assumptions</aside>

Ethnography and interpretive case study both involve live contexts and breathing research subjects, and that may take you into fieldwork of one kind or another as an 'observer', on the observer–participant continuum. The observer/researcher has to find ways of being as unobtrusive as possible, while recognising that the research participants are aware that the research is taking place. This can be both easy and difficult: young people really absorbed in classroom activity can quickly forget about a quiet observer or a video camera in the corner as they focus on more important matters, just as they can blot out noises outside the classroom window or even irrelevant classroom happenings. On the other hand, much 'workshopped' activity or small-group work is about debate and performance. The third-party researcher or camera can be an audience to be self-conscious about, or alternatively one to be played up to. Any effect that your presence has on the research site is part of the data and this must be acknowledged and documented. Especially if you are doing contemporary ethnographical research, you may be deliberately creating a relationship that will deeply affect the context. Working effectively involves developing a bond of trust between the subjects and the researcher(s). You should tell them about what you are researching and why, so at least they lose both their curiosity and their fear of you, removing two important destabilising factors. Many researchers, rather than creating a proactive relationship, will try to become part of the normal pattern of the research site—part of the classroom furniture, for instance, so that

<aside>observer/researcher</aside>
<aside>trust</aside>

they disrupt the normal process as little as possible. In such cases, the very trust that you create can be a two-edged weapon, as many researchers trying to be unobtrusive observers have ruefully found. The very confidence that their neutral adult presence generates encourages their research subjects to come running up to engage them in conversation, confidences and requests for advice.

Generating data

■ change-oriented methodologies

As we have stressed, change-oriented methodologies, such as action research, design research and much experimental research, involve some kind of fieldwork, where you focus on an aspect of the research context, impose a change from the norm, and collect data on what happens. In itself that is not hard, but it does presage two problems. One problem is generating too much data, which not only clouds the central research topic but can be difficult to manage. Another problem is that the data collected is likely to include unexpected elements as the result of unforeseen variables.

■ unforeseen variables

> Common examples of collecting unexpected data are:
>
> • changes in behaviour that might be the result of the research intervention or equally of a host of other factors
>
> • other unexpected and unplanned organisational changes. For instance, in schools, timetables are notoriously unreliable, and teacher and student absences always a hazard; in corporate workplaces, restructurings, staff turnover and market forces are daily pressures
>
> • unplanned and unsolicited interventions, either from people wanting to be helpful, or from negative stakeholders seeking to question or disrupt the research.

■ preparation

This is why it is essential to prepare thoroughly in advance, in order to anticipate your needs, remove as many of these uncontrolled variables as possible, and choose carefully from the possible data-collection instruments. Remember, you can never collect all possible data on human behaviour, and so you just need to gather the data that will be the most helpful in testing your hypothesis. Here you do have to be judicious, because you cannot risk missing a key source of information, and it is never easy to add a data-gathering tool later. You can't video a lesson or a community or organisation-based presentation retrospectively. Even a task like setting students a reflective or assessment task that will provide their view of events, if you have not planned for it in advance, is usually too hard to arrange *post hoc*. It may also entail a change to your ethics approval, which can be drawn out and problematic.

■ modification

Sometimes diverting to collect further data, or modifying the instruments you are using, is unavoidable. This is especially so in action research, where each cycle involves documentation and data collection, and is dependent on what has happened in the previous cycle. In this kind of research, it is wise to include in your preliminary plan—and in your ethics proposal—a wider range of data-collection instruments than you expect to use, covering at least the predictable exigencies. Then you can pick the instruments that seem best at first, and those that could only be used if planned in advance, while keeping up your sleeve one or two that could be implemented practicably if the occasion arises. As a beginning action researcher, called Hamlet, observed, 'The readiness is all.' (Pity he didn't take his own advice.)

▨ exigencies

Part of that readiness may be to take the participants into your confidence and endow them as co-researchers. Not only does this give them some power in the process, as we discussed in Chapter 2, but it gives them a personal stake and ownership of the research that usually makes them more enthusiastic and flexible in contributing to it. They may also have their own unique sources of data, such as personal diaries, blogs, Facebook pages and SMS networks, otherwise unavailable to you, that you can very usefully tap into.

▨ co-researchers

▨ participant data

Experimental research, particularly comparative investigation, is more severe and unforgiving, as it is always impossible to vary the data collection once it has begun. Varying one set of data by introducing new variables will invariably corrupt another or otherwise render it unusable, as we discuss under participant data (see p. 123).

▨ experiments

◥ NEGATIVE DATA AND SILENT VOICES

You also have to find and disinterestedly record data that challenges, contradicts or confounds your hypotheses and expectations. This is what we might call *negative data* and this is what separates the sheep from the goats—the genuine researchers from the advocates and those with personal agendas, in disguise as researchers. Negative data is just as important as positive data, but more easily overlooked. In properly constructed experimental research, this data will automatically come up, and usually jumps out at the researcher. Then the test is in the data analysis: to interpret the negative factors and findings and accord them their appropriate weighting.

▨ negative data

In qualitative data collection, this task is much harder. You have to counter your natural instincts and actively go looking for negative data. Very often it is hard to find because it consists of silent or silenced voices (literally or figuratively). These silent voices include:

▨ silent voices

- the stakeholders, positive and negative, who you have neglected to identify and include in the research

▨ overlooked stakeholders

- often literally silent, the quieter, more passive, timid or otherwise less assertive participants

▨ unassertive participants

- those who find it difficult to articulate what they represent or believe, either in words or images—for example, very young children and people with disabilities

▨ inarticulate participants

- dissenters, who may be reluctant to spoil the research by voicing their reservations, intimidated by the researchers or the scale of the research project, or gagged by the rest of the participants, particularly if they are a small minority.

▨ dissenters

The last three groups are easy to miss in participatory research, where 'group-think' is an ever-present danger, and the majority of participants often collude with the researchers, consciously or unconsciously, to provide them with what they are looking for.

▨ group think

In the corporate world, most staff are keeping an eye on their employability and promotion prospects, which can construct an organisational culture of compliance, as we discussed in Part A. In schools, young people, when onside, are naturally helpful and, especially if they have an interest in the successful outcome of research, want to maximise its chances of success. In contrast to these two groups, the incompatible or dissenting opinions, while essential for the 'friction' that is needed for traction across the ice, can destabilise research for participants and researchers alike if its importance is overblown.

Alert researchers will have the foresight to anticipate this. Sometimes the silent voices can be encouraged or persuaded to make themselves heard, by your valuing and validating their contributions. Sometimes you must be shrewd, subtle and indirect. In observing or otherwise collecting data from participants, you must read the subtexts with your eyes and ears. In interviews, when the verbal text is in conflict with the non-verbal signals—the 'paralanguage'—you should invariably believe the paralanguage, and try to find a way to assist such interviewees to reveal their real thoughts and reservations. In reading student or participant journals, you must read between the lines. In both interviews and participant writings, you must actively look and listen for what is *not* being said: the omissions caused by politeness, fear or inarticulacy. In classroom activities, you can force yourself to look beyond the heart-warming sight of the engaged participants in the forefront of your vision, to deliberately scan the rest of the action (and especially those participants off focus) for paralanguage of reluctance, disengagement, hostility or just nervous lack of involvement. Then you must follow that up again to find a way to allow the participants to articulate their lack of engagement or dissent. This may be quite simple, such as by ensuring that the participants are being interviewed by a research assistant who is external to the project, and guaranteed anonymity for their responses.

Sometimes you must be even more indirect, not to trick the participants, but to permit them to reveal their true attitudes without being aware of your own central objective. Two examples from the same research project show techniques of respectively allowing participants to reveal attitudes that they might be reluctant to acknowledge directly, and gathering information that enthusiastic participants might be eager to augment or overemphasise.

■ paralanguage

■ data omissions

■ indirect data

One of the action research projects that comprised 'cooling conflict' was designed to discover the effects, if any, of a combination of drama and peer-teaching on intercultural conflict among secondary students (O'Toole and Burton 2005b, p. 274). In advance, the participants were asked to complete a survey of their attitudes towards conflict. Direct questions of the 'Tick if you have racist attitudes' type would not be likely to elicit true responses. Students with racist feelings know from early schooling that those ideas are directly counter to official school policies and teacher ethos, so therefore certainly to a group of researchers investigating intercultural conflict. Accordingly, the questionnaire did not call attention to questions of racism, but invited opinions on conflict types, protagonists, gender, how the respondents themselves handle conflict and other more value-neutral matters. The questions included several based on hypothetical cases — 'If you were … what would you do?' Two of these actually dealt with racial conflict:

> If it was announced that for the third year running the school captain was to be a Chinese student, would you:
>
> - be proud?
> - think it was unfair?
> - not care?
>
>   Explain if you like.
>
> If you were suddenly to find out (however far-fetched it may seem) that your great-grandfather was Aboriginal, would you:
>
> - be pleased?
> - be sorry?
> - not care?
> - have a different or mixed reaction?
>
> Would you tell people at school?
>
> - Yes
> - No
>
>   Explain if you like.
>
> (O'Toole and Burton 2005a, p. 383)

The responses to these questions were, on the whole, candid and revealing.

Following the action plan, a key question the researchers wanted to know the answer to was: 'Has what you have learned in this program had any effect on the way you deal with conflict *beyond* the project classroom?' The research team had engaged the students as co-researchers, the drama and peer-teaching had been for nearly all the students a very exciting and satisfying experience, and there was a warm relationship between the students and the research team. As a result, the team were concerned that the students would be keen to validate the research. This could well include answering all such questions in the affirmative, with wish fulfilment playing a part, and some might even embroider their experiences. Accordingly, the students were interviewed by research assistants who had not been part of the action plan and were strangers to them. These assistants were given explicit instructions *not* to raise the key question with the students, or lead them in any way towards it, or respond with significant emphasis. By giving these instructions, the team realised that a great deal of positive data on the real effects of the program was likely to be lost when students did not happen to bring the subject up by themselves. As it was, over 50 per cent of the students did volunteer unsolicited information and anecdotes clearly indicating that they had used their new-found conflict literacy in dealing with real-life conflict differently than they would have previously. The research team interpreted this finding as much more reliable than any directly elicited information would have been, and a strong affirmation of the program's transferability into the students' lives beyond the classroom.

BACKGROUND DATA

■ documents

For some research, part or all of the data is derived from documents; this is the norm for historical research looking back more than a lifetime, where the people who contributed to primary sources are all dead and research sites likely to be changed beyond recognition. Documents may also be an important component of contemporary research. The past and the present can be vigorously linked, as this example shows.

> Catherine (Yongyang)'s PhD explored the teaching of Chinese as a foreign language (TCFL), using Chinese literature (Wang 2008). She identified rich background data on how Chinese literature has been used in such teaching, both for 'insiders' and 'outsiders': 'it has been used for conducting moral-political education, for language education, and for professional development. I have argued that the influence of the Chinese intellectual tradition is readily apparent in the TCFL curriculum, and have demonstrated this influence in my analysis of textbooks employed for teaching Chinese literature to non-Chinese learners' (Wang 2008, p. 247). For Catherine, the past is shown in 'the large body of canonical "heritage" literature in the local Chinese curriculum which plays an important role in citizenship education and ideological indoctrination that is underpinned by China's long-standing historical and hagiographic tradition'. She traces this back to Confucianism. The recent past and the present is a contrast: 'TCFL is a recently established tradition, having only 56 years of history, including almost 10 years suspension due to the Cultural Revolution' (Wang 2008, p. 247).

■ permissions

Just one very important warning—permissions are essential. You must ensure that either the documents are in the public domain (like the textbooks in Catherine's example), or that you have permission both to access the documents and, if you are intending to quote or refer directly to them, to cite them in your research report (as with some of the unit outlines). And, of course, you must be scrupulous in the way you use and reference them. If the documents are private, the owners must be apprised of the reference you are intending to make and the amount you are intending to quote, if that applies. This

■ sensitivities

can be a sensitive issue, if the research is revealing findings that might be critical of the owner or writer of the documents. That must be dealt with tactfully. You must recognise that your rights as researchers are subsidiary to the common law rights of the owners.

> Catherine used her extensive research into TCFL to come up with a new 'reading practice', which is 'not just a matter of different content, or an expanded repertoire of sources, but a matter of integrating cultural awareness and language learning in a form of pedagogy that is derived from appreciation of a non-Chinese learner's needs

and perspectives' (Wang 2008, p. 248). This does not require abandoning the past—its rich canonical texts—but rather will embrace 'marginalised, avant garde and diasporic writers', so that the complexity of China and the Chinese in the twenty-first century can be more fully revealed. This is at the heart of the humanistic ideal, in research, and worked for Catherine's project because she was able to locate her analyses in the 'textuality' of textbooks themselves. In her PhD's 'social semiotic' approach, she relied partly on Roland Barthes, when she claimed, in her literature review, that in the reading of literature, 'meanings are created by the reader' (p. 36), more than by the writer(s).

In the corporate world, to give another (this time hypothetical) example, if the fieldwork had uncovered evidence of organisational or individual malpractice and the researcher had reported that in his research findings, he might be accused of defamation or face other threats of litigation. Even with public documents, there could be issues of copyright and/or intellectual property—if for example, the research became a commercially published book or DVD illustrated by the company's posters and named company products.

PARTICIPANT DATA

Direct participant data

The research participants can of course provide the most directly authentic data, particularly about their behaviour, feelings, attitudes and thoughts during fieldwork episodes. This can be collected in a number of ways, some direct, some oblique, some synchronous with the fieldwork, some retrospective.

Often the best way to collect rich data from the participants, and to motivate them to produce it, is to invite them to become co-researchers, where from the inception, what they produce and their thoughts about it will be recognised as important data. For adults, this is usually necessary initially. For instance, busy teachers or other professionals may consider the task of writing a journal or log of what they are doing an onerous and unwelcome extra job. When they actually engage in the activity, they find themselves reflecting on it, and for their own satisfaction and sense of achievement, they usually want to assist the research to come up with useful data, which obviously includes their opinions.

Participants' journals

A regularly kept log or reflective journal is always a very valuable source of participant data. Although, like anything else, some skill is necessary to make it really useful to the researcher. Some research participants will, of course, already be familiar with writing a journal from previous studies. However, students and even professionals do not automatically understand how to create and structure a reflective journal so

reflective journals

that it *is* reflective. The automatic response of a beginner to the task is either to just describe the explicit action in a simple narrative, or to dive into unstructured stream-of-consciousness personal feelings about the experience. Reflectiveness has to be taught. Instead of a continuous journal, it may be more useful to ask the participants, after each session, to write a response to a specific question framed by the researcher, which actively demands reflective thinking about what has happened.

FOR YOUR JOURNAL

During today's session, you were asked to suggest interventions in a case study based on a real historical conflict.

- Which, if any, of the interventions that were tried or suggested did you think were likely to have been most successful in de-escalating the conflict?
- Which of these strategies, or what other strategy, would you have chosen?
- Why do you think that, as history tells us, the conflict was allowed to escalate into war?
- Write up to half a page on each of these questions.

Some participants may not be able to articulate well enough on paper to complete a journal, or there may not be time available, or the ambience may be wrong. There are other ways of collecting useful data. An oral journal, usually in the form of a taped structured interview (this could be as simple as asking for a retelling of the story) following the experience, can be useful. Photographs can form an important kind of participant journal, and the practice of giving research participants cameras (or even video cameras), asking them to photograph aspects of the experience you are researching, and then writing an interpretive commentary, or taking part in an explanatory discussion with the researcher, is becoming quite commonplace. Particularly with young children, drawing or painting can be figuratively as well as literally illuminating, providing you can find a visual arts educator who can interpret it.

▤ oral journals
▤ visual journals

A large-scale study by one of the authors compared the effect of a story (*The Songman and the Pest*) when enacted in participatory theatre in education (ten 'program classes') or read by the class teacher (ten 'control classes') (O'Toole 1977, pp. 146–58). This was measured by asking the children to retell the story in writing, and to do a drawing, both of which, when collated, provided valuable, different yet compatible data from two sets of three hundred children. What the data revealed, and the missed data-gathering opportunities, will be described in Chapter 8, when we look at data analysis.

Assessment items

When working with school students, often the easiest way of collecting useful feedback data is in the form of assessment items. Those journals or memos can serve a double function. So too can an exam, where cognitive knowledge can easily be tested; like the story retellings on page 126 in the example, exams and tests can provide both statistics and qualitative material.

■ assessment as data

It is important to reflect on the relationship between performance assessment and research. Does a practical approach to assessment work in non-school settings? We are all now involved in annual or at least regular 'performance assessments' as part of our work. In complex professional and organisational contexts, it is increasingly common to be asked in annual 'appraisal' interviews creative questions like: 'What are you most proud/pleased/satisfied with in your work over the past year?' and 'What would you most like to have done differently?' Looking to some future assessment, the questions then move to 'What plans can we agree are worth resourcing, for the next year?' and 'What obstacles are there to achieving …?' While the implicit contractual grip of these questions may chill you to the bone, it can't be denied that they have a way of focusing staff on strategic, documentable outcomes. This is one implication of competent performance (Beckett and Hager 2002, pp. 56–9).

■ performance assessment

Whether or not for assessment, back in schools and community settings, the products of fieldwork are themselves valuable data.

> The script and performance of a group-devised play can be analysed for all sorts of things: what they reveal about the pedagogy of a particular teacher (Sanders 2003), the effectiveness of a reflective practitioner in a complex or problematic context (Lovesy 2003), factors of gender or culture in schools (Hatton 2004), or all of the above (Donelan 2005).

Products, too, do not necessarily mean end-products, since in all these contexts, early, experimental jottings; improvised training notes; 'dot-points' briefings; the ubiquitous PowerPoint presentation; the even more ubiquitous post-training 'happy sheets' of evaluations; and any personal follow-ups are all process-driven data. They help shape outcomes. The leader's reflective thoughts within such processes can be equally revealing—the reflection-in-action, as Donald Schön would put it, as we outlined in Chapter 4.

■ process-driven data

Creative conventions as research tools

Creative pedagogies abound in opportunities for subtle and indirect forms of data collection. Here we make no apologies for introducing a range of these techniques from our own home territory of drama pedagogy. Learners of any age, in schools and non-school contexts, can undertake *in-role writing*. Not only is it an excellent way for

■ in-role writing

learners to understand and develop character, diversity and empathy, but it can also be used to analyse many other factors in learning holistically: the level of engagement, comprehension of the whole context or particular elements, understanding of the theme or the dilemma, imaginativeness in response to a challenge. In-role writing can take the form of letters to governments, friends, relatives and newspapers; diary entries; articles and newspaper features; or poems written in the first person. And the oral complement to in-role writing is another of the techniques common in experiential learning: *hot-seating* and its more well-known pedagogical partner, *simulations*.

■ hot-seating, simulations

Variants of these techniques in the collection of participant data are other creative learning experiences:

- *time jumps*: inviting participants to jump backward or forward significant distances in time, allowing for more distanced responses to a situation or character
- *role on the wall*: drawing the outline of a person under scrutiny, and then inscribing within the outline some of the attributes of that character (this activity has variations)
- *role changes or reversals*: using role changes or reversals to give participants a different point of view, then asking participants to comment on the situation or character from this other perspective
- *combining strategies*: using a combination of these, by jumping the action into a wholly different setting and asking participants to comment, for example, from the viewpoint of archaeologists far in the future coming upon some of the artefacts or relics previously created in the learning space, and speculating on their meaning.

■ normal conditions

A final caveat, already a common refrain throughout this book: when using any of these participant techniques, you must ensure, as far as possible, that the task of collecting research data does not interfere with the 'normal' operation of the site. For instance, the participants may be so aware of the data-collection purpose that they write or carry out their tasks with that in mind rather than the learning context. Sometimes, and especially in the corporate and professional world, the double function of assessment and research puts unfair pressure on the participants. Do staff feel they 'must' participate to keep themselves employable? Here is the implicit 'compliance' concern that we first raised in Part A. In deliberately involving participants, do we seek their allegiance, through Foucauldian 'surveillance', to non-research outcomes? The salutary lesson here is that an eye that looks like it invites compliance from participants, may, also, need to keep an eye on ethics. There could be official clearance procedures that may be necessary, such as if confidential documents are needed by researchers. Looking both ways can compromise both the participants and the researchers. Taken further, are the participants explicitly involved in debriefing? Participation should itself be holistic.

■ pressure
■ compliance

Interviews

One of the commonest forms of data collection from participants is the interview. This can take many forms, and there are many useful handbooks and book chapters on how to structure interviews, so this summary will only note some of the more important considerations.

If you are considering interviewing research subjects, there are at least seven dimensions that you must carefully consider. These are outlined below.

Are they worth it?

Interviews are very time-consuming, for researchers and subjects alike. They are sometimes quite complex to set up. Finding appropriate times and spaces can be a problem in some research sites; subjects may not be immediately willing; the interviews may need ethical permissions. They will usually require transcribing—and transcription can only capture the words, not the gestures and paralanguage, the emotional subtexts that may be more important to the research. Video recording will partly overcome that, but cannot pick up what a live interviewer can by way of eye contact and so on. Recording equipment can go wrong, and there are usually words or even sections that are inaudible. This is particularly likely if the subjects speak in accents and dialects that deviate from the transcriber's, or if they are not very articulate. Most important of all, interviewers need to be skilled and attentive listeners, and skilled at questioning, too. This is as necessary to convincingly and demonstrably confirm expectations as it is to hear or elicit the unexpected and to encourage the silenced voice to speak. So the first thing to decide is whether the interview is worth all that effort. Could the information be obtained in some other, simpler way—from observation, subject journals or questionnaires, for instance?

demands and drawbacks

alternatives

If you decide the game is worth the candle—that the effort is worthwhile—you need to decide how many of these time-consuming encounters you need; perhaps it's better to think how few you *really* need. Remember, data is like rabbits: unwanted proliferation is an ever-present peril.

In some forms of research, interviews are *de rigueur* and one of the principal methods of data collection. Some anthropological studies and ethnographies are entirely built on the witness statements of community members; and many developmental case studies, for instance, depend on sequenced interviews. In longitudinal research, too, re-interviewing subjects over a period of time, or in retrospect, can provide vital information and even statistics.

ethnographic interviews

Who do you interview?

Sometimes—especially in a group learning situation, from a sports coaching clinic to a training orchestra—it is not easy to decide who to interview. Again, you must decide exactly what information you need and can expect. There may be a case for interviewing everybody, but think of the transcription and analysis burden. If you want to know, in general, how a group (for example, an audience or a class of students) reacted to an event, can you choose a sample group? Usually yes, but you must have clear criteria for choosing your sample, particularly if you want a true cross-section. You must take into account factors like gender, age, education or familiarity with the genre, or the context of the event, even perhaps socio-economic or geographical factors. Anyway, is a cross-section what you really want? Might you get more from targeted interviews—say

samples

cross-sections

targeted interviews

the coach, conductor or teacher, and the audience or class members who were most engrossed and contributed most actively, or were most articulate? Oh, but don't forget that valuable negative data: the subject whose eyes wandered a lot, or the group that became disruptive at the back … or the child who did not speak once—what was she really thinking?

> In Melissa's PhD study of HACC (home and community care assessment) staff, the sheer diversity of jurisdictions across Australia—involving local, state and federal agencies and employers—made her 'scoping' of the field very difficult (Lindeman 2006). Older citizens needing health assessments live everywhere! Yet she managed, eventually, to target representative interviewees just in Victoria.
>
> However, in Stephanie's PhD (we first met Stephanie as an MEd researcher in Chapter 1), interviewing based on the depth and nature of experience was essential (Lockhart 2013). In her study of deaths in nursing, she had to build in an interview cohort of midwives—for whom neo-natal death is rare and, therefore, experienced as atypical of nursing work. Yet for nurses in chronic or acute adult nursing, it is a fairly typical workplace experience.

Who does the interview?

This is a very important decision, particularly if you are a participant-researcher. The subjects may already know you through the event you are researching or through some other involvement in their lives. The decision over who conducts the interviews is significant—it may either validate or corrupt your data. (Note, the term 'corrupt', or corrupted, data is very common in research contexts, and is less alarming than it sounds. It does not imply blackmail or extortion to gain the data, just that some unexpected factor or variable has got tangled up in it and makes it less valuable or usable.)

Doing the interviews yourself brings very clear advantages and drawbacks. The first advantage is trust and confidence. If they know you, the subjects will be at ease talking to a familiar person; they will be even more comfortable if you have already taken them into your confidence as co-researchers, or kept them in touch with what you are doing. They will probably be keen to help you add to your data. Whether or not they know you, your own familiarity with the context will also enable you to elicit more specific answers and check their responses and understandings, although care must be taken not to steer the interviews too much towards the findings that you want. Doing the interviews yourself is also cheaper and usually easier to organise, and to deal with rearrangements.

On the other hand, subjects' familiarity with you can alter the data they give you. Cooperative subjects will unconsciously collude to give you the answers they think

■ corrupt data

■ researcher-as-interviewer

■ familiarity issues

you want to hear; uncooperative ones may be silenced, or give misleading or careless responses. There may be vital information that they withhold from you because they think it might upset you or because they are concerned about consequences or implications elsewhere arising from your familiarity with them. Moreover, you yourself may have a strong personal investment in the interview topic, which shows, and students consciously or unconsciously react to that. Indeed, because of your investment, you may avoid asking questions that may result in you hearing what you don't want to. It's worth remembering that conducting interviews might be difficult or challenging for you too— you may hear responses to your own work or your project that are confronting, critical or simply disappointing.

You may need to ensure that the interview data is free of any of these potentially 'corrupting' influences. If so, it will be necessary to arrange to have the interviews done by outsiders, or even an outside agency, and provide guarantees of anonymity. The drawbacks and advantages of this are the converse of those above. There may be initial constraint or embarrassment in talking to strangers. The interviewers will be less familiar with the details and the context or your research interest, and may miss opportunities to press for specific or deeper responses. Organising external interviews adds another level of expense and complexity to your research management. On the other hand, the data may be cleaner and more neutral, freer from corruption, and less subject to collusion or silenced voices. Of course, some respondents might not easily speak to a stranger, so that might silence them! No method is perfect, and sometimes you have to decide between swings and roundabouts. Below are three brief examples of different choices that researchers made in projects:

■ outsider interviewers

- In some classroom research investigating the combination of live drama and internet-based activity, the children were interviewed by their teachers, one of whom was the researcher herself (Dunn and O'Toole 2008). What she wanted to collect were the children's ideas about the comparative advantages of drama and internet activities, and the possibilities of combining them. As the teachers had used both forms of activity in the lesson, the information would not have any consequences beyond the classroom. Since they wanted to probe and prompt imaginative responses based on the experience they had shared with the students, they decided to carry out the interviews themselves.

- In Cheryl's art studio with adults with intellectual disabilities, interviews with the 'subjects' never carried the primary focus of the data collection: photographs and original artworks were the focus, to which a variety of interviewees responded—most of them not the artists (Daye 1998)! In this way, Cheryl was triangulating aesthetic experiences without compromising the integrity of the artists' own experiences by an inappropriate focus on what could not be articulated in conversation.

→

> • In the first interviews of student peer teachers of conflict management, the researchers needed quite specific information (O'Toole and Burton 2005b). It had to be probed for and understood only by people familiar with the research, but it also had to be resistant to student collusion. Accordingly, research assistants were briefed to observe the peer-teaching episodes but not become implicated, and then conduct the interviews, again with guarantees of anonymity.

■ indirect interviews

A rather different approach to the problem of silenced voices is for the interviewer to divert the central topic of the conversation to something apparently neutral but revealing. This might be asking the subjects to respond to a stimulus, such as a photograph, a story or even an anonymous case study, where the attention is therefore on external material rather than the interviewees themselves, or their relationship with the research.

> A very elegant example of this was devised in Margaret Barrett and Heather Smigiel's widely known study investigating children's responses to art, where children were encouraged first to take photographs themselves of what they considered art, and then they were interviewed about those photographs (Barrett and Smigiel 2003).

Solo interviews or focus groups?

■ group interviews

Focus group is the name given to interviews with small groups. Solo interviews may not always be possible, and focus groups are a way to collect the voices of larger numbers of informants. They have a valuable dynamic that is quite different from a solo interview. A group of people interacts not only with the interviewer, but with each other, and there is a level of endemic prompting and probing that often provides rich and profound insights and observations from the interviewees. The participants bounce off each others' ideas, light fuses for each other … or alternatively (and sometimes simultaneously) argue and

■ contestation

wrangle, releasing valuable contestatory data. However, there is a very real danger in focus groups of silenced voices, often because somebody cannot get a word in edgeways and sometimes because a dissentient voice might be intimidated or even dissuaded by the strength of group opinion. A further extension of this danger is, as we have emphasised

■ group-think

already, 'group-think', where, quite unconsciously, a group takes on particular opinions and emphases, reshaping their responses and therefore your data in unconscious solidarity. If they all want to keep their jobs, can you blame them? Transcribing focus group interviews can often be quite difficult too, even for you, because people tend to talk over the top of each other, and voices cannot always be identified where it would be important—for instance, seeing if a particular line of argument is confined to one speaker or more widely shared.

One potential approach to focus groups, especially with adults, that is perhaps not sufficiently used, is the possibility of conducting an interview entirely without an interviewer—just switch on the tape-recorder, give them a question or discussion topic to start them off, then shut the door and leave them to it!

How much structure?

Interviews can be conducted anywhere along a continuum of questioning that is usually simplified into three categories: structured, semi-structured and unstructured.

Fully *structured* interviews are most useful where statistical information is needed, with large numbers of interviewees, who are all asked exactly the same questions, in identical or similar contexts—that is, with as many variables removed as possible. The answers can then be collated and directly compared as part of the analysis. This is where interviews contribute usefully to statistics. Devising a structured interview demands great attention to detail, and to the phrasing of the questions, to ensure that they will be heard and interpreted exactly the same by all respondents.

▩ structured interviews

Where you seek more qualitative information, and varieties of response or opinion within a common framework, some degree of structure is needed to ensure that there is a proportion of common data. A *semi-structured* interview gives the opportunity for the unexpected insight to be collected, and for the interviewer to seek clarification, invite expansion or explore a response further. The pre-interview brief may consist of a set of five or ten questions that the interviewer will raise with all subjects. The interviewer then has licence to listen and record subjects who stray or digress down potentially useful pathways, or to probe for depth or expansion.

▩ semi-structured interviews

Unstructured interviews are useful if you wish to give your subjects free rein to discuss what interests or concerns them, and not constrain their thinking or expression by imposing external frameworks. Some ethnography demands that freedom, for instance. It is always useful to have a few starter questions up your sleeve, which can prompt discussion or recollection. On the other hand, unstructured interviews sometimes happen quite spontaneously, as Jo Raphael (2003) recounts wryly:

▩ unstructured interviews

> Towards the end of my time in the field some other participants executed a real coup when they effectively took over my final interview with them, on the bus as we travelled between venues. This was not a scheduled interview and I am so pleased that I had the presence of mind to take out my tape recorder. When listening to this interview later, I was struck by the passion in the voices—and that my interview had been hijacked by three of the participants. One of the first voices heard is Robert's as he grabs my recorder, 'Hang on, can I do the interviewing? I know how to hold the tape.' Sally's voice is heard ordering, 'Me first, then you, then her.' Robert proceeds to ask the questions of other participants. Neil is also heard taking control of the interview for a time and proceeds to turn it around and question me. 'Who is the researcher now?' I wonder.

How long, when and where?

Calculating in advance the likely length of time needed for an interview or focus group can be quite tricky, but is important in any prearrangement. Interviews can last anything from three minutes to over an hour. When you have decided what kind of interview you intend

▩ interview length

to conduct, and the questions you will ask or start with, it is useful to have a rehearsal with an informed colleague who takes the role of the research subject, and time it.

interview timing

If the interview is in response to a specific event, you should, if possible, give consideration to the time lag between that event and the interview. An interview immediately after the event will certainly be fresh and spontaneous. It can carry some of the residual excitement or emotion of the event and will probably focus on details; it may even take on some of the immediate verbal outpouring that is an inescapable human response to excitement and is, in fact, the first part of the reflective process. Sometimes, the interview can be the opposite: an anti-climax for the subject(s). An interview conducted after a significant time lapse is likely to gather a more collected

interview location

and reflective response, with more 'big picture' perspective. On the other hand, time is an enemy to accurate memory, which can easily be overlaid by newer, stronger experiences, or embroidered by wish-fulfilment urges. Logistically, this can prove a problem, particularly for part-time researchers, who may have to conduct interviews at varying distances from the event.

The location of the interview should be considered in advance. Ideally, you should find somewhere with an appropriate, quiet ambience, where the interviewee(s) can concentrate unselfconsciously and not be interrupted—not always easy in crowded, busy schools and workplaces. Take care, of course, to avoid locations that might compromise the subject(s), you or the research.

Responsibilities of interviewers

ethical responsibilities

Interviewers have very important ethical and legal responsibilities, especially when dealing with underage subjects. We remind you that this book contains fundamental guidance on ethical principles in Chapters 2 and 5. Putting the principles into practice means you have to get written permission to interview minors. Usually as part of a research ethics application, you will have to draft a set of interview questions in advance, and not depart from them—very far, at least.

There is one strong research tradition that demands that whatever their age, before you use anything your subjects have said in any public forum—whether a conference, a thesis or a report—you are duty-bound to show them what they have written or said, for them to verify it and agree to its being used as their words or ideas. This is

member checking

sometimes called 'member checking'. In this tradition, to be absolutely scrupulous, you should send a transcript of every interview you do to the subjects for them to verify and alter if they wish, before you even start analysing it. Often, of course, this is quite unmanageable and unnecessary. You need to use your common sense according to the circumstances, the sensitiveness of the material or the subjects, and so on. There are times when member checking will be crucial and perhaps a condition of the interview. It may not always be very palatable, as you will find transcripts that you sent for checking in good faith coming back much altered or bowdlerised, as the interviewee on

deletions

rereading the interview clearly had second thoughts, and deleted or revised the original accordingly.

In Part A, we mentioned Rod's PhD on civics and citizenship education, which depended greatly on a limited number of key interviews with important stakeholders in national debates on government policy (Wise 2000). The researcher and his supervisor were disappointed to receive an angry phone call from one such stakeholder the day after the (semi-structured) interview, stating that it had drifted from the agreed topics. Eventually a much revised interview transcript was agreed to.

We also mentioned, in Part A, Therese's nursing education PhD, which ran into trouble at the point where the quantitative study became qualitative (Anderson 2001). One key stakeholder heard a 'work-in-progress' conference paper, and inferred that her 'position' was being misinterpreted. Litigation was threatened. Eventually the data was restructured to overcome this stakeholder's concern.

Both researchers in these examples were surprised at the stakeholders' reactions, as the interviews did not appear particularly contentious or inflammatory. However, the research had to proceed without those tantalising gems.

There is another minefield laid for educational researchers by recent trends in care provision in educational settings for minors. Most states now have laws about disclosure, particularly in matters of family violence and abuse. A child may reveal something to the interviewer in the confidentiality of the interview (may even choose this friendly stranger to confide in) that the law now demands be officially disclosed, whether the child wants that or not. This can put you (or any teacher and caregiver) in a very difficult position. If there is anything potentially sensitive in your research topic, or likely to come up in interview, you should check beforehand on the prevailing laws, on the local regulations of the school or other institutional context, and on the procedures to deal with disclosures, such as how to file a report. You may be able to put yourself out of harm's way by having a school counsellor sitting in on the interview, or by getting somebody with power in the situation to conduct the interview.

■ disclosure

Allira, who was researching the effect of certain workshops on survivors of child abuse (Power 2004), was not even allowed to interview the subjects unless they spoke to her spontaneously, as sometimes happened within the sessions. However, she was able to formulate questions for them that one of the official counsellors would include in a regular post-session interview. The counsellor would then pass the responses back to the researcher for the study.

When interviewing, if you are wide enough awake to the perils of your subject straying into this minefield, you can very often head off the danger in time. Unfortunately, it would be improper to suggest that if all else fails, selective deafness and a speedy finger on the tape-recorder's off button might be a useful last resort. Given the current laws throughout Australia, you may well not be able to act judiciously in what you believe may be the interest of the respondent.

Questionnaires and surveys

These words are sometimes used interchangeably, and so they can be. Strictly, a survey is what you do—you conduct a survey. A questionnaire is the instrument consisting of the questions you ask, either on paper or in person—you administer a questionnaire. A survey may also use other instruments. Sometimes, of course, a survey consists solely of a questionnaire! So it's really splitting hairs. Questionnaires are among the most popular and widely used data-gathering instruments in educational research. There are many useful books on how to design effective questionnaires, not only in the educational research literature but in marketing and management textbooks too. So again, we shall just be making introductory comments, from which you would be wise to go to the literature for detailed instruction.

▪ qualitative data

▪ quantitative data

The great virtue of surveys and questionnaires is that they can collect both qualitative and quantitative data at the same time from large numbers of informants. Their great utility is that this is relatively easy to set up and manage and they are quickly collated and easily analysed. There are many firms, now usually online, that will design, manage

▪ survey limitations

and collate your questionnaires. Their underlying drawback is that you can't totally rely on them, as you can rarely check the veracity or the reliability of the informants. With a questionnaire, you can't interrogate or have a discussion. This can be very tantalising, where the responses cry out for further information …

> … as in the case of the anonymous child respondent to a post-project questionnaire on 'cooling conflict' who wrote—contra the positive responses of most of the thousands of children who filled in the same questionnaire—'as a result of this project I have lost all my friends' (O'Toole and Burton 2005b, p. 275). Our hearts went out to this untraceable child, and our researchers' noses smelt a valuable source of negative data, now lost forever.

Surveys need to be used judiciously, as people quickly tire of filling in questionnaires of doubtful use for research that they may themselves have little stake in. We all fill them in for so many other purposes already—market research, course evaluation, accommodation or service satisfaction, and so on. What's more, researchers at all levels, who ought to know better, almost invariably underestimate the amount of time and effort they will take to fill in. 'Just ten minutes of your time and no effort', as you will yourselves know too well, usually turns out to be about forty minutes, at least twenty of which were spent racking your brain over the deceptively simple-sounding 'comment if you like' sections of the questionnaire.

▪ trust

Some of the underlying principles of good questionnaires are the same as those for interviews. There should ideally be trust and motivation: an understanding of what the completed questionnaire will be used for and what incentive there is for the participants, either personal, or in terms of feeling satisfied to have helped in a worthy cause. There is another trust factor, too: the participants must have absolute confidence that the data will remain confidential, not tampered with, and only used for the purposes for which it is given. Some ethics clearance procedures already demand full statements in plain language to accompany questionnaires, detailing the exact purposes of the questionnaire, and how the results and the copies will be stored.

Even more than a structured interview, the questions should be very precisely framed and carefully worded, to ensure that they will be heard or read and interpreted exactly the same by all respondents, some of whom will surprise you with their propensity to grasp the wrong end of the stick.

precision

As much as possible in your planning, you should give attention to exerting some control over the location, ambience and timing of the taking of the questionnaire. This may often be difficult to arrange, especially for posted or internet surveys, or ones otherwise administered remotely. It is nonetheless important to ensure that the subjects are in an appropriate frame of mind, are willing to collaborate, able to concentrate and that they have enough time to complete the questionnaire. If some school-based questionnaires, for instance, are given in a designated time with a helpful administrator, while others are dished out at the end of school as students are running for the bus or otherwise diverted, there will be serious disparities in the data and, therefore, in the trustworthiness of the results. There will probably also be some colourful but unreliable comments from the second group.

location
timing

Other factors to consider include, first and foremost, the logic and sequencing of the questions. The subjects should normally be led through what is a clear and sensible sequence of ideas, where answering one question naturally leads on to the next. It is sometimes tempting to consider questionnaires that lead subjects to reveal unconsciously aspects of their attitude or taste while ostensibly answering a questionnaire about something else entirely. Market surveyors love that kind, where questions about, say, car owners' attitudes to particular marques and models (especially the brand that is paying for the survey) are embedded in a range of more or less irrelevant questions about shopping, media, holidays and so on. Occasionally this kind of deception is unavoidable:

> In the drama and peer-teaching study it was necessary to identify how many of the subjects had racially discriminatory attitudes. It was not possible to ask them directly, so those case study type questions, 'If you …?' were embedded in other more neutral ones (O'Toole and Burton 2005b).

Then of course there is an ethical issue to be considered, about whether and how far it is justifiable to lead your subjects up the garden path in the interests of your research. Once again, it puts them at the wrong end of a power imbalance.

Quantitative surveys

There are a number of ways you can gather useful quantitative data—which becomes statistics. The great virtue of data gathered this way is that statements we make, supported by quantitative data, can be easily defended as 'evidence-based'.

So much of the data we need to collect, however, is less amenable to simple, one-dimensional metrics such as, 'How many times last year did you watch live sport?' We are dealing in subjective fields of attitude, feelings and taste, which are multidimensional. Quantitative surveys can still be useful, particularly in the common form of the *Likert scale*, which was originated by management and leadership guru Rensis Likert in 1932. This scale adds a second dimension, and forms a (still fairly primitive) way of measuring perceptions, judgments, attitudes, opinions or tastes as points on a linear continuum. In the words of one of the dozens of websites that give useful information on this hardly ground-breaking technique, the Likert scale is:

> A psychometric response scale primarily used in questionnaires to obtain participant's preferences or degree of agreement with a statement or set of statements. Likert scales are a non-comparative scaling technique and are unidimensional (only measure a single trait) in nature. Respondents are asked to indicate their level of agreement with a given statement by way of an ordinal scale. (Bertram 2013)

Although the five-point scale is the most common, for example,

I think rock musicians should go out and get a proper job.
Strongly agree | Agree | Unsure/neutral | Disagree | Strongly disagree

a Likert scale may have as few as three or four or as many as seven or eight points on the scale. More points are able to capture a finer degree of discrimination on the continuum (how often have we wanted to put a tick *between* the boxes?) but may be more difficult to manage in terms of analysis or reduction to usable metrics.

Qualitative surveys

Surveys are obviously also useful ways of collecting qualitative data from large numbers of people. Identical questions can be asked of large numbers, and people's verbal responses can then be collated for interpretation. As we have already indicated, the information we want to collect can be elicited directly or indirectly, and occasionally it may be necessary to use a degree of subterfuge, so that we can examine the subtexts rather than the responses themselves.

Wherever possible, surveys should be interesting, giving the subjects an enjoyable experience, and however tenuous, a sense that they have a stake in the outcomes. Obviously, a questionnaire that is targeted to its subjects' area of special interest or concern has a head start, and if you happen to squeeze people's emotional triggers, you face the prospect of an overflow of data! Another incentive to increase motivation for survey completion (apart from a lolly or a set of steak knives) is to ask interesting questions, or ask them in an

■ Likert scale

■ interest value

interesting way. Questions should be phrased as simply as possible. That aside, the 'case study' or 'hypothetical' question can be very productive.

▦ hypotheticals

 # EXPERIMENTAL DATA

Comparative studies

There are almost as many types of experimental instruments as there are experiments, but among the most common kind used in Education are comparative studies. These are widely and effectively used in all fields of education where mathematically inclined and scientifically trained administrators and educators are in charge, and they form a major element of policy setting and monitoring at the systemic level. Although there is the same wonderful diversity of research methods and data-collection instruments equally available within arts and humanities research, in our opinion it is a great pity that there are not more comparative studies.

> Honourable exceptions are two experiments led by Madonna Stinson in Singapore on the value of experiential pedagogy for second language (English) teaching (Stinson and Freebody 2005; Stinson 2009). There are lots of statistics on English language levels and acquisition in Singapore—it is one of their regular standardised tests. This research team did not even have to find a control group: they merely singled out a number of classes for intensive workshopping techniques, used the standard English language tests at the end of the experiment, and compared the results with comparable students. The interim results of the first are 'evidence-based' gold for advocates of such a pedagogy, although the research was not set up just for advocacy—it might have backfired by providing negative or inconclusive results. The second experiment produced much more equivocal results, which have proved equally useful in a different way by identifying teacher inexperience and resistance as crucial constraints on the success of that experiential pedagogy.

In Chapter 4, we briefly canvassed the classic technique of stating a *hypothesis* that can be tested in practice, such as a particular pedagogy or teaching technique mode. Properly managed, with sufficient attention to the controllable variables, this kind of research can provide really valuable 'evidence-based' quantitative data, and usually a great deal of valuable anecdotal qualitative data as well.

▦ hypothesis

We need to identify a sufficiently large and suitable experimental sample group to test the hypothesis on, find a comparable control group that will not have access to the new pedagogy, then devise an appropriate instrument to test both groups to find out the differences between them.

Statistics for the faint-hearted

If you are among the many arts or humanities educators referred to above who are more at ease with words and actions than numbers, take a deep breath, and seriously consider whether the use of statistics might give your argument some muscle. Many such educationalists often shy away from this consideration, partly because we know that statistics can be one step beyond damned lies. Also because the early days of Education research, especially in America, were littered with the bones of attempts to quantify human behaviour—proving statistically that innovative pedagogies increase vastly complex attributes such as self-esteem was (and still is) a particularly favoured stamping ground. Partly too, if we admit it, many of us are scared of the maths, and the graphs. These authors must admit it too. How much more convincing some of our research might be with some attention to proper statistical analysis. This will be critiqued in more detail in the next chapter.

■ strengths of statistics

If you consider that your investigation of the Research Question might be significantly improved by statistical data, then you should be ready to collect it from the start—which again means foresight and pre-planning. One of the preliminary barriers is the jargon, so we will give a brief glossary to help. Statistics are just sets of figures—often expressed in the form of a scale or table that can be depicted visually, numerically or verbally—that describes something that can be measured. The scales can easily be put together out of data collected through questionnaires, or assessment and examination results, or school records, or other simple data-collection instruments, so long as we think of them in advance. The most common scales that you might wish to use are outlined below.

■ pre-planning

Although it is often used to mean 'token', the word *nominal* comes from the Latin word for 'name', and a *nominal scale* is simply one that uses words, numbers or symbols to *name* a quality or level. A Likert scale, which we have already encountered in this chapter, is a very simple nominal scale that we might express in the form of words: 'Strongly agree < > agree < > unsure < > disagree < > strongly disagree', or numbers: 'Express satisfaction on a scale of 1 < > 5'. The statistical analysis you can do on a nominal scale is limited, because the descriptors of whatever elements you are measuring are only names—though you can, of course, add up the quantity of responses under each heading.

■ nominal scale

■ Likert scale

A variant of this is the *ordinal scale* that we use to rank our elements. In an ordinal scale, we order information into 1st, 2nd, 3rd, etc. (these are ordinal numbers). Every teacher is familiar with this kind of scale. It's what we use when ranking our students from first to last on a particular assessment item, or what state examination boards use to provide tertiary entrance scores. There is not much arithmetical manipulation possible here, either. But it can provide normative measurements, such as the 'bell curve' (or normal curve) that often raises its head in educational contexts, usually to standardise results for administrative purposes.

■ ordinal scale

The *interval scale* is merely the term we give to measure the distance between a series of elements. A typical interval scale is a set of ages grouped into say, ten-year intervals.

■ interval scale

The most useful scale is the *ratio scale*, which contains the characteristics of the three previous scales. The ratio scale is manipulable completely through arithmetic—if you have the arithmetic for it. This scale has a common baseline, which is usually expressed

■ ratio scale

arithmetically as zero, so that every measurement can be taken as a deviation from that common baseline. An example frequently favoured, because it is simple and goes up in multiples of one, is the Kelvin temperature scale, where no heat at all is registered as (absolute) zero, and 150 is exactly half of 300. That is unlike, say, decibels or the Richter earthquake scale, which have what is called a logarithmic ratio, based on multiples of ten—so that 1.1 decibels is actually twice as loud as 1.0.

logarithmic scale

Statistics expressed in these scales and derived from data-collection instruments such as questionnaires, interviews and tests can be used for a number of purposes, which we shall examine in more detail in Chapter 8. Here's a quick overview of some of the purposes statistics might be used for (which will also be discussed in more detail in the next chapter):

- the *frequency count*—the number of times something occurs

frequency count

- the *central value*—this is what we mean when we refer to something as being 'normal', when our view of normality can be translated into statistics. That's the 'bell curve' again—not named after the inventor of the telephone, or anybody else, but because the most normal curve plotted on a graph looks a bit like a bell (actually more like a jellyfish, if you look at Figure 8.1 in the next chapter, but somehow jellyfish don't have the *gravitas* for research)

central value

- *variability*—that is, *standard deviation* from a known norm

variability, standard deviation

- *correlations*—comparison between two sets of measures that can be from the same group at different times, taking different tests, or different groups using the same test.

correlations

A little imagination, or advice from scientifically minded colleagues, will quickly suggest areas of your own research where the collection of statistics can lead, like any good data, to significant understanding, insights and conclusions.

DOCUMENTING DATA

Your own documentation is likely to be among your most important data. In most of the approaches used by practising educators who become researchers, you will probably position yourself on the observer–participant continuum within or alongside the research—the participants or phenomenon you are studying, as we described it in Chapter 3. That means that you are in the strongest position to observe and document what is happening, using your comprehensive inside knowledge of the research topic and Question, together with the background and other literature you have been studying. If you are a central research participant—as in most reflective practitioner research, and some action research, arts-based enquiry, etc.—your own testimony will often be at the centre of data collection. To document and comment objectively is, in this new world of tentative knowledge (as we also showed in Chapter 4), harder to justify, but your biases of philosophical and methodological positioning can be counterbalanced by effective triangulation or crystallisation.

Researchers' personal documentation can take basically three forms:

■ commentaries

- journal(s) or commentaries

■ case notes

- field notes and/or case notes

■ reflective memos

- reflective memos or essays.

Reflective memos are composed during the data collection, but are effectively also a first stage in the data-analysis process.

Journals and commentaries

■ research journal

Ideally, researchers should always keep a journal from the beginning through to the end of the research. In some forms of research, such as case study, action research and reflective practitioner research, it is imperative. In this, you first of all record what you do, and when you do it. The journal should include a dated log of all meetings you have in connection with the research, including those with your supervisor if you are a student researcher; also, meetings with participants and visits to the research site. You should also note briefly any major outcomes of those meetings and visits. The time and nature of any unexpected factors, opportunities or obstacles that arise should be noted, and, especially, any changes in the focus of the Research Question. All this will be needed for any final account of the research, and for its accountability, whether in the form of a research report or a thesis. Meetings and sudden opportunities or changes of direction usually seem crystal clear and memorable at the time. It is tempting for a busy researcher with a challenging full-time job and a family crisis, and a bunch of kids at the staffroom door demanding attention, to think you will certainly remember this key moment … but key moments quickly blur into the complex texture of the whole project when reviewed six months or two years later.

■ composite journals

Some methodologies, such as action research, may dictate a particular form for the journal. At least in the particular way we use action research, the journal is in three sections. Along with a time-and-date log of the whole project, the first main section will normally consist of the detailed analysis of the context—the pre-planning phase. The second section will be the longest, and divided into subsections for every cycle, each comprising the field notes, observations, evaluations and replanning, documented through each phase of the cycle. The third section will chart and reflect on the progress made through the whole set of cycles.

■ exegesis

A critical commentary—known, if you are working in arts-based enquiry, as *exegesis*—is really a variant of the ongoing research journal, but whereas journals are just raw data, to be drawn from and to inform the data analysis, an exegesis usually forms a substantive part of the final thesis. That means that you must approach your research journal from the beginning with an eye to its being 'presentable'. The notes must not be so rough and raw that they cannot be tidied into a linear narrative or other discursive form that can be read by an outsider. Combining your field notes with very regular—say, weekly—reflective memos is one useful approach.

Case notes and field notes

The central data of almost any case study research is the researcher's case notes. These take as many forms as there are types of case study. Their commonalities and disparities are too complex to go into here—there are good preliminary readers on various forms of case study research that explain their documentation processes.

⬛ case notes

Any project that incorporates fieldwork will probably have many sources of data, but one of the keys to its success will be the researcher's field notes. Regardless of the size and scope of your research project, if you are observing an activity of participants in specific contexts, you need to keep clear field notes as a record of your observation. As a rule of thumb, you should always transcribe notes within twenty-four hours of taking them so that you can faithfully and authentically reconstruct your observations. The longer you leave them, the more generalised they become. Field notes are an excellent way of storing not only the actions of participants, but your reactions to them, as well as recording any relevant methodological points about your role as observer–participant.

⬛ field notes

There are really three components to effective field notes, and it may be useful to use separate pages or even notebooks, though sorting the notes into those three components may sometimes best be left to the phase of transcription in tranquillity. Taking field notes can sometimes be a flurry of writing, scribbling notes, codes, shorthand and frustration. Dictating into a pocket tape-recorder or electronic memo does not always ease this—the hurried manipulation of electronic aids is more subject to accidental obliteration than paper. Upon entering the research site, remember to limit what you actually record: filter and focus what you are watching or taking part in through a selective frame or lens, which comes as directly as possible out of the Research Question.

⬛ field notes procedures

1   Through your selective lens you describe what you see happening. This forms the core of the field notes for the session.

⬛ selection

2   It is useful also to record your immediate reflections and responses, feelings and thoughts about what is happening, as they occur to you. The comments can be as informal or formal as you want or have time for. There will be moments during the session when you make links to other ideas, data, images, documentation and literature; other moments of sudden insight into the Research Question or the underlying philosophy—those 'Aha!' moments. Moments of doubt too, and the sinking feeling that something is undermining your whole hypothesis or you might be going off the rails, or … Those moments are important negative data.

⬛ 'Aha!' moments

⬛ negative data

3   However centrally and subjectively involved you might be in the fieldwork as participant-researcher, you should also always 'keep a cool strip' and use the notes to describe and comment on the methods you are using to gather the data. Disruptions to the method, and unexpected factors arising from the site or the participants that might modify the fieldwork or the data-gathering, should be recorded and acknowledged.

⬛ comments

Reflective memos and essays

While you are concentrating on coolly and faithfully recording fieldwork observations and keeping up (or catching up) with the ongoing literature, your own brain will not have gone to sleep. Besides those Aha! moments, your growing knowledge will be bringing you insights that are not final, but are scaffolding your understanding in a crucial way. These

■ provisional insights insights are, at the moment, partial; they may even be wrong, so they are very provisional, but they are worth pondering critically and recording discursively. This will take the form of an essay, in the true meaning of that word: it is a 'try' or try-out of your position. In this essay you discuss what you think is happening at the research site and what you think you are seeing—it's a way of thinking aloud. If the reflective discussion is short, say one or two pages, it is usually called a reflective 'memo', or reminder to yourself that will jog your memory and place you back in context when you approach those field notes again, perhaps many months later. Because these memos follow the sequence of the research and should be dated, when it comes time for you to prepare the research dissertation, report or publication you will be able to chart your own meta-thinking about the research, and pinpoint moments of insight (and disruptions and hiccups) as they authentically emerged from the data. That's why they are also the first stage of the data analysis.

Third-party observations

As the researcher, you have an agenda and perhaps a hypothesis you are hoping to prove, so it is nearly always helpful to have an outside eye present during fieldwork, providing

■ outside eye that this does not clutter the fieldwork site with observers who change the dynamic significantly. There is a limit to the number of outsiders who can watch and record a small-group discussion, for instance, without making the participants extremely self-conscious. Then, participants either become silent, or play to the gallery—either way, the authenticity of the data is lessened.

■ disinterested observer
■ professional research

By an outside eye, we mean somebody who is disinterested, though not uninterested, in the research. If you have plenty of money, you might try hiring a professional research company, who can carry out their own observations, interviews and so on. There are quite a few of these, usually with a strong social science research orientation, and more used to doing research into retail, media or sociological issues than education, but therefore likely to come up with quite different and independent perspectives on the work.

> Peter and his New Zealand 'Everyday Theatre' team developed a whole-day, participatory intervention program for educating students about domestic violence and abuse. The program was held in schools with social disadvantages and a high proportion of students who would have experienced violence and abuse in their own lives. This exceptionally sensitive and delicate program required—and the Department of Child, Youth and Family demanded—a concurrent, completely independent research presence. Both a professional company, and also an education researcher familiar with drama education, followed the project and reported on it for its first two years (Holland 2009, p. 534; O'Connor 2009, p. 471).

For most of your research, especially beginning research, that kind of spending would be out of reach. However, it is usually possible to find a thoughtful friend or colleague, known as a 'critical friend', who can come into your research context—perhaps not for the whole of the fieldwork, but for one or more key sessions—to provide that outside eye. A major research project may even attract one or more research students to assist.

critical friend

research students

> In Part A, and earlier in this chapter, we mentioned Cheryl's PhD on art programs for adults with intellectual disabilities (Daye 1998). Cheryl is an expert in this professional field of practice, but she needed to widen the fieldwork, since her research 'subjects' (the adult artists she taught) were limited in their ability to articulate (as research data) a comprehensive account of their studio experiences. 'Third-party observations' therefore included the artists' families—as their primary carers—and also a variety of 'arts workers', who could respond to the pedagogies of the studio but also to the aesthetic qualities of what is known as 'outsider' art. For Cheryl, the more 'eyes' the better.

It is necessary to consider how far outside the 'eye' should be, where it will provide an appropriate level of knowledge to the observer. You will be tempted to 'fill in' your observer with plenty of background to the project, and what you are looking for. This may be appropriate, so that the observer may pick up what you miss, and will understand and interpret the key issues and moments. On the other hand, the observer, particularly if a close colleague, will then really just be duplicating your work, and, if given less information in advance, might come up with quite different observations. Throughout, it is essential to maintain that spirit of critique that gives research traction on the ice.

degree of familiarity

> In a classic research exercise in Australia in 1981, British sociologist and arts philosopher Robert Witkin led an audience of thirty to forty humanities teachers in a series of observations of lessons (Haseman 1981). Surprisingly for all concerned, he did not ask the teacher in advance to explain his or her objectives for the lesson, but asked the group very specifically to record exactly what they saw.
> At the end (again to everybody's surprise) he did not ask the teacher for his or her comments or explanation of the lesson, but sent the teacher to a quiet corner, from where Witkin silenced every attempt by the teacher to join in the discussion. Instead he asked the group what they had seen. Most of the observers tended to start with, 'I think [the teacher] was …' or '[The teacher] set up a situation where …' or '[The teacher] should have …' and he ruthlessly cut them off with, 'Don't tell me what you think the teacher was doing, or intended; tell me what you saw'. Gradually, a quite different picture of the lesson emerged, very much a worm's eye view—and certainly
> →

different from the teacher's picture of the lesson. And different too, from how the audience were originally conceptualising what they saw, which was highly coloured by their empathy with the teacher, and also immediately evaluative. Finally, Witkin permitted the teacher to state his or her perception of the lesson (one of the authors was one of those teachers, and remembers how lame and unobservant his explanation of his own objectives and processes sounded). The booklet of these workshops is well worth reading.

Covert observation

Wouldn't it be nice, especially for case study and ethnographic research, if we could just observe the participants without their being aware of us, in other words, totally naturalistically? That way we wouldn't have to make allowances for our presence or even for the research. What about trying to find one of those observation rooms with one-way mirrors that they use in cop shows for identity parades and interrogation? Well, yes, this is not entirely out of the question, but there are some obstacles. First, there is the ethical question, about the propriety of researching people who do not know they are being researched. This, you will remember, involves issues of unequitable power

■ permissions

relationships. It also raises formal issues of permission, directly with adults (which automatically cancels out their unawareness) and indirectly with children through their caregivers—and is problematic when approaching any formal research ethics procedures. There is a very long tradition of covert observation, particularly in child psychology research, and also in such fields as criminology, psychiatry and medicine. But ethics committees are usually hard to persuade about the benefits of this kind of clandestine surveillance. They are also particularly reluctant if the research field does not traditionally use these techniques, or the field is still not always seen as a serious research discipline.

There are such facilities, however, and permissions too, if you know where to find them and can mount a convincing case for the need to observe covertly. A few educational establishments—for example, those attached to universities as demonstration or experimental schools—have such a space, where students and researchers often come to observe the children in their normal environment. The authors' own university runs an Early Learning Centre with a classroom equipped with a one-way mirror wall. Part of the agreement with the parents and guardians who send their children to the centre is that the children may be used for this kind of observation and research. Access to that space also means that it is only a 'normal' teaching space for those children who normally use it, so for any other research subjects it would change the physical context and ambience of the research site, thus again lessening the chance of seeing the research naturalistically (which is, of course, the whole point of covert research).

Electronic recording

A video camera or audio recorder is a very valuable tool, and still the most effective way of capturing a permanent record of the action of your fieldwork. The considerations below are mainly true for both forms of recording, but perhaps more problematic with video, so we will concentrate on that. Electronically recorded data, properly handled, can be invaluable when analysing and interpreting what happened in the field, and is dealt with in some detail in the next chapter, along with the problems of effective video and audio analysis. Since the usefulness of such a record is self-evident, we will concentrate on the problems, to help you use and manage electronic data collection effectively and productively:

- Perhaps the first thing to bear in mind is that video especially is very time-consuming to process and analyse, so be careful before deciding to video or record everything. On the other hand, a comprehensive record can be a valuable compendium from which you can select what you want to watch … but only if you log it and label it carefully and thoroughly. — time problems

- Second, the camera is obtrusive (a microphone perhaps less so), especially if it is being operated by professionals. They will usually want the space set up for their needs, with lights, camera and sound operators, and may even make demands for set-up time, long pauses and intervals for special shots and repeat takes. — intrusion problems

- A more common and cheaper form of recording is the use of a single camera. Here again, choices must be made—a wide-angle camera set on a tripod will capture a holistic record. After the first flush of interest and attention, it will usually be ignored by the participants. But it will not capture any detail, and although directional microphones are now very efficient, usually much of the sound is lost. A roving camera may capture vital detail, and even close discussion, but will not get the whole picture, and will be correspondingly more intrusive and disruptive. — data-collection choices

- The researcher must make a further decision: whether to operate the camera or recorder yourself. If you operate the device, you can choose what to focus on, and where to rove, and perhaps the recording may be less of a novelty. If you have a technician operate it, it's more efficient, leaves the researcher hands-free and less subject to interruption, but the stranger is another disruptive dynamic and may make very different choices about what to video. — operator choices

- Much experiential classroom work—especially spontaneous or improvised work, or discussion of any kind—will be disrupted by recording, regardless of whether the researcher is doing it, or a third-person observer, whose involvement inevitably changes the nature of the research site and the data. There are two ways of countering this. The first is to try and minimise the disruption—by giving the participants time to become used to the camera or recorder, even time to play or experiment with it themselves to get over the novelty. The second is to ensure it is managed as unobtrusively as possible, with a small hand-held digital camera on the tripod in a corner. — disruption problems

There are other, more imaginative ways to use the research camera. Perhaps the simplest of these is to enlist your participants to help you. There are many research contexts where student co-researchers can be willingly organised to record important segments of action. Another is to build it into the fieldwork, by harnessing and using the tape-recorder or research camera as an active participant in the teaching context. This can be used in some action research and case study, though with more difficulty in ethnography. Large and quite small research programs can equally benefit from this technology.

▪ co-researchers

▪ participant camera

> At the authors' university, David Clarke's (2013) international studies of classroom-based pedagogical interactions transcend their original significance in science education, and are now making an impact in other discipline and practice areas. Current use of this technology to map the skills of highly experienced 'accomplished' geography teachers in three states of Australia is of national significance, since the aim is to identify professional standards for teaching. Similarly, small-scale video observations and debriefings of how medical students can improve their hospital-based skills in clinical diagnoses can help shape standards of professional accomplishment for those entering medical practice.

Where any such proactive intervention occurs, the researcher must define and acknowledge, as clearly as possible, the nature and effect of the intervention when reporting on the research. There can also be side effects to the research that are quite unexpected but significant.

> Julie, studying the dramatic play of pre-adolescent girls, found a way of creating a context where what is normally a private activity, hidden from adults, could be studied and video-recorded (Dunn 2002, p. 279). The researcher tried to help the participants forget the camera by letting them play with it, then placing it unobtrusively. The girls remained periodically conscious of it. They came to treat it as if it was a camera recording them for Hollywood auditions—which made it a meta-character in a meta-layer of dramatic fiction. Mostly they just ignored it, but occasionally they acted up to it—and after a while begged the researcher to let them see their work on screen. Very reluctantly, she did ... to their horror. They had been visualising themselves in their play as glamorous characters in full imaginary *mise-en-scène*. Instead, they saw a bunch of little girls running around a hall full of chairs. They did not ask again to see the filmed episodes. This, however, and their later interviews and focus group discussions with the researcher, provided her with another very significant insight into the phenomenon under study.

? REFLECTIVE QUESTIONS

1 What would a 'mix and match' methodology look like as fieldwork? What data would you collect, from whom? And how could you bring diverse data together to tell one story?

2 How would you capture the experiences of a group of people at your work site who seem to elude traditional methods of research? What ethical issues are raised by this exclusion, and by your (hypothetical) plan to include them?

3 The 'Aha!' moment. Outline a plan to document these vital insights in research participants' practices—such as for the nurse educator in the operating theatre when a new procedure is effective, or for the music classroom in Taiwan when the new electronic keyboard kicks in.

WIDER READING

Burton, D. and Bartlett, S. 2005. *Practitioner Research for Teachers.* Paul Chapman Publishing, London.

Dunne, M., Pryor, J. and Yates, P. 2005. *Becoming a Researcher: A Companion to the Research Process.* Open University Press, Maidenhead, UK.

Moss, J. (ed.) 2008. *Researching Education: Visually—Digitally—Spatially.* Sense Publishers, Rotterdam.

8

DATA ANALYSIS AND SYNTHESIS

 CHAPTER OBJECTIVES

After reading this chapter, you should be able to:

- plan and implement ways to reduce data to patterns
- select from either or both quantitative and qualitative methods in synthesising data
- show how rigour in fieldwork can be built into data reduction.

⬊ A NOTE OF ENCOURAGEMENT

The meat of any research project requiring fieldwork is the analysis of the data and its synthesis with the literature and with the Research Question and/or hypothesis. In fact, this is the point when we are throwing you back on your intelligence. Certainly, we will identify some of the key principles and techniques to help you approach your analysis, but your own resources, your intellect, your knowledge, your sensibility and your intuition will be needed for most of the hard work.

■ own resources

There are some other practical reasons for this chapter not taking the prescriptive route. First, each of the distinct research methodologies has its own standard forms of data analysis and you will really need to consult the Wider Reading lists at the end of our chapters, on whatever methodology you have chosen, to follow the system of analysis that is recommended. Second, with much of the Education research we do, the data we collect is not available for collection according to standard scientific and methodical principles. In Education, being a social science, our data lies in the natural world, by which we mean the ordinariness of life, in contrast to a 'non-natural' environment like a laboratory. Furthermore, given this natural messiness, and especially bearing in mind the messiness of professional practice (a fine source and focus of research, as we argued in Chapter 3), it is likely that quite a few readers will choose or be driven to find mixed methods, for which some mix of analysis systems may be needed. Therefore, you may have to modify, reinvent or even invent new kinds of data analysis, new lenses through which you can find new perspectives and not just outsights and overviews, but insights.

■ messiness

■ mixed methods

Because this, too, is a lengthy chapter, here is an overview. Next is a section on preparing the ground for analysis: think of this as a way to immerse yourself in the data. There is no substitute for intimate familiarity with the data, be it quantitative or qualitative, so do dive in, as it does follow from balancing yourself on the springboard, at the end of the literature review (see Chapter 6). After that, twin sections take this immersion further: as we urged in the Introduction, you dive into the pool of beginning research, as a reflective practitioner (whether or not you are using that named methodology), and Schön's model requires reflection 'in' (amid) action, so we propose analysis 'in' action, then reflection and analysis 'on' action (with hindsight). Then, more twins: analysis of quantitative and of qualitative data. Finally two sections on the outcomes: the mediation of data, and its synthesis.

Notice the way immersion in the data, from the very beginning, leads quite naturally (we mean this literally—you will find this a natural experience) to an intuitive distillation of the raw data you have collected into 'patterns' of some kinds. This search for commonalities will lead you to draw together the evidence for patterns in the data, but also quite sensibly to generalise from that data, and thus to disregard forthwith what is extraneous to those 'patterns'. The patterns are 'findings' and can lead into synthesis, as this chapter shows towards the end. This is also called 'data reduction', a term that would describe this chapter equally well. (However, just a brief clarification, as the word 'reduction' also has a very different and much more assertive meaning in research, more associated with scientific research and connected with our old friend William of Occam. 'Reductionist' research seeks to cut out all the uncontrollable variables and pare the research and its findings down to the barest minimum that can be 'proved' … rather than, like much artistic and creative research, mapping and celebrating the richness of those variables, and then 'reducing' the evidence to manageable proportions and useful insights, which is what we are talking about.)

▥ patterns

You bring to this identification of 'patterns' in the analysis of raw data your intelligence and intuition as we stated at the outset. You can back hunches, as data analysis unfolds, that there are, indeed, particular commonalities emerging that you rather like, or even expect. But the sensibility of a researcher, not an advocate, is paramount. Whatever your passion, or the commitment to a topic, perhaps even when it is all the more compelling by this immersion, the one value that is front and centre is that data reduction be done with integrity, and with every bit of systematic objectivity you can muster. Look for the rough ground, by all means. Wittgenstein reminded us (in Chapter 3) that we need it for friction, and researchers need friction to make traction with their Research Question. But look fearlessly for the *evidence* for it—and, by contrast, look for evidence in the slipperiness of the ice as well.

▥ sensibility

◥ PREPARING THE GROUND FOR ANALYSIS

It may sound like begging the question, but the kind of data you have collected will largely determine how you analyse it. We will explore that little knot throughout this section. First of all, just as the teachers among us talk about the 'learning-readiness'

▥ readiness

of students, and that elusive 'teachable moment', so you must be sure you are 'analysis-ready'. This means that you are ready to:

- explore the data as coolly and neutrally as you can, in order to make interpretations and inferences from it
- sift each data set, and then cross-reference them, to provide corroboration, confirmation, contestation and contradictions, problematisation, answers (occasionally), triangulation, resonances and so on.

▦ sifting
▦ corroboration, contestation

▦ distance

For these, you need a stance that is both engaged and critical: that is, usually letting some time elapse between the data collection and data analysis, particularly if you are a participant researcher. At this point too, you must remember and implement strategies you might employ for giving distance to your data.

Dealing with the unexpected

▦ negative data

You will usually learn plenty, sometimes much more than you anticipated, from research that has not gone to plan, or that has suffered setbacks and unexpected constraints, or that has not achieved the positive outcomes you had hoped for. From research that goes entirely as intended you will only learn what you already thought you knew, or expected to find—which may be important or comforting or both, of course. Engaging in research that encounters glitches, gets partly derailed, or comes up with negative data may well have been painful when the unexpected occurred. Your hopes and expectations may have also taken a battering. However, as the Chinese have it, a crisis is the same thing as an opportunity. It allows you to use much more penetrating questions to interrogate the data.

Madonna Stinson's second investigation into drama in second language teaching was a follow-up study to the smooth and harmonious pilot research project that we described in the last chapter (Stinson and Freebody 2005). That project had clearly indicated that process drama workshops in the hands of experienced practitioners measurably improved the oral communication skills of English as second or other language (ESOL) students. The researchers set out to investigate an important corollary: how far non-drama-trained teachers could achieve the same ESOL improvement, and what conditions were necessary for their professional development to help them achieve it.

From the start, the project was subverted by a quite new set of unexpected and largely uncontrollable variables (Stinson 2009). The teachers were not, as had been promised, volunteers, but conscripts pressed into the project by the enthusiastic school principal, resentful of the extra time demands made on them, and under the strong influence of a head of department who was also inimical to the whole project. This context, and other unanticipated constraints, meant that the project appeared very unlikely to give the clear, positive reinforcement to the first Research Question—

whether process drama would still lead to improvement in oral communication—that the research team had earnestly hoped for. Moreover, it guaranteed a difficult, often stressful and depressing implementation of the project. But in terms of identifying the *conditions necessary* for the professional development of general teachers to enable them to use process drama (the second part of the Research Question) the data, properly analysed, was pure gold.

Identifying with the participants

Some actors, when approaching the task of acting unpleasant or unsympathetic characters, find it helpful to identify and learn to respect the character's integrity. They try to understand those character traits, attitudes and motives that drive the character, which are, of course, entirely justifiable from the character's standpoint. It is equally important for researchers to apply this as a principle to their real-life subjects—to recognise that, however incongruously a participant or participants may have behaved towards the project, they had their own integrity: motives, constraints, character-traits, attitudes and reasons that led them to behave as they did, and that must be respected. ▨ respect That will allow the data they provide to reveal more than whether or not they conformed to the project's parameters. With proper analysis, it can also illuminate more about the research topic, site and structure.

This reinforces the importance of keeping some emotional distance from the research data.

> In the second Singapore project described above, periodic tensions arose, not surprisingly, between the teachers and Stinson's research team (Stinson 2009). The research team themselves became frustrated and sometimes resentful of what they interpreted as white-anting of the project, or minimal cooperation. Remnants of those tensions were still present as they addressed the data. Very properly, they started to identify the questions with which they would interrogate the data by deliberately looking at the project through the eyes of the teachers, and identifying the attributes the teachers brought to the project, the difficulties and frustrations they would have faced, and how the research topic and site must have presented itself to them. This allowed the researchers to address the data much more even-handedly, particularly the teachers' first-hand witness accounts through journals, interviews and video reflection. They could then understand it much more clearly and in a less polarised light.

Checking below the surface

In reading data of human behaviour, it is crucial to remember the *subtext*. This is equally ▨ subtext true for journals, field notes, interviews, and even some quantitative data and surveys. People say or do one thing (the surface text), but may mean quite another (the primary

■ multiple subtexts

subtext), or may mean that one thing but also a whole lot of associated and conditional other things (multiple subtexts). This is where the real intelligence of data analysis comes in. First you have to spot and interpret those subtexts, and then you must go one level deeper and check your own analysis to ensure that the subtexts are really there and are not being erroneously inferred by the researcher. For this, you don't need a degree in psychoanalysis, just effective cross-referencing. If you think you sense something in the data that is not being said, or that it is not what it seems, turn to other data sets to check and corroborate or cancel out your hunch—that's why you collected a range of complementary and contrasting data sets, remember?

> From the same ESOL project, there was an interview between Stinson, the chief investigator, and the school's head of department, right at the end of the project. This interview was never going to provide cool, intellectual reportage. Both parties approached it with great residual tension and a range of negative emotions—anger, resentment, defensiveness, guilt, betrayal, frustration. Nonetheless the researcher decided to carry it out herself: she had inside knowledge she needed to check and validate.
>
> The surface text of the interview transcript is polite throughout. The quality of the head of department's language, however, immediately betrays some of her subtexts: in places she is evasive, in others she is by turns incoherent, self-contradictory, repetitive, illogical, erratic, strident and lost for words. This is plain at the first reading of the transcript, plainer still when revisiting the audiotape where some of the vocal and timing dimensions corroborate and give added substance to the reader's inferences. In this instance, it was very important that the interviewer-researcher not be the only reader of the transcript. Two sources were accessed. A critical friend—O'Toole—offered a more dispassionate reading of Stinson's questions and responses. The (Singaporean) research team offered a more practised cultural reading of the head of department's responses than the researcher herself, a foreigner, had been able to read or adapt to in the interview and, who, as you can probably tell from this account, was far from dispassionate, even months later when revisiting the data. With these extra dimensions of inference and understanding, this interview revealed yet another very important component of the research: the researcher's own emotional subtexts, and the impact they had on the interviewee's responses (adapted from Stinson 2009).

Subjectivity and emotion

■ subjectivity

■ reliability

Don't be afraid of your subjectivity, or try to deny your emotional involvement with your subject. What you must do is acknowledge it, chronicle and plot it as best you can, and then tally and compare what it is telling you for *reliability*, *credibility* and *triangulation* with other analyses of the data, some of which need to come from outside the researcher. As we implied at the beginning, new markers of validity for research have come to join reliability and triangulation as watchwords. Especially if you are using qualitative instruments that invoke or demand a subjective component, you should certainly keep a constant eye throughout your data analysis on the following checking questions, which will also ensure some level of objectivity, or at least distance:

- *Credibility*: is your research outcome believable in its context, based on what you know or knew before?

- *Resonance*: how does the research resonate with the context itself, with other research in the area, with what is already known?

- *Plausibility*: even more than its credibility, you must ask yourself what is there in the analysis that will make *other* people believe it?

- *Transferability*: the demand that the results be generalisable, which was once an imperative for valid research, cannot be met in a lot of qualitative research. However, for all but the most myopic piece of action research or case study, you will hope that it might be usable in other contexts, by other people; therefore, who else might find this analysis useful, and will its results have currency beyond the end of this project?

Achieving distance in participant-researcher data analysis must start with you as the researcher, and must start during the data-collection process. Just writing up your field notes and your journal will begin a process of transformation and distancing of the data, conveying not only what you are seeing, but your thoughts and feelings about what you are seeing—it is your first chance to 'think aloud' and identify the difference. You will find yourself making links to other ideas, data, images, documentation and literature from the field.

Just writing the journal or field notes is not all there is to it, of course. We'll come back later to what you do with it after the action is over.

Preparing to analyse in depth

You have an ocean of data, and are wondering where to start fishing. Let's follow this oceanographic metaphor for a while. When in doubt, as always, go back to your Research Question and start there, baiting the hook in terms of asking what you might fish up from the data, and where you are likely to find it. It may be that you already have some sub-questions attached to your main Research Question. These now become crucial, but only as a first toe in the water. You need to prepare a depth probe. In other words, by questioning your questions, each time you will find a new set of questions to take you deeper. The Research Question is your little boat on the surface of the data, on the first level, which you have positioned as best you can from what you know and have read. We'll use the example of the Singapore research project described above to illustrate how your trawling will get down to deeper levels till you can map the ocean floor and find the big and unknown fish.

> Our sustained 'deep-water fishing' metaphor was both collaboratively coined for the occasion and applied to the second Singapore project, by one of us (O'Toole) and the research team. In fact, it formed the preliminary systematic frame for the analysis of the whole project. The metaphor was as useful as the organisational plan in keeping the analysis focused.
>
> $\rightarrow$

Margin notes: credibility · resonance · plausibility · transferability · generalisability · transformation of data · fishing the data · depth probing

Sea-level (Research Question):

How does process drama impact on oral communication?

First depth-level (sub-questions):

What do we need to know from the data that will help us identify the impact of process drama?

One example from six identified was:

What were the student responses to the project?

- Data to be fished: Students' focus group interviews; videos of lessons; researchers' field notes.
- Trawling through the data in pursuit of answers to this sub-question, one of the first findings was that there was very considerable diversity in their response. This finding prompted a new level of questions.

Second depth-level (sub-sub-questions):

What factors might account for this diversity?

- Data to be fished—the student focus group interviews.
- The researchers identified fourteen further factors, including:
  - What was the significance to the students of process drama as a new pedagogy?
  - What was the significance of the students' level of English?

In trawling the student focus groups for these sub-sub-questions, a previously unidentified generalisable factor became evident: that there was a noticeable *shift of response* in some students between their first focus group interview (end of first semester) and their second (end of second semester).

Third depth-level (sub-sub-sub-questions):

When did these shifts of response occur, and how can we account for them?

To answer this sub-sub-sub-question, the researchers had to make some choices, which led to a sequence of decisions on setting a new course for their data fishing:

1. to restrict their searches to a sample of students who manifested these shifts
2. then to go back to the student focus groups, revisiting the second-level questions
3. then also to access other data such as their own journals and field notes to see if these shifts were chronicled there
4. next to access the teachers' journals and the videos of their classes, correlating the identified student focus groups with the particular teachers
5. finally to examine the quantitative test results of the individual students, and of their class and teacher.

↘ ANALYSIS IN ACTION

Preliminary analysis and reflection-in-action—the participant-researcher

If you are collecting qualitative data, you will almost certainly have already made a start on its analysis long before you finish the collection. Methodologies like action research and reflective practitioner research demand it formally. In any case, your brain will not have remained in neutral as you went through the data-collection process. Data analysis that is strictly post-collection is really only necessary for quantitative instruments, and for experimental research, where, of course, the experiment must run its course, and not be pre-empted.

Two whole movements in research are actually based on the principle of analysing the data as you go along: *grounded theory* and *reflection-in-action*. Both have already been mentioned in Chapter 4, and grounded theory, in particular, is replete with a suite of widely recognised data generation and data reduction techniques, so we refer you to the more encyclopaedic texts on our various Wider Reading lists for details of these. Briefly, in analysing data towards creating grounded theory through *grounded analysis*, the key to the approach is constant comparison of the data as it is collected—compare surveys with interviews, and interviews with each other. Theoretical ideas will begin to emerge (as we described in the previous chapter). These, in turn, might suggest other forms of data that would be useful to collect, and you continue to analyse the data by comparing it with the theory as that grows and changes, as the following example, described in the researcher Brad's own words, demonstrates:

▪ grounded theory

▪ reflection-in-action

> As it was decided to investigate by examining the lived experience of successful teacher educators in the arts, *Grounded theory* was selected … This … was attractive too because, as a form of social criticism, clear and practical guidelines for effective implementation of change can be set down at the conclusion of the investigation.
>
> During the first six months research was conducted in a number of institutions operating teacher education programs. This involved visiting six lecturers in tertiary institutions in England. Each visit enabled data to be collected on the program, the students and the institution. While the data gathered came from observing students at work and collecting program outlines, student reading lists, assessment outlines and the like, the principal means of gathering data was through an interview with the lecturer selected.
>
> Grounded theory requires that the actual business of data collection remains responsive to the emerging theory. This required the interviews to be scheduled far enough apart to allow for sufficient time for data analysis, thereby enabling the emerging theory to evolve from the collected data. (Haseman 1991)

▦ elaborated theory

In recent years, other researchers have expanded on this notion of grounded or data-responsive theory-making, such as Diane Vaughan, who dubbed it *elaborated theory* (Vaughan 1992, p. 173).

▦ reflection-in-action

If you have read any of the works of Donald Schön or his followers (or read Chapters 3 and 4 of this book), you will be familiar with his concept of 'reflection-in-action'. This is a necessary part of various forms of participant-researcher study, such as reflective practitioner research, and often of action research, arts-based enquiry and case study. This kind of reflection has the great advantage that it incorporates the emotional—and even sensory and kinaesthetic—components of cognition, together with the sense of immediacy that consists of still being directly involved in action as you are beginning to process it. Often the hardest part of reflection-in-action is capturing it in writing or some other recording device, quickly and spontaneously enough for it still to be reflection-*in*-action, rather than reflection *on* action.

▦ reflective memos

The next step in ongoing action pre-analysis is the reflective memo. This is that pause that allows you to collect your thoughts and feelings, and begin to shape them. You may be gaining new or reshaped perspectives, you might have had one or more 'Aha!' moments, or something from your literature keeps forcing itself on your attention, as being either confirmed or contested by the action. The series of reflective memos, if you use them, will be the next stage of the preliminary analysis, and will then themselves form important data for cross-referencing later. Perhaps the most significant aspect of

▦ emerging themes

this concurrent pre-analysis is that some theme or themes, or the beginning of what might be a pattern, will emerge. This is well worth capturing in a reflective memo when it happens, as that is the beginning of your real data analysis.

ANALYSIS AFTER ACTION

Reflection on action

Of course, as a way of beginning to analyse fieldwork, reflection *on* action is just as valid as reflection-in-action. The passing of time fades the immediacy of memory, but permits distance and the introduction of other perspectives; distance permits action to resonate with other experiences. This introduces a sense of proportion and a measure of objectivity. It does not necessarily cancel or preclude the subjective

▦ objectivity

dimension, or emotion—which will also be transformed by the distance, however. David Wright (2005) invokes the poetic phrase 'the dance of understanding' to describe the 'interweaving of mood and explanation' that happens in reflection on

▦ resonances

action. Such *resonances* are also the stuff of poetry. We have elsewhere explored the nexus between research and arts. Perhaps the only difference is that researchers can socialise the resonances, anchoring them in a living, concrete context in education, where the insights gained can be offered to the audience/viewer/reader as 'outsights'. If we are contributing anything by our research in, through and about education, surely it is not in drawing a nominal distinction between knowledge and wisdom, but in knowing what questions are wise to ask as Part A makes plain, we hope, right from Chapter 1.

Retrospective analysis—preliminary processing

Most of your data analysis will, of course, occur retrospectively. You will certainly have a space-consuming pile of physical data, and probably a megabyte-consuming pile of electronic files, such as journals, field notes, figures and graphs, photocopied documents, interviews, videos and photographs, which fill boxes, baskets, filing cabinets and your hard drive. The first thing to do is to get it into order, ready to sift. You should sort out each type of data separately, and probably chronologically, in the first instance. Interviews, focus groups, questionnaires and journals give quite different kinds of information. Then each form of data needs preparing for use, at least checking that it is ready. These sorted collections are known as your *data sets*. We are assuming that any researcher today is at least minimally computer-literate, because word-processing and spreadsheets for numerical analysis save countless hours (and prevent the disfigurement of walls!). There are also a number of qualitative data-analysis software programs available to help you get and keep your e-data sorted, which we will look briefly at below (as well as any number of quantitative and statistical ones).

physical data

e-data

data sets

Gather all your notes together, and if they were handwritten, you should have them electronically stored, for easy access, sorting and cross-referencing. Make sure that they are complete, and in a sensible order. It is a good idea to devise a code for yourself for easy retrieval, and so that you can quickly cross-reference with other relevant data, for example:

field note coding

> Field notes at school A, visit 1, 28 May: FA-1–29/5
>
> Field notes at school A, visit 2, 30 May: FA-2–30/5
>
> Field notes at school B, visit 1, 29 May: FB-1–28/5
>
> Field notes at school B, visit 2, 31 May: FB-2–31/5
>
> Journal book 2, 27–31 May (Week 4): J-2-W4/5

If possible, you should number every line of every document (your word-processing program will have this facility, as will any research software program). That will make it easier for your retrieval, and also for when you are reporting; you can easily refer to a document in an appendix.

line-numbering

If you find data is missing, or has been mislaid, this too must be noted. You must then be aware that you are working from an incomplete record (and possibly declare it in your methodology section).

missing data

Interviews and focus groups, of course, have to be transcribed, and the lines of these numbered too. This is one of the most time-consuming parts of any research project.

■ transcription

■ self-transcribing

If you can afford it, an experienced typist can usually be found to transcribe interviews, especially if you made sure they were recorded on an appropriate machine. Though this will save you a great deal of time, it is not always the best idea. Transcribing your own interviews can be more than just a tedious chore. In listening, you will recall the key pauses and the interviewee's changes of expression or intensity, the nervous fidget or unexpected gesture, and only you can properly interpret whether the little giggle was amused or tense (you can even add them as 'stage directions' to the interview transcript). Your transcription will be likely to be more accurate, too. External transcribers, however acute, cannot know the full context and may not be familiar with the interviewee's accent, and words and phrases will be inaudible to them but quite clear to you. You know your own voice and often those of the interviewees. Transcribing your own interviews also gives you a far more intimate knowledge of your own data—very useful when refining themes for later analysis.

■ quantitative data collection

■ transcribing surveys

■ statistician

■ spreadsheets

Quantitative data is usually relatively easy to put together ready for analysis, and, in fact, is easier to analyse. If you have set up an experiment, or set out to collect specific figures or statistics, you know what you are looking for, and why—at least in the first instance. For example, questionnaires and surveys are easy to collate and it is usually better to have them externally collated if you can, for speed and convenience and to preserve anonymity and probity. There are then plenty of ways the statistics can be analysed, and we will introduce you to a few of the simplest. Beyond these, go to the literature or consult a statistician. To further prepare for analysing quantitative data, we strongly recommend that you become familiar, if you are not already, with your computer's ordinary word-processing and spreadsheet software, which will give you the tools to do most simple numerical analyses yourself. Spreadsheets offer calculating tools for simple to quite complex tasks, if you can learn the formulae that help you not only to collate, but to cross-reference, compare and reclassify the statistics in dozens of ways. Any recent word processor contains graph-making tools for line graphs, pie charts and most other visual diagrams you are likely to need.

◤ ANALYSING THE DATA—QUANTITATIVE

Formulating the criteria

■ patterns

Data lies around in large numbers of bits! We believe, like most researchers in Education, that close attention to what patterns these may have necessitates a working knowledge of statistics—ways we make these bits 'count'. After all, even the most intensely meaningful accounts of experience (such as 'pain' in childbirth) can be, as ethnography, much enhanced by evidence that some or most or all new mothers reported the same feelings. Once you start counting responses in the search for patterns, you can quantify data (e.g. '33 per cent of the mothers reported …'). You can mix and match this with data that intensely qualitative data methodologies such as phenomenology generate, if you are driven by the reform of an educative program for antenatal classes. Alternatively, you can tell a different sort of research story (such as a causal story about the efficacy of pain relief medication). So, at the most basic level, the results of numerical data analysis may be self-evident, and easily interpreted from simple percentages.

> Students in a range of classes were taught through workshops to identify three stages of conflict: *latent, emerging* and *manifest* (O'Toole and Burton 2005a). Immediately following the workshop, a questionnaire to most of the classes tested their recall of this classification. Nearly 100 per cent were able to recall and name accurately the three stages. The questionnaire was administered nearly three months later to one class where it had been overlooked by the teacher. This unplanned piece of data collection indicated that still over 90 per cent were able to recall in order the three stages at that distance.

Both these pieces of data analysis proved very helpful in developing more sophisticated tools of analysis. For example, the extent to which the students were able to identify the three stages of conflict accurately in further activity work was explored through more quantitative survey data, and whether they actually ever applied them in real-life conflict contexts was addressed through qualitative data in the form of unprompted interviews, which we have described in Chapter 7.

Wherever interpretation of numerical data is involved, it is necessary to formulate very clear criteria for analysis, very early on. You need to know in advance exactly what you are looking for, and build your research design to include, say, an experiment or a survey, to find out just those factors, with as few uncontrollable variables as you can. You can always supplement or complement this with other data collection, as the 'pain-in-childbirth' example on page 160 shows.

analysis criteria

Ask yourself: what do you want numbers to do for you? Different purposes, or criteria, for statistics are listed in Kervin et al. (2006, pp. 147–8). They can:

- summarise data and reveal what is typical and atypical within a group
- identify the relative standing of individuals within an identified cohort
- show relationships between and among variables
- show similarities and differences among groups
- identify error that is inherent in a sample selection
- test for significance of findings
- support the researcher in making other inferences about the population.

Each of these purposes is essential in making evidential claims from data. They help make patterns, and relationships between them, more or less defensible, so they are often, and quite rightly, at the heart of data collection, and analysis. Education, as a social science, invites measurement. The first issue is: how is it to be done with *precision*? The second, more important issue is: how is this done with *accuracy*? Precise measurement is always desirable (Babbie 2002, p. 136), but once we have a statistic, what work does it do? Does it measure accurately what we want? There is always a crucial

relationships

precision
accuracy

■ judgment

element of interpretation and judgment among the various purposes of statistics, and different types of techniques that arise once choices have been made. We survey some main techniques shortly. For the present, here is an example of a very basic reliance on statistical precision in the service of fieldwork accuracy (as it should be).

> Percentages proved a useful baseline in the theatre-in-education experiment, already referred to in Chapter 7, where twenty classes of children experienced a story ('The Songman ...'): ten program classes through teacher narration, and ten control classes through theatre-in-education (O'Toole 1977). This story was constructed to contain nine distinct narrative elements, in a linear sequence. The children were asked to write a summary of the story, and to draw a picture of their own choice, relating to the story.
>
> The summary was analysed by identifying how many of the key narrative elements were mentioned in the retelling, and their sequence. The program classes scored slightly but significantly higher in both the elements and the accuracy of sequencing, and tended to write fewer words—i.e. more succinct retellings.
>
> Analysis of the drawings showed more marked differences. The program classes' drawings were realistic and accurate, and usually filled the whole page. The control classes drew much more schematic and fragmented drawings, often with a lot of unfilled space left on the paper, and where there was detail, it was often decorative and unrelated to the story. A professional art educator shown a selection class by class, but not knowing which were control and which were program classes, easily identified them all. He noted that the program class drawings showed on the whole 'more spontaneity, exhilaration and enjoyment'. There was a tendency in the program class drawings for more movement, more people, and those people to be more individualised; the program classes' work also seemed to reflect a stronger *class* experience—their drawings were more coherent and 'of a piece'.

As can be seen from this example of beginning research (the experiment was for a masters thesis), although all the above can be expressed in the form of simple graphs,

■ interpretation

some of the analysis goes beyond direct *statistical* collection into *interpretation*. The summary was pretty straightforward, though it was necessary to have two readers (more would have been even more reliable) since with the children's limited and varied writing capacities, it was not always clear whether they had, in fact, recorded some of the narrative elements, or whether the students' memory of the sequence might in some cases have been clearer than their ability to express it in written form. Even here, interpretation was becoming important in deriving the bare statistics, so we were already out of the realm of 'objectivity'. In fact, we were right into the realm of subjectivity, since

■ subjectivity

one of the readers was the researcher himself, who had an inbuilt bias, not declared or even properly recognised at the time, to look harder for success from the program classes than the control classes... The analysis of the drawings was more reliable, since it was carried out by an expert in children's art, who was also more disinterested.

This example indicates quite vividly, and again, the way in which *interpretive* analysis is by no means incompatible with *quantitative* experiment, nor insusceptible to at least some numbers. In the end, the major limitation of this experiment was not that it was unreliable. The uncontrollable variables had mostly been very carefully taken account of in advance, and thoroughly acknowledged in the analysis and the reporting. The criteria for analysis were as clear as they could be for both summary and artwork. The dramatic/literary material that formed the basis of the experiment had, in fact, been written very specifically to elucidate those criteria for the participants/listeners. The real let-down of that piece of research was in how much more potential it had to provide valuable and telling results than it achieved. Two golden opportunities for precious data analysis were missed.

The first failure was methodological in origin. The mainly quantitative data derived for interpretation would have been far more valuable if it could have been compared with other rich *qualitative* data from a much wider range of sources: teachers' journals from the twenty participating teachers; observation by an outsider who watched some at least of both program and control class sessions (nobody in the whole project did this even once); individual or focus group interviews with selected children; preselected children for case study; longitudinal follow-up interviews or test instruments with classes or individuals sometime after the event. None of this data was collected, so the figures remained shrouded in much more mystery than necessary.

■ uncollected data

The second was a failure of analysis. The figures gathered, while a little wobbly, were still quite substantial, with nearly six hundred children involved in the experiment. Ignorance and fear of statistics kept the analysis over-simple. Any of the basic statistical tools below could have offered opportunities for interrogating the figures and understanding their significance far better than was achieved.

■ inadequate analysis

Useful statistical instruments

At the end of the last chapter, we looked briefly at the kinds of statistical instruments we might use, and this section is only marginally less brief. If it interests you enough to consider using these tools, you should find out more about them; there are numerous websites, even more numerous books, and probably quite a few colleagues, from which and whom you can learn enough for your purposes. How about checking out some help from your science colleagues (if you are a teacher or in a tertiary institution) or the technical or accountancy staff (if you are in an industry or community agency setting)?

■ statistics
■ resources

Descriptive statistics are usually frequency counts, that is, the number of times something occurs, whether people, events or material objects. They have limited value and are usually confined to situations where a simple census is all that is required. However, they can be useful, as they were in the Singaporean ESOL example described earlier. We all unconsciously use this kind of statistic in our everyday language when we refer to something as being 'normal', translated into statistics as the majority view or the most usual result. When a series of events or a collection of people are selected at random, the resulting score will invariably translate to a curve, in which the majority of

■ frequency counts

■ bell curve

members of the distribution are in the central 60 per cent. This is the so-called 'normal curve' or *bell curve* (more accurately referred to in this book as the jellyfish, and more formally known as Gaussian distribution).

FIGURE 8.1 Gaussian distribution or bell curve

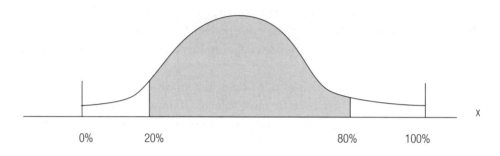

■ 'normality'

■ probability

Formally or implicitly, we usually use versions of this distribution when determining grades in education. Although test results cannot be said to be random, they still tend to conform to such a curve in the case of large populations. Studies that take advantage of this factor test whether or not an individual or subgroup is a member of the 'normal' population or is outside the majority of the curve. The results of such studies are usually reported as a probability; for example, there is a 99 per cent chance that the group are not members of the normal or control population.

> How useful a bell curve would have been in O'Toole's 'Songman' story research to show the contrasting simple distribution of the program and control classes in terms of the number of elements recalled.

■ standard deviation

Another immensely useful statistical device is the *standard deviation*, which is a measure of the *variability* (dispersion or spread) of any set of numerical values about their arithmetical mean.

> This would have been a useful way to explore in more detail: the spread of recall of the elements of the 'Songman' story; which elements were most recalled; and a more detailed comparison of the spreads between the program classes and the control classes.

Most advanced uses of statistics are based upon this measure. It is specifically defined as the square root of the arithmetical mean of the squared deviations. If everyone scores the same, the spread is 0. (There is no comparison with a normal curve.) If the spread is wide then you need to be able to compare the width of the spread with that of your control group as well as the overall distribution.

A further valuable test to bring to the basic data is an *ANOVA* (*analysis of variance*). It compares all the scores of all the groups and tests to see if there are any significant differences between one or more groups, or one group from the rest of the groups.

▦ analysis of variance

> That too could have been employed in the 'Songman' research, particularly because it would have helped to identify any of the controllable (dependent) variables that were not fully under control, or any unexpected uncontrollable (independent) variables.

Correlation is a comparison between two sets of measures. These can be taken from the same group at different times taking different tests, or different groups. The results are also expressed as a measure of probability that the two scores are the same. An important point to realise is that there can be no expectation of causality between the scores. For that, the researcher has to rely on other forms of data to put up against these correlations.

▦ correlation

> The 'Songman' research did attempt some basic correlation, but again, much more could have been possible. Wouldn't it have been both useful and revealing to have used the teachers' journals and the notes of the independent observer along with the scales that were presented?

The further you are prepared to delve into statistics, and have the kind of data sets to allow you to do so, the more you will be able to discover both correlations and patterns that are reliable. A common analysis tool is *regression analysis*, whose purpose is to see how some kind of change in one of the *independent variables* affects the *dependent variable*. An extension of this is *path analysis*, which often computes into picturesque (and informative) 'molecular' diagrams for the visual thinker. This can help to identify the causal connections between data where some correlations have already been discovered.

▦ regression analysis

▦ path analysis

> With more effective monitoring of the quality of the story reading in the 'Songman' control classes, and the consistency of performance in the experimental classes, either of the above forms of analysis might have thrown up very useful understanding about the quality of the teaching and learning experience and the students' learning and retention. This was yet another missed opportunity.

The sins of omission that are now so evident in the research project mentioned above underline how important it is to have our wits fully about us at all times in research, especially at the outset. This includes thinking laterally and with foresight—so much more could have been achieved with more imaginative and knowledgeable planning.

▦ foresight

▦ planning

■ detachment

■ the unexpected

When going through the data provided by quantitative instruments, it is necessary to keep your minds focused on your criteria and your purposes for collecting the data. But it is also very valuable to 'keep a cool strip', slightly detached from the central data-crunching. You can very often see in data (particularly in numerical data) patterns emerging that you had neither expected nor planned for. As we stated in the overview to this chapter, this is the exciting part of the 'friction' generated by the rough ground of research. To repeat: you get much traction from friction.

> In research on the nature and extent of cultural capital provided by major performing arts centres, the researchers were collecting some preliminary data on the artists associated with one of the centres (Ferres et al. 2006). In just collating the personal details of the artists, some quite startling patterns emerged, relating to the gender and socio-cultural profiles of the artists employed by and associated with the centre. Further scrutiny through *path analysis* revealed further significant employment patterns. These patterns then influenced the next stage of the process and criteria for selecting interviewees, in contrast to the much more limited and individualistic criteria that had originally been formulated. Even the nature of the interviews themselves was modified in response to these unexpected patterns.

■ aberrant patterns

In the above case, the aberrant patterns emerged early enough to be incorporated in the research without any change to the Research Question or the structure, which the patterns actually enriched. In many cases, however, such patterns offer a tantalising dilemma: they are not strictly within the terms of the Research Question, and so to incorporate them entails modifying the Question … and that means altering the structure, shifting the emphasis or modifying the lens of the analysis. The researcher must decide if *that* game is worth the candle. The answer is usually no, especially in beginning research. Don't be deflected. Make a note of the emerging pattern, resolve to look at it again one day when you've finished this research, and return with fortitude to your stated criteria.

■ proof

A final reminder: even in quantitative research you can never 'prove' anything. You can provide indicators, and you can go some way towards confirming or disproving something, but you can never know if another experiment next year is going to provide quite different results, as those uncontrollable variables, lying hidden in the long grass (which covers the rough ground), strike again.

↘ ANALYSING THE DATA—QUALITATIVE

Addressing the criteria decided in advance

■ criteria

Analysing qualitative data is quite different from analysing quantitative data, and often rather harder. That is particularly the case with methodologies where there are no predetermined criteria, no given or prefigured lens through which to filter the data.

This is where you might be in danger of being unnecessarily confused by vocabulary and semantics, particularly if you have been reading literature from a range of paradigms and methodologies. You will note that we have been mainly using the term 'criteria' to describe those factors that form the basis of your analysis process—the way you identify, classify and group what is important to your Research Question from the raw data. In other words, before you can have findings, you have to know what it is that you might have found. Many other terms are used to label this categorisation process: *categories*, *themes*, *indicators*, *key concepts*. Some descriptions of the process are more metaphorical, like the *lenses* that we have ourselves used several times. Each of these has its place in its own methodology, and some carry subtle distinctions of definition that could, on occasion, be important. Because we cannot deal in detail with all the analysis processes, we will use the word *criteria* as our main label, with apologies to those for whom it may not be strictly the best term.

▤ defining criteria

▤ categories
▤ themes
▤ indicators
▤ key concepts
▤ lenses

If you are working to a hypothesis, and your criteria have been laid down in advance, say in a case study looking for very specific evidence of learning or behaviour change, then what you need is patience, to sift through the data according to your criteria, one at a time, to find evidence of that criterion. After each cast through, you need more patience *and* a strong will to counter your natural instincts, and to go through again specifically looking for evidence that contradicts or contests the criterion—the crucial negative data we have stressed so often. This whole process means that you need to comb the data many times. We have suggested that sanity is at risk, and certainly the time-scale of the project, if you collect too much data. This is why, when you are working out your criteria, you should not end up biting off more than you can chew.

▤ evidence
▤ patience
▤ contradictory evidence

Identifying the criteria to be decided

This section is for those who are working in one of these fairly open methodologies. If you are an action researcher or a reflective practitioner, you will only know what you have planned in the first instance in order to solve your problem, achieve your vision or improve your practice, and the data you collect will help you to identify whether and to what extent your planning is working in action. You cannot plan in advance the criteria by which you will interpret the unplanned. That's why grounded theory and reflection-in-action were formulated. Even more so, if you are an ethnographer, you are in honour bound to accept the data that you gather, virtually without making any kind of pre-judgment on any of it. This means that after collection you have to identify the criteria by which you will make sense of the data.

▤ ethnography

If you are a researcher working in one of these open methodologies, you must have even more patience than those who have been able to work out their criteria in advance. You will have to work your way through the data once or more to establish your criteria, and then again just as often as those with already decided criteria do to apply your emergent criteria throughout the data! You will also need to use your intelligence more shrewdly, because you have to start by finding what you don't yet know you are looking for. This is not magic, but like detective work, it will involve a lot of painstaking and

■ intuition

■ back brain

sometimes repetitive scrutiny and also what is variously called 'intuition', 'the back brain' or terms more mystical. The very complex intellectual processes of classification, analysis and synthesis that elsewhere we label 'perceptiveness', 'great intelligence' and 'imagination' do not all happen consciously, or neatly in the order in which we are consciously pursuing the research. As Yeats (1939) described, what we might call the project research preparation of a couple of highly successful action researchers, Julius Caesar and Michelangelo: 'Like a long-legged fly upon the stream, his mind moves upon silence'. Just as the Globe Theatre's timelines indicate that Shakespeare's plays must have been at least partly ready-made as they poured out on the page so quickly, and as countless writers testify, some of the processing of any data happens according to intuited calculations. The least of us occasionally surprise ourselves with the elegance

■ revelations

■ deadlines

and coherence of our own apparently spontaneous revelations. That is scary, because it seems unscientific, and we would certainly not recommend trusting the back brain to do the whole job. Moreover, the back brain does not always work on the same timelines as the front. Uncharitable supervisors, university examiners or grant systems sometimes pre-empt the readiness of the back brain to proffer the synthesised article, by demanding interim reports or chapters, or even publications (about which we have more to say in Chapter 9), before you have any coherent analysis to show.

To cut a long story short: now (right at the start of the data analysis) is often the place to trust your back brain. You can do worse, if you do not have any other starting place, than to reread your Research Question minutely and commit it to memory. Let it fire you up again with the enthusiasm that got you involved in this project in the first place, then dive into the data following your nose, or your instinct. Your job is to identify some key criteria, factors that are so important that they are essential to your making any kind of meaning pertaining to the Research Question. This may also work well in tandem with your use of computer software for data analysis, if you are thinking of trying that. A brief description of what that can do is below.

■ thick data

As we said before, data of open forms of qualitative analysis is often known as 'thick' data because it is complex and textured. You need to recognise and welcome its complexity, though your initial reaction may be to wish it was simpler and clearer … Remember, you did not choose this open methodology because it would provide reductive or minimal data. As you read through or otherwise start to examine the data, your front and back brains will be looking for connections, for something that makes

■ patterns

the data coherent. You may have some specific factors or patterns that you are looking for in the first place. Good, but don't only look for those, or you will miss everything else that the data might offer. There will be rudimentary structures of analysis in your head somewhere, and your attention will be called to them in the first instance by what

■ emotional response

seems interesting, or affirming, or surprising. This emotional reaction is worth trusting, because what seems interesting *is* usually relevant, in some way. So the next step is to interrogate not so much the data as your reaction: why do I find this interesting/ affirming/surprising? Can I identify where it *might* fit in with my Research Question? Make a note of the piece of data, in your code, so that you can easily retrieve it, together with a first note about why you thought it might be relevant.

Just a warning: at this point, don't cling to the literature or to your own expectations based on what the literature, those thick books written by other people, has told you. You need your data to speak directly to you. In fact, you need to converse with it, unmediated by what you think you *might* be supposed to be saying to each other and looking for.

Soon you will have a lot of these second-phase notes, and the glimmers of something coherent: themes or patterns of repetition, even maybe criteria will be emerging—probably many more than you will eventually be able to deal with. Bind yourself to the mast of that Research Question, just to make sure you are not being led off course by the blandishments of data, like the Sirens beckoning you to a desert island too far off for you to return to your odyssey. You may find it useful at this time to write the occasional reflective memo, to test whether there is something substantial in what you think you are seeing.

▩ emerging criteria

▩ diversions

When you have completed at least one preliminary cast through the data, step back a little and look through your notes, and the patterns and themes. It is often a good idea to discuss these with somebody knowledgeable and sympathetic, but actually outside the project—your supervisor (that's what they're for) or a colleague. This is crunch time. You have to make decisions that will provide a clear focus for your study, and also close doors that may have led to other vital enquiries but are beyond the scope of yours. See if you can sort your themes into some kind of order or sequence. If you have a strongly visual approach to thinking, now is the time for playing with diagrams and flow charts. Be playful, don't just grab at the first shape that seems to make some kind of sense, but keep refining it until it (probably) falls apart and then try a completely different shape. Even if you are more word-oriented, simple sets of visual axes or continua can be quite helpful. By making your data two-dimensional you will certainly be oversimplifying it, but you are also making it manageable and clear.

▩ organising themes

The decisions that you need to make here are tough, because you will have to pass over much that would be valuable and relevant if you are to cut your coat according to your cloth and your timelines. You may even be faced with realising that the study is more limited than you had hoped.

Following some very exhausting, dangerous and time-consuming DEd fieldwork in Peshawar, north-west Pakistan on teachers' professional performance criteria, Wahid (we first met Wahid in Part A) went through his first, informal data-sifting process, and came up triumphantly with twenty-eight quite separate themes, which with great effort, he pruned to about fifteen (see Hussain 2008). After discussion with his supervisor, he realised that too many themes meant examining all the data more times, and then condensing his analysis and reportage on each to tiny slices of one or at most two chapters. He heroically brought down the number to five … but then realised that the intensity and focus that this would give him demanded a more sophisticated approach to the fieldwork itself, from which he had already learnt a lot. By returning to, then broadening out, the literature, Wahid was able to take a more global perspective on his themes, animating them more vividly. The results were spectacularly clearer; the thesis had more impact, with richer recommendations for reform in Pakistan.

sifting

casting

quilting

bricolage

crystallisation

You will find the preliminary data-sifting processes and the identification of the criteria called by various terms, some colourful or metaphorical—like *sifting* (flour) and *casting* (fishing-rod) or even *quilting*. None of this terminology need be feared. Postmodernists like the term *bricolage* for the whole process. Laurel Richardson's (2000) *crystallisation*, like bricolage, applies to the whole data-analysis process, not just the preliminary cast-through, but seeing the cognitive coherence emerging and growing like crystals from all the various data sources.

Electronic data analysis

More and more, researchers are turning to electronic tools to help them analyse qualitative data. In their early forms, these were rather mechanistic, complicated to set up and transfer data into, and hard to use for those with diverse, complex and sensitive data. Recent upgrades have made electronic tools much more user-friendly and adaptable, and much more simple to set up and manage. Basically, they all help you to do the same things that were traditionally done manually and laboriously: storing, sorting and coding data, and helping retrieval. They can also help you to make and follow connections that might often be overlooked, as they can display data simultaneously in a number of forms and formulations, and cross-reference your key ideas more easily than by covering the floor and the walls with sheets of paper or post-it notes. There are a number of sophisticated programs that are commercially available, such as NVivo, QDA Miner, Xsight and ATLAS.ti. Some, such as QDA Miner, have the capacity to marry quantitative data analysis with statistics.

storing

sorting

coding

electronic
opportunities

What one user said about the first well-known version of these (NUD.IST, the now-superseded precursor of Nvivo) still gives quite a realistic idea of what they might do for you. The user might not have been disinterested, and it might not have been *quite* as simple as it is made to sound, but the comments are still valid.

Computers can't crunch words as if they were numbers and NUD.IST won't analyse your data for you. What then can you expect of the software? NUD.IST will help you manage your data as you analyse documents such as interview transcripts, field notes, journal articles, papers, e-mail archives or any other data you can save as a text file. It will also facilitate your management of other data formats such as video and audiotapes. You can search and code your data and automate many of the coding, searching and reporting tasks. You can write memos and add context-sensitive annotations to your data. As you progress through your analysis you can use NUD.IST to document your analytic process and reflect on your role as a researcher … Perhaps most significantly, NUD.IST allows you to fracture and reorganise your data in ways that simply aren't possible with traditional software applications, and thus develop new insights into your research. When you begin your first research project with NUD.IST you will find two particular features of the software to be especially reassuring. First, and perhaps most important, is *context*. NUD.IST, at all times,

> enables you to remain close to your data, even closer than if you had hard copy at your fingertips! You never need to worry about coding selections of your data and later not having access to the original context of the data. You can code data and go back to it days or even weeks later, and you're only one keystroke away from viewing the coded data in its original context. The second important feature of NUD.IST is its *flexibility*. You can develop and easily modify your coding structure 'on the fly' even during the initial stages of your project when your analysis and/or cognitive style are themselves fluid and changing. (Kerlin 2002)

Since then, such programs have been made more genuinely user-friendly, and expanded some of their facilities, particularly to deal effectively with contemporary text and data. At the time of writing this second edition, NVivo, NUD.IST's successor, is now into its tenth version:

    contemporary text

> NVivo is software that supports qualitative and mixed methods research. It lets you collect, organise and analyse content from interviews, focus group discussions, surveys, audio—and now in NVIVO 10 social media and web pages. (NVivo 2013)

Like NVivo, some of its competitors are alive to the challenges of marrying quantitative and qualitative data.

    mixed methods

> QDA Miner qualitative data-analysis tool may be used to analyze interview or focus group transcripts, legal documents, journal articles, speeches, even entire books, as well as drawings, photographs, paintings, and other types of visual documents. Its seamless integration with SimStat, a statistical data-analysis tool, and WordStat, a quantitative content analysis and text mining module, gives you unprecedented flexibility for analyzing text and relating its content to structured information including numerical and categorical data. (QDA Miner 2013)

You will see from the promotional statements on their web pages that the software designers are highly attuned to the fluid and evanescent nature of our research, as well as to the needs of beginning researchers. Just so that you don't either get carried away by all their blandishments, or entirely daunted by the jargon, you can remember that like all technology, these packages are good servants but bad masters, and really they are only as good as your skill and confidence in operating them. As the old statement on NUD.IST reminds us, the human being still does the analysis. Artificial intelligence is still some way off from replacing human intelligence. You can always go back to the colour-coded post-it notes and papers all over the wall.

    caveat emptor

MEDIATING AND MEDIATED DATA

Impermanence of data

The very word *data* sounds solid and definite, doesn't it? Well, it's not. One very important factor to remember in your data analysis is that data is actually as impermanent and unstable as everything else in our shifting and protean world of research. First, let's consider just how many destabilising factors you've already encountered:

■ uncollected data

- You've already made decisions, based on the scale and focus of your research methodology, that have led to the non-collection of vast quantities of data that might have been relevant.

■ contingencies

- Unless you have developed very effective methods of cataloguing and coding your data, you have probably already lost some en route, or just not had good enough equipment to capture all you wanted, or had your data-collection context interfered with by unpredictable contingencies—absent students, interrupted interviews, sound tapes accidentally wiped, and so on.

■ lost data

- Unless you are very careful, data can actually deteriorate, particularly in a long project: pencilled and some photocopied and coloured text can fade in time; computers can crash and lose or corrupt files; video and tape recordings can deteriorate, especially in hot storerooms; cheap photo album sleeves actually eat the photographic surface; mice can get at the paper records; rain, coffee and Coke can blot the butcher's paper and student assignments.

Mediation and interpretation of data

However, the chances are that you are still left with quite as much data as you can deal with. Your job is to analyse it, but your brain is already ahead of your intentions, mediating that task for you and changing the rules. Data rarely comes in an entirely unmediated form, and in storing and retrieving it, you are transforming it. A sound recording of an interview you made is an impoverishment of the original face-to-face encounter, because the whole paralinguistic dimension is missing. Transcribe that sound recording, and you also lose the vocal intonation, pitch and energy cues. Your response to what you read is very different from your response to the original interview, not least because of the emotional dimension of your relationship with the interviewee. Some of that can be recalled, especially in the sound-tape version, if you transcribed it yourself. However, if, in the interests of objectivity, you are reading a transcript from an unknown respondent, who was interviewed by a third-party interviewer, and which was transcribed by another, you will only be presented with a fraction of the interaction. Your intelligence is absolutely essential in interpretation (although of course it can also lead you astray). Like any good critical audience, you must look for the subtext, make inferences from what you are presented with, *and* bear in mind how it has been mediated.

■ transforming data

■ interpretation

This applies just as much to your own personal data components as it does to received data. Before you start to go through your journal or field notes, let a bit of time elapse, to give you some perspective and emotional distance from the event; then approach the text a little as if you were reading the journal of a stranger, trying to read between the lines. You will often see things that you were not consciously aware of when you jotted them down. It's crucial at this time to compare your journal with whatever other sources of data you set up. What do the other participants in the event say about it, and in what ways does their perception of what happened differ from yours? If you had another observer in the room, what did they see that you didn't? Use this to interrogate your journal: why did you miss the things that they saw or found important?

distance

comparing data

Video is a massively mediated form of data, and this has both disadvantages and advantages. You will probably find when you watch it that the event that was rich and momentous as it took place in the moment now seems flat and curiously lifeless. It is in two dimensions now, for a start. Video doesn't seem able to record the energy and excitement of real-life action; this is because it literally can't. Videos and films that we watch which have 'life' and 'energy' about them, whether for entertainment or edification, are the product of effective editing: the cutting and jumping, the changes of angle and focus are what provide the energy. Usually, video taken for research purposes is single-camera, often fixed in space and focal length. Nevertheless, because of that very limitation, video can provide very valuable data for analysis, particularly of an event that you were part of. The video's point of focus does not waver and jump in the directions yours did, so it will reveal things that you did not see, or did not notice. Most of all, it can reveal new and negative data, those relevant things that you were not looking for. Analysing video is probably the best place in a research project for using a *critical friend*.

video transformation

critical friend

- Watch the video yourself, and retrieve from it what seems important to you.
- Choose a segment that seems to be rich or interesting in terms of your Research Question or criteria.
- Give some context of the event to your critical friend, and let him or her watch—preferably without you hovering.
- Then have a discussion, which you record, about what you both saw.
- Next try watching it together, with both of you having access to the pause and rewind buttons—still recording your dialogue.
- Now transcribe the sound recording of your dialogue and analyse that.

> Some people make excellent critical video friends.
>
> The late Paul Stevenson, a retired educator, almost made a new career of it: he was used for well over a decade in this generic fashion, *inter alia*, to view interviews with young police officers, episodes of children's play, and work in African Theatre for Development. There is an excellent example of how he operated in Julie Dunn's account of her dramatic play research (Dunn 2002, pp. 81–3).

Even simple data must be mediated and processed. There is more to analysing numerical surveys than just collating the data and presenting it. The numerical results have to be related back to their context, and inferences made about the factors that produced those results. Sometimes having a large number of responses allows you to identify common themes or preoccupations that people might not be keen to see elicited. Where the responses are verbal, it is usually not too difficult to deduce what the driving factors in people's opinions are. 'I think rock musicians should bloody well go out and get a proper day job' tells you about how that respondent classifies the job of musician, the genre of rock and the status of the profession. It also tells you something about the emotional strength of the response and the respondent's attitude to this art form. In conjunction with other replies from that or other respondents, you may also make some inferences relating to their context, which presumably is what you chose these respondents for. Where you have used both numerical and verbal responses—say in a Likert scale with an invitation for comments underneath—you have to take particular care. The two sets of differing data will certainly allow you to make inferences, and will shed some light on each other. However, the verbal responses will almost never exactly reflect or match the numerical results, because the people who take the trouble to write comments are those who have the strongest emotional reaction to the question, either positive or negative, and they may not reflect the majority that shows up in the numerical results—in fact, they can be quite untypical, so any inferences you make must be with caution and all your powers of shrewdness.

Which brings us once again to what is something of a refrain in this book: remember the negative data! What the data doesn't say is just as important as what it does say, and now is the time to identify it. For instance:

- Your *journal*: interrogate it for the gaps. What didn't happen? Who wasn't quite as enthusiastic, or was right off-task, or left early? Why? Is there any of your other data that suggests that some participants might have different viewpoints about what you documented?
- In the *interviews*: Who chose not to be interviewed, or who gave bland replies? Why?
- On the *video*: Who hung back or hardly appears on the screen, or was fidgeting a lot? Why?

Especially if you are not using formal triangulation of data, this is the way you provide some rigour to your research to balance your subjectivity. To pick up Richardson's elegant metaphor: a true crystal shows its impurities in its areas of cloudiness and the seams and fault lines of alien compounds that run through it. For crystallisation to occur effectively, any theory must incorporate the negative data.

Your ability to interpret your data is what lies at the heart of all qualitative research. That means not just to reiterate it, but to make shape, pattern and meaning out of it, tie it to your key themes and criteria, and thence back to illuminate your Research Question.

■ processing surveys

■ common themes

■ Likert scale

■ negative data

■ rigour
■ balance

■ crystallisation

⬊ DATA SYNTHESIS

Round about now, you will start seeing the light at the end of the tunnel. Though the final section of your thesis or research report will be the most important for the reader, namely, deriving the results, conclusions or emerging insights, it is unlikely to be the hardest. The leg-work has nearly all been done, and you are about to reap the rewards.

▦ conclusions

Re-examining the literature

When you have clarified your criteria and done the bulk of the analysis, you are sure to start seeing patterns. Some will just appear tantalisingly then disappear under the next wave of data or a crushingly contradictory piece of evidence, but others will recur and solidify. Your interrogatives will begin to turn into statements. That so-familiar Research Question will now be illuminated so that you will feel you know its dimensions and proportions inside out. Indeed, looking at it from outside, you will now have a sense of proportion, and from inside, you will have emerging insights. The next step is to check your data against your literature, which is laborious but can be quite exciting, and this time you should address it with confidence. If you remember, we warned you earlier when starting to deal with your data to put the literature aside so that you could concentrate on your analysis. Now welcome it again: you are now meeting it as an equal, bringing your own hard-won offerings. Look at how the research and analysis you have done sits with the literature. You will probably find that much of your work agrees with the literature you trusted most. Your first response will be to seek out and recognise that with relief. That should not be your only response, however heart-warming and reassuring it is. This is not the key to new knowledge, only to confirming old knowledge.

▦ patterns

▦ emerging insights

▦ reincorporating literature

▦ old knowledge

Now look to see how what you have found extends what you originally gleaned from that received word, the literature of previous research. It may be only by a subtle shift of emphasis, or perhaps adding an important new factor (one or more of your criteria). It may do more, by casting doubt on some assertion—opening a door to possibilities unseen by the previous writers. Occasionally, it may signally contest what they say, and you can balance and compare what you have found with what they thought they knew. Now you can start feeling a little empowered (probably it's the first time for a while!). Judgment is in your hands: do you trust your data enough to open up the debate, join the field of serious scholars in the topic, or even challenge the received wisdom? Are there points still open to contestation?

▦ new knowledge

You do need a little bit of time and brain-space during this phase for the old-fashioned business of ruminating (metaphorically chewing the well-regurgitated cud for one last time). Provided you have been trusting your back brain or at least permitting it to operate, you can now reasonably expect that it will start delivering. As if by magic, you will make connections with phrases you have read and thought you had forgotten that resonate with your data: data resonating with other data. If you are using a computer

▦ rumination
▦ back brain

▦ resonances

data-analysis program, you will find you are beating it to the connection. Remember, it's not magic—just the power of the brain that the age of rationalism and positivism forgot about.

collaboration

supervisor

critical friend

One of the strengths of collaborative research is that the reflection can be collaborative, too. Now is the time for you to ruminate together. If you are a solo student researcher, now is probably a good time for a defining discussion with your supervisor. It is another good time to sit down with your critical friend, if you are still speaking after the video analysis! Discuss your findings, with others or yourself, and start thinking about how you are going to frame and state them. Here are a few ruminative general questions to help your cud-chewing:

claims

- Do you have finite results from an experiment, and if so, what claims or interpretive statements can you make?

grounded theory

- Have you developed theory that is sufficiently grounded to stand the test of matching up with the literature, or the practice?

new knowledge

- Above all, what new knowledge can you identify? This does not need to be absolute truths, merely 'holding positions' that nobody has actually articulated before, which have now stood the test of some analysis.

validity

- How confidently can you articulate new conclusions, and how valid are your provisional insights?

contradictions

- Can you identify the remaining pressure points? What remains unsatisfactory, inconclusive, contradictory, and does this matter?

incompleteness

- Can you identify what unfinished business there still is? Can you accept the incompleteness of the synthesis?

The following account by a successful beginning researcher, Anna, of her data analysis from go to whoa in her PhD research beautifully encapsulates much of what we have been proposing in this chapter.

> For me, one of the most difficult aspects of completing a doctoral thesis was how to effectively analyse the data. I found myself standing in the middle of my lounge room, the floor of which had disappeared under a mass of paper, which I warily surveyed.
>
> The conundrum I found myself in—which I was comfortingly told was entirely normal—was what on earth should I do with it all before I was completely overwhelmed? Procrastinating was not an option, yet I was unsure how to begin—how to manage the data in a way that was productive and would allow me to reclaim my lounge room floor. This process—or what I technically referred to as the 'yucky' stage—involved thrashing around in the research, trying to be as open as possible to any findings that emerged. To avoid getting 'bogged' down by the sheer amount of data, I began by wading through the piles of interviews, observation notes etc., highlighting items of interest—anything that took my fancy really. I also took note of items that deviated from recurring

patterns, because findings that do not correlate with initial perceptions should be actively sought rather than dreaded or ignored.

Ongoing analysis actually eased the management of the copious amounts of data I had gathered. I began by reading then re-reading my journal and reflective notes, as well as the students' journals. I then made notes of the themes and ideas that seemed to be emerging. It was important to try and stay as close as possible to the data as originally recorded to enable it to speak for itself.

As I progressed and tentative themes began to reveal themselves, being a visual learner I simply used different colour highlighter pens to distinguish between various themes. Not very technical—but effective enough! I then literally cut up each segment of data, to form piles that were the same colour. For me, this made the process more manageable, and made me feel more in control. I chose pieces from each colour-coded pile, whichever I felt best represented the theme I was portraying. It soon became clear which pieces of data were repetitive, or were not as clearly expressed as others. When I couldn't decide, I would ask not only my supervisors, but also family and friends for their opinions. At this stage, the generation of data, its analysis and interpretation were not mutually exclusive activities.

This process did get easier! In fact, distinguishing exactly what was relevant and pertinent became clearer and more manageable as the research progressed. This is because the spirits of logic and enquiry required me to be constantly open to my Question's redefinition. Significantly, this also means the literature included in the thesis becomes more focused. I did not utilise a large amount of my data and my reading in the end, but it was all still useful in getting me to the finishing point.

Overall, whilst analysis took place from the very moment I entered the field, the process of quiet contemplation, of turning my experience into a meaningful whole, was one of the most difficult tasks, but also the most valuable. To think critically and reflexively was also one of the most important research tools I learned to use. Although a 'finished' construction or interpretation of that meaningful whole is presented in my doctorate, it is possible to question, with Fitzgerald, whether ethnography actually ever ends. (This story refers to Plunkett 2003.)

What about failure?

It may be that after all your efforts, you have failed to achieve any significant results or answers to your Research Question: to discover what you wanted, solve your problem or achieve your vision. You cannot prove your hypothesis, or you may have even had it disproved by the evidence of the data. Depending on your context, of course, this apparent failure should not be terminal, at least if you have carried out your research efficiently. After all, if you remember Occam's razor, that is what hypotheses are for: to be tried and if possible disproved. You have merely been carrying out a sophisticated version of the oldest learning method of all: trial and error. You've come up with the error, and you have done the world a service by holding the trial and providing new negative knowledge!

▪ Occam's razor

▪ trial and error

▪ negative knowledge

■ falsification   If you are a student, do not under any circumstances try to play down your lack of success, or pump up those parts of the research that did appear to answer your Research Question. It will be tempting to make as much as you can of what you have achieved (both for your self-esteem and for the consequences on the successful completion of your thesis), but you must not join those who obscure rather than add to human knowledge—that dishonourable list at the top of which now stands one of Korea's most distinguished geneticists, Hwang Woo-suk, who cancelled out his mighty achievement of cloning the world's first dog by falsifying figures. Nor be unduly humble in your conclusion. Just state, calmly and honestly, what led you to the conclusion that your research has not succeeded. If possible, point the way forward for other researchers, who may find another way of addressing your Research Question, or rephrasing it more productively. Then trust the probity and intelligence of your examiner(s). Just like the primary arithmetic teacher who is more interested in how the child arrives at the answer

■ examining process   than whether the answer is right, the job of the examiner is to scrutinise your process as well as your results. And as in arithmetic, the answer to any problem can be a negative quantity.

If, on the other hand, your research is not a student thesis, but a grant-aided research project, your prognosis is probably not so good, but you must honour the process, regardless. Certainly, much contemporary research is driven by sponsors who want particular, positive results—either for implementation or for advocacy—and so failure to come up with the goods can mean you kiss goodbye any further grants from that

■ fudging   sponsor. Nevertheless, the ethical requirement is absolute. No fudging. If you are very clever you might persuade your sponsor that now you have got the previous hypothesis out of the way, you can concentrate on another one with a refined Research Question that will have much better chances of success. If not, there are a thousand other projects in Education needing and waiting for what you know in order to get them done, and the experience you have gained on the last project is the most valuable thing you could possibly have, whether your results this time have succeeded or not.

Further research

Your final task is really a corollary of what this last section has discussed: whither next, for you or others? The real satisfaction to be gained out of provisional construction of knowledge, as opposed to the discovery of absolute truths, is that whatever you have discovered, positive or negative, will actually point the way to new research projects, new questions to be addressed or new ways to ask the original Question. Having put all this work into reaching your now thoroughly educated standpoint, you really have a responsibility, and the singular position, to open the gate for the next person to investigate the field, or for your own next project. Your conclusions should normally finish with some indication of new directions for research in the future. This may be very specific: your research could turn up something that cries out for immediate study; alternatively, the possibilities for future research might be more speculative and beyond your scope entirely.

NEW QUESTIONS, NEW PROJECTS

In the project already referred to extensively in the last two chapters—on addressing conflict in schools through various forms of drama and peer-teaching—after five years' experimentation in schools the researchers were led to three new burning questions (which formed part of the conclusions of that phase of the research):

- Would the same drama/peer-teaching structures used to create 'conflict literacy' be applicable to 'bullying literacy' in schools?
- What would be the most effective forms of in-service to engage and assist the teachers to contribute to and sustain the program?
- Could school administrative systems sustain the program sufficiently to allow the students to change the culture of conflict and bullying in their school?

These questions proved interesting enough for the sponsorship of another research project concentrating on them. At the end of another three years, all of them had to some extent been addressed, the first affirmatively, the second mainly affirmatively, and the third leaving very equivocal results. This time, two exciting new questions, more generic and speculative, arose:

- Could these techniques be applied to related but not identical concepts, such as postwar trauma, domestic violence or suicide prevention?
- Could they be applied in contexts other than schooling, such as adult workplaces or correctional centres?

Armed with those questions, the research team marched resolutely into its second decade of research in this area (Burton and O'Toole 2005).

❓ REFLECTIVE QUESTIONS

1 What does 'measurement' mean to you, now you have read this chapter? How is it apparent in a qualitative research design?

2 How would you establish what is 'plausible', 'credible' or 'trustworthy' about your research? (In other words: what integrity does it have?)

3 What steps can you now take to reduce your raw data to patterns, which the literature review could then animate?

WIDER READING

Babbie, E. 2002. *The Basics of Social Research.* Wadsworth Thomson Learning, Belmont, California. Part 2, The Structuring of Inquiry; Part 4, Analysis of Data.

Drew, C., Hardman, M. and Hosp, J. 2008. *Designing and Conducting Research in Education, Part III, Data Analysis and Results Interpretation.* Sage, Thousand Oaks, California.

Foreman-Peck, L. and Winch, C. 2010. *Using Educational Research to Inform Practice: A Practical Guide to Practitioner Research in Universities and Colleges.* Routledge, London.

Kervin, L., Vialle, W., Herrington, J. and Okely, T. 2006. *Research for Educators.* Thomson Social Science Press, Melbourne. Chapter 8, Analysing Data: Techniques and Principles.

REPORTING RESEARCH

☑ CHAPTER OBJECTIVES

At the end of this chapter you should be able to:

- write confidently for the readership you intend
- closely shape your writing to avoid common errors, and to target specific strengths, for example, the first person voice
- feel that your courage in getting your research message out is reinforced.

 PLANNING YOUR REPORT

Identifying your readership

This is the last chapter only because, logically, reporting your research is the last thing you do. But it is certainly not the last thing that you should consider. There are two major connected imperatives that really mean you should be contemplating it at the outset of the project. The first of these is that your research will impact on the outside world in whatever form you give it, and you need to bear in mind throughout the appropriate forum and form to communicate your outcomes. The second is that as Marshall McLuhan reminded us, and every educator well knows, 'the medium is the message'. The form cannot be entirely separated from either the content or the participants' responses, and your report should not only clearly and accurately but *truly* reflect your research quest in a way that the chosen readership will find appealing and enlightening. So even the title of this chapter is contestable: you can indeed 'report', but you can also write to 'interpret' what you have done (the message sets out a new story in itself), to 'constitute' what you have done (the message makes up the story) or to show how these first three intentions play out in 'practices' of various kinds. This fourfold range is set out well by Beth Graue (2006, p. 516) as she discusses writing Education research. She goes on, 'Writing is more than description and even analysis: it is an elaborate performance of identity that connects an author and his or her work to a community … rather than being merely researchers or social scientists, researchers who write are also authors who work through language.'

You will already almost certainly have discovered this from earlier chapters. In writing we have the most intimate manifestation of the *ontological* (our state of being,

impact

the medium is the message

form and content

authoring research

the ontological

the epistemological

or identity) with the *epistemological* (knowing something). Their reflexive relationship was outlined earlier in Chapters 1–4 of this book. So Graue is correct: how I write is both a reflection of and a constitution of my self and my practices (in this book, in Education). In using 'reporting', we wish to bundle up all these four intentions a researcher may have in getting the message down—and getting it disseminated. All four assume that writing is indeed a social practice.

The question of how to write the report may to some extent have been pre-empted by your chosen methodology—if you are using narrative research or arts-informed enquiry, then presumably some of this will form part of the substance of your final report. If you have decided on ethnographic performance, you will already have given much thought to identifying your audience and how best to reconfigure the data to engage them. In more conventional methodologies, too, there are some standard formats that make it easy to appeal to some audiences.

primary audience

secondary audience

stakeholders

participants

So what is your chosen readership? Or are there a number of such groups? Yes, in fact. There is the primary audience: the people or group that the thesis or report is actually written for, and will be the first people to see it. Then there are the secondary readers, or audiences. Those are other people or groups that are likely to be interested in it. Some of them will even have a stake in its results, such as people in your field or those who want to consult your research because it is relevant to their own research or practice. Then there are the participants in the research themselves. There are usually multiple secondary audiences as you get deeper into research. Ultimately, you may find yourself serving more and more masters, each of whom is looking for something different.

Student research

examiners

thesis modification

PhD by publication

Student research has the simplest audience to identify. The primary audience is obviously the examiner(s), and all efforts must be focused on identifying exactly what they want. You may expect that your research will have a life, or some usefulness, beyond your study: you might find yourself implementing some aspect of your emergent findings or giving advice based on what you are discovering before the thesis is completed; you may even want to, or be expected to, publish while you are engaged in preparing your research report. But these outlets are very definitely your secondary audiences. In order to present your research to secondary audiences, the form and format of your report to the examiner—that is, your thesis—will need to be modified or significantly changed. Advice on how to do this is given later in this chapter. Normally, don't expect that you can satisfy competing and diverse audiences at the same time—your first responsibility is to your examiners. There is, as usual, one exception to this rule: some universities in Australia and overseas are starting to award PhDs based on refereed journal publications. Any student taking that path (not yet a common one, nor widely available) should start by considering their primary audience as the readers of whatever journals they hope to publish in. More on this later; for now we'll return to the more orthodox student research report.

As a beginning researcher, you would be wise to be familiar with the standard format ▪ thesis format
for theses. Unless you have a good reason not to, aim to conform to the standard. Here is
a typical format—none of them vary in their essentials:

- statement of authorship and acknowledgments
- abstract
- introduction including statement of thesis or hypothesis and Research Question, and explanation of the shape and contents of the thesis
- background to the research
- literature review
- methodology (which will include a brief explanation of the data collection)
- description of the fieldwork and/or data collection
- analysis of the data
- findings
- conclusions
- bibliography
- appendices.

This list incorporates all the elements that you will need to address in some form or another. Your examiner(s) will be familiar with this format, which is the first step in appealing to this rather peculiar audience. If you decide to go with this model, stick to it carefully, because there is a logic to it that works both for the researcher and the reader. For instance, be careful not to incorporate your findings or conclusions in your introduction or during the discussions within your literature review, even if you continue reading well after your data analysis is started. That will only confuse the reader, who wants to know:

- what you are doing and why (the introduction)
- where the research comes from and why it is important (the background)
- what is known already about the topic, and what you know and think of that (the literature review)
- how you are going to go about finding some new knowledge or carrying out your investigation (the methodology)
- how and where you find your data (data collection)
- how you go about making sense of the data (data analysis)
- what you discover (findings)
- what you make of that, and what's next (conclusions).

Think very carefully before you venture into the territory of experimental formats. ▪ non-standard thesis
Do you have the necessary literary or performing skills to generate effective research and formats
art simultaneously? These can generate tensions or block each other, as we discussed in
Chapter 4.

Within Education, however, theses are not always totally straightforward; you may
in fact *have* a very good reason for not conforming. There is no law to force conformity,
and you will not be penalised, providing you have included the necessary components,

even when not using the standard order or terminology. Just remember to give your examiner signposts to show where you are departing from the norm, and where to find your methodology, your literature review, your findings and so on.

Publishing student research

You may find yourself tempted, invited or even expected to publish some aspects of your research while you are engaged on it. First, universities are increasingly making PhDs (mainly) available 'through' or 'including' publications. There are many research cultures where an assembly of peer-reviewed publications can be book-ended by chapters that make sense of the whole series of published papers, and are therefore worthy versions of a thesis. In this way, such research productivity is rewarded on the way through—by being published—and also, with the thesis as an outcome.

Second, however, we think that the increasing expectation of universities that students *will* publish most or all of their research before it is finished needs to be carefully scrutinised and pondered. Unless your study is of the above kind—by publication— writing up your research in a publishable form will take time out of the study itself. We examine this dilemma in the last section of this chapter; if you are in this position, you should read that section carefully.

On the other hand, conference presentations before you submit can be worthwhile or even essential, to road-test your research. A dialogue can take place between you and your audience, either during the session or following it. Also, it may be in your interests to give your work an airing, to get input from leaders in the field, and possibly discover cognate researchers or potential collaborators who can add to your research. That is the great value of the regular graduate seminars and colloquia that most universities hold. If your establishment doesn't hold these, find one that does, as they are usually open to outsiders, and Education researchers are normally only too willing to share their labours.

You will in all likelihood have to go a little bit public with your research before it is complete. Most Australian universities now demand a preliminary or confirmation presentation early in your research, even as a hurdle or qualification requirement; and many also invite or expect you to present your work on or near completion. The audience for both will be much the same, including your supervisor(s), other graduate students and/or academics, perhaps a few outside eyes and even a possible future examiner. They will all be looking at it through the eyes and ears of that primary audience, your examiners. In the early seminar, you should not try to dazzle them with your vision or what you've already achieved. Concentrate on clearly, modestly and succinctly spelling out:

- the context and purpose of the research, and how and why you got into it
- what the current literature says and what you need to read (very briefly: you will not be expected to have read it all, nor to go over it in detail)
- the research question and how you propose to investigate it (your methodology— again briefly)

Margin notes:
- signposts for readers
- publishing student research
- publication
- conference presentations
- graduate seminars
- confirmation seminar

- the fieldwork if there is any, and any research visits or other collaborations you may undertake
- your expected timeline
- what you have done so far (don't skite).

That is all you will probably have time for. However, if you are brave enough, you might want to mention (if there is one) any difficulty, tension or problem you foresee; it will not count against you, and in that audience there will be people who can give you valuable advice. This is the main point of that introductory seminar (much more than assessing or judging you). When you have made the presentation, *listen* carefully, and make sure you document the comments, discussion and questions. Avoid the terrible temptation of trying to answer all of the questions on the spot to show how knowledgeable you are—a few may be seeking more information, but most questions are being asked in order to help you focus and enrich the research, and you'll just make yourself look like a goose if it appears you think you already have an answer to them all!

▨ admitting difficulties

A seminar on completion is a quite different event, and in Australia, usually much more informal (unlike under the European system, where all candidates have to go through a formal defence of the thesis, which includes responding to one or more formal antagonists, appointed by the university to try and shoot down your research and its findings—an Occam's razor gang, if you like). In this presentation, don't waste too much time on what formed the bulk of your confirmation seminar—just sketch out briefly the background, your interest, the research question and how you approached it. By all means mention the difficulties and 'rough ground' you have traversed. Make sure you have plenty of time to talk about your findings, your 'new knowledge' and insights. Point the way forward to where this new knowledge will or may find a use, and to further research that now needs doing but was beyond the scope of your project.

▨ completion seminar

When your research is finished, you can take stock of it, and consider your supervisor's advice and possibly the opinions of your examiners, who are often asked by the university to indicate whether in their opinion the whole or parts of the research are publishable or in some other way worth making more public. If you wish, you can now forget about the strictures we have made in this book against advocacy, and the discouragement we provide in this chapter about premature exposure, and go for it (see page 200 for how). However, do so with the understanding that you are now going to have to do quite a lot more work on your thesis to turn it into an article, articles or a book that anybody will want to read.

Funded and commissioned research reports

Reporting funded or commissioned research for the primary audience, the funding body, is usually a fairly simple matter, as most research funding schemes have report pro-formas that indicate very clearly what they want. The rules are always the same: be clear, be succinct and don't fudge, even if the sponsor would be happier to hear other news. However, if that is the case you may need to be diplomatic, particularly if there are different sets of interests represented in the sponsorship. One potential minefield is

▨ funded research reports

ARC Linkage grants

industry partners

tensions with partners

sponsored research

collaborative grants. At the time of writing the major provider of these is the Australian Research Council Linkage grant scheme between universities and industry partners. The expectations and demands of industry partners are not always compatible with disinterested research. This can cause tension in the research process, the results and particularly the reportage; for instance, if the research process found gaps or problems in the industry partner's practices.

For sponsored research, your secondary audiences are very important, and both necessary and worthwhile. In your submission, it is likely that you were asked to identify possible outcomes of your research, and if you were sensible, you would have identified one or more sources of publication. Your own scholarly community needs to know of your research and its results—even if it did not achieve its intended aims, or achieved something else entirely.

This brings us to the next section, which we believe is compulsory reading (or at least consideration) for everybody.

AESTHETICS AND STYLE

The aesthetics of reporting

artistry

If you work in Education, and not exclusively in arts and humanities, you are concerned with art and artistry. 'An elegant experiment' is high praise in science, and it is natural that we should all try to manage our research 'elegantly', which is partly to say aesthetically, and document it accordingly as we have discussed in Chapter 2. We can look at the documentation in a little more detail here.

monologue and dialogue

research as conversation

The first problem is the form in which we are usually expected to present our research, and in which the vast majority of research is presented. A thesis, final report or research journal paper is a written monologue. That is unlikely to represent truly the dynamic dialogue and emerging discovery of your research itself. In previous chapters we have constantly referred to the conversational or dialogical nature of research and to the provisional, complex and ambiguous nature of many of our findings. A monologue is unrepresentative of much research in Education. Indeed, some of our colleagues in the Melbourne Graduate School of Education have recently published a book on how visual and spatial research methods can permeate methodologies more broadly. The editor, Julianne Moss, states in her conclusion:

> All of the researchers in this book have become knowingly entangled in the games of truth that constitute education research. Taking up various points of participatory, critical, postmodern inquiry and post postmodern inquiry [tends to disturb]the relationship between researcher as author and researcher as text producer, between doing research and reporting on it. (Moss 2008, p. 230)

We fully agree. There is both style and substance at stake in how these relationships unfold on the page, and in what is available for 'seeing' on the space of the page. Whether visuals merely complement the writing, or they speak directly as texts in their own right (write?) is itself worth interrogating. We invite you to do so. The research thesis and journal paper are very simplified summaries of the complexities of your research journey, as they have to be for both the reader's sake and yours. They are *literally* monological, doubly so. In structure, they recount the researcher's single line of reasoning (mono-*logic*) from Research Question to the answers or findings about that Question. In surface form they are indubitably also a static and unchangeable sequence of printed words directed to the reader by the author (a mono-*logue*). Literal dialogue is occasionally just possible, say through the paper's placement in a themed journal that encourages responses (such as *Educational Philosophy and Theory*), but only at a glacial pace.

summary of complexity

The essentials of elegance

If you are a beginning researcher, especially a student, and dealing with a fairly orthodox piece of research (such as action research, experiment, case study), you would be unwise to depart from the written monologue. A Bauhaus-type simplicity is quite appropriate: clean lines that emphasise the straightforward functionality, and a balanced design that will be easy and stress-free for your reader to follow. Above all, you want it to be clear, though not appear simplistic. It need not be colourless, however, though once that would have been *de rigueur* (see 'Writing styles', on page 189). Clarity is in itself aesthetically pleasing. It is quite possible to write a doctoral thesis, for example, so crisply and elegantly that no footnotes or endnotes are required.

simplicity
functionality
balance

clarity

Of course you want your report to be engaging—you need your readers to want to read it, and to finish it. You may want them to feel some of the emotional commitment that started you off and greeted your findings, but you also want them to comprehend the findings fully. If your research report has an explicitly aesthetic component, you will also want to set that off in the most effective way that is compatible with clarity and authenticity. Once upon a time there were very clear and unbreakable rules for research reporting, but these are now much more negotiable.

engaging writting

Metaphor

You will surely have noticed that this book is *infused throughout*, or *liberally peppered* with metaphors (themselves a couple of meta-metaphorical verbs, which differ depending on whether the reader feels that the metaphors we have been using add to the intrinsic *nutriment* of the meal or are just for *seasoning and garnish*). That is partly because these authors both enjoy and feel comfortable using metaphor, but mainly for much more important reasons, both of substance and style. Metaphor is important in all the hierarchy of intellectual levels that embody a research project. Throughout the book we have been stressing that the philosophical paradigm that underpins the book's point of view is constructivist, and that the knowledge and meanings we are identifying are provisional, negotiable and founded on other knowledge and meanings we have made. Part A set this out in some detail. We have also stressed that literal, rationalist thought and language do not fully or accurately express the range of human behaviour and motivation, or even cognition. That then gives us not only the right, but the need

constructivism
provisional knowledge

lenses

and responsibility, sometimes, to express our research using metaphors. That may even mean to conceptualise it, and certainly to carry it out and report on it, through metaphorical *lenses* (there's another meta-metaphor—it's actually impossible to avoid them). The following account of Prue Wales's PhD research (2006) is a vivid example of how a thesis can be reconceptualised through metaphor.

> Well before I began the writing-up phase I was thinking about a suitable metaphor I could use to run through my PhD thesis. The metaphor needed to be something that would connect all the elements together to produce some sort of coherence, or act as a spine. I played around with some familiar metaphors for a while but they were so well used they had become clichés. I wanted something that would not only capture the essence of what I was looking at but also support the post-structuralist form of my methodology. During a chance conversation with a friend I rambled on about how I needed to find something that conveyed the balancing act, the constant juggling, tightrope walking and playfulness of drama teaching. I needed her to tell me it sounded like I was talking about a circus.
>
> I divided the thesis into acts, each one denoting an aspect of the circus and its associated sideshow attractions and symbolising a facet of the participating drama teachers' experiences. Framing this was *The Big Top*, which could be a metaphor for the education system, a school or performance space. Notions of the marginalisation of the drama teacher are explored in *The Freaks*, while *The Hall of Mirrors* highlights how drama teachers' early memories 'reflect' their subjectivities. *The Fortune Tellers* explores the place of the past (childhood memories) in shaping the construction of subjectivities in the future. Since the participating teachers' memories of drama were such liberating experiences these stories are situated in *The Aerialists*; however their negative memories of education are found in *The Lion Tamers*. After all if children are considered animals what then are teachers? Playful and subversive, the metaphor allowed me to generate layers of meaning that captured the binary nature of subjectivities in rich and powerful ways.

serviceable
metaphors

To be serviceable, a metaphor does not have to be strikingly original or never-before-thought-of, but it does have to structure or convey thoughts and feelings with a richness that literal language cannot achieve. This metaphor of a circus may not be the most original description of human behaviour, or even of schooling, but the researcher has used the strong basic commonality of circuses and drama teaching (both are playful and performative) to provide a sustained analogy that does by its detailed consistency avoid the clichés she feared. The metaphor helps her first to structure her understanding—to give it coherence, as she says. Then it assists her to express its multiple relevance for her, with correspondences that can be expected to resonate with an audience familiar with circuses. Writing the above paragraphs, it was very difficult, in fact, not to drop into metaphors, albeit more or less dead ones ('drop into' and 'dead', there are another two). Did she 'tie the metaphor into' her thinking, or did she 'anchor' her thinking upon it; did it provide a 'building block' perhaps; well it certainly gave 'coherence'—yes, even that's

metaphor as
structure

dead metaphors

a metaphor, to do with stickiness. Our language is imbued with metaphor down to its very roots (there we go again), and we cannot avoid it even if we want to.

We shouldn't try to avoid metaphor, but we should be aware of what we are doing. The 'fishing' metaphor used in the extended example of data analysis in Chapter 8 was not an indulgent conceit to decorate the example; it actually helped the research team to formulate and manage an important element of the data-analysis process. Metaphors are very helpful in marshalling the holistic nature of human experience into a readily digestible narrative, often with profound metaphysical significance. For example, the 2012 film *The Life of Pi* and the 2001 book it is based on use an extended visual account of the lifeboat, the tiger and the young Indian male, to investigate fundamental human destiny, situated in earlier accounts of Islam, Hinduism and Christianity. The writings of many contemporary research scholars, and the practices that underlie them, are similarly imbued with metaphor, none more so than Laurel Richardson's. There is quite a noticeable assertiveness among qualitative researchers to use metaphors cheekily drawn from arts practice; two current standard texts both use dance to describe research processes: *Dancing the Data* (Bagley and Cancienne 2000); and 'The Choreography of Qualitative Research Design: Minuets, Improvisations and Crystallisation' (Janesick 2000).

metaphorical substance

Wales, in her account above, was wise to be wary of clichés. Some metaphors are so old and hackneyed that they have really run their race (ow!), and to try and create new meaning out of them is just flogging a dead horse (if you see what we mean). Research as a 'journey' is one of the corniest and worth avoiding, on the whole. It is particularly hard to get away from, and we hope the reader has forgiven our own recurrent use of it. Wittgenstein's 'back to the rough ground' emerged in Chapter 3, then again in Chapter 8 … Both the 'journey' and the 'rough ground' are still to make one final appearance in the book. Describing a thesis structure using the quasi-dramatic terminology of 'prologue', 'epilogue' and sometimes even 'acts and scenes' is becoming similarly tiresome. Yes, smart readers will also notice that we have done that too, and only defend it on the grounds that *our* epilogues are indeed a quasi-dramatic dialogue. In fact, we need to give a warning here that goes beyond the externals of metaphorical phraseology. The idea of using metaphor to structure either your thesis or your expression of the results will be very enticing, now you have been given permission. It can be a trap. Be careful not to reach too hard for metaphor, or work too assiduously to find one that fits. What you fabricate is likely to be laboured and probably clichéd, and may easily just obfuscate your well-constructed, logical and clear thought line through the whole report. We're aware that effective metaphor comes from the back brain, and is usually dependent on long experience in both thinking figuratively and laterally, and expressing oneself in sustained metaphorical forms. If you are not a ready user of unexpected juxtapositions of thought and colourful figures of speech, you are wisest, yet again, to K.I.S.S (Keep It Simple, Stupid).

clichéd metaphors

Writing styles

There was a time, not long ago, when research reports tended to be very dull reading. When researchers pursued 'objectivity', one measure of the success of research was how dispassionate the reporting was. The style mattered a lot, but engaging the reader was

traditional research reports

not part of the writer's aim. On the contrary, researchers had to avoid at all cost anything that engaged the emotions, of the writer or the reader. The research tradition assumed and expected that research findings were not only objective but rational, emotion-free and generalisable. The research depended on effective application of method, not individual acuity and intelligence (especially not 'emotional intelligence' or 'the intelligence of feeling', which are both phrases now widely used in our trade). Therefore the personal element should be ironed out. The word 'I' in particular, was taboo. So too, of course, were any attempts at colour or worse, metaphor. The aim was to write clearly, neutrally and as simply as possible.

■ rationality
■ generalisability

■ impersonality

■ neutrality
■ clarity

The first of these characteristics, clarity, was and still is the primary guiding principle. Ironically, the pursuit of neutrality in language often made both clarity and simplicity harder to attain. A so-called 'Academic English' style emerged, which encouraged some very bad habits such as an endemic hesitancy or reluctance to say anything outright, which in turn encouraged extreme circumlocution, and other infelicities that you will discover in the following paragraphs. We are looking back at our Academic English past, partly because its residues are still with us; usually unconsciously, many of us feel constrained by what we believe to be its salient features, and cultivate a special academic language. Partly, too, because those bad habits and constraints do not just pertain to the style—they infuse the whole work.

■ Academic English

To build for yourself effective academic writing from scratch, the first factor you can look at is, yet again, your positioning. By now, you will have positioned yourself in terms of the research, and acknowledged that position—and perhaps indulged in a little meta-research reflecting on the peculiar impact of that positioning on the research site. You can and should acknowledge this stylistically, in two ways. First, you can use the first-person pronoun, 'I' or 'we', naturally and as often as you need to. The words 'this researcher' or 'the research team' (when repeated often) deaden the impact of your report, as does 'it may be postulated that' instead of the much more honest 'I think'. In fact, we have used the phrase 'one of the authors' a few times in this book, but for a specific reason, that there are two of us represented here, so it is a way of signalling when we are quoting the previous work of just one of us.

■ positioning

■ meta-research

■ researcher as 'I'

You can also make a real effort to get rid of the insidious and very misleading use of the passive voice, which actually conceals the agency of the verb, of who is responsible.

■ passive voice
■ hidden agents

> 'In the 1990s, unusual attention was given to such mundanely routine
> occasions as …'

Who gave this unusual attention? If we are lucky, we may be able to deduce it from the context, but this apparently innocuous verbal form permits the doer to remain anonymous or hidden.

■ anonymity

> 'However, it is important to stress that his views were not treated as definitive.'

By whom? The researchers, of course. There is a self-importance, too, about this grammatical construction, which gives a kind of spurious validation to the action (in other words what the researchers did with 'his views'), which really just meant they took them into account but acted on their own opinions.

Although it is usually done unconsciously, there is a similar kind of concealment in the reification of action (*res* = a thing, in Latin; so, to 'thingify'). When the writer transfers agency from people to things, it gives the impression that action is generating itself rather than happening at the hands of any human agent (usually the researcher).

▪ reification

> 'The project set out with the intention to investigate the effect of particular workshops on literacy, and the particular school site was chosen because it encouraged traditional teaching styles.'

No, the researchers set out with that intention, and they chose the school (another of those pretentious passives) because *either* the teachers *and/or* the principal encouraged traditional teaching (it might be very significant which of those alternatives provided the encouragement that the writers' abstraction omits to distinguish).

Sometimes these apparently living nouns even cluster together into strings, which sound even more important:

▪ noun strings

> 'Interaction development processes could be identified in operation for the entire duration of this activity by the research subjects'

rather than 'We watched the children learning group skills while they were doing this activity'. (The four quotations above are all taken—no, *we* have taken them—from a contemporary research report. Out of politeness to its authors, we leave them anonymous.)

You may be able to identify another common piece of obfuscation in that last quotation starting 'Interaction development processes', one that is just as toxic to clarity as the relentless use of passive voice and nominalised verbs. If you know about the derivation of the English language, you will know that the vocabulary is a palimpsest—a layering of a number of languages on each other. One of the bottom layers is Anglo-Saxon, still the real basis of our language and most of its commonest words. The language is characterised by short basic word forms. The Norman conquerors imported French— with characteristically longer, already much more modalised word forms, from its Latin origins. They also brought new legal and class systems. For some time the two languages existed side by side, with the defeated speaking Anglo-Saxon, but having to deal with French law and officialdom, and the victors speaking French. Gradually the languages amalgamated, but still with the vocabularies of law and the bureaucracy (and more recently, science, medicine and education itself) heavily imbued with Latinate forms, and Anglo-Saxon words still tarred with rather more lower class associations. We can demonstrate this as we explain its significance to your writing.

▪ Anglo-Saxon English

▪ Latinate English

Compare:

- *Anglo-Saxon 'root'*: Let's say, you might like to think of and choose a few words alike in meaning, put them together and see which are on the whole shorter, clearer and more to the point, and which are more uncommon, or just harder to understand.

with:

- *Latinate 'origin'*: To exemplify, you might recall and select a restricted number of synonymous expressions, make an investigative comparison to identify which in the majority of circumstances are the more economical, lucid and succinct, and which are the more recondite, or veritably virtually incomprehensible.

We guess you've got the point. While the language that came to us through law and science does sometimes permit a precision and complexity that the common phrase cannot achieve, it also encourages obscurity and pretension. Once again, in the wise words (or letters) of that American grandfather of acronyms: K.I.S.S.

Reports, especially a thesis, should not shy away from the vivid. Our practice and our research are both full of audacity. The conferences where we share and exchange these, imbued by our living pedagogy, are sometimes far more exciting and stimulating than those of other non-educational disciplines. Our writing too should lead from the front: like teaching itself, inspire, provoke and demand immediate reflection, not limp halting and laboured behind, dragging bundles of scholastic bric-a-brac for the reader to scavenge through … the power of the form should be evident in the text.

That said, the first priority in reporting research is clarity and the second is precision of expression. George Orwell's essay *Politics and the English Language* (1946) is still the very best style guide we have ever come across, in terms of the clear, precise use of English, and it's free to read online from a dozen sites. Since Education and its documentation are just as imbued with pompous and impenetrable jargon as the corporate and political worlds, we also gratefully refer readers to the trenchant advice of our own Don Watson's *Death Sentence: The Decay of Public Language* (2003) and *Dictionary of Weasel Words* (2004). There are, too, many appropriate and much more up-to-date style guides than Orwell available—most universities have produced their own, invariably useful and sometimes salutary, to remind us, however experienced we think we are as writers, of the good habits to follow, and the solecisms we commit. This is just a brief summary of some of the major considerations.

Structuring the report

In structuring your report, you must make sure you have a clear thought-line through it for the reader to follow. In the case of beginning and student research this should be firmly (and clearly) based on the Research Question. That will entail referring or alluding to this at each key point, particularly if you are apparently heading away from it. When you become more experienced you may wish to develop a less linear, more postmodern or literary approach. The same principle holds, however. The Research Question is an

Margin notes:
- inspiring writing
- clarity
- precision
- George Orwell
- style guides
- Research Question
- non-linear reports

immovable peg providing a clear line from the Question through whatever structure you choose. In this way you defer to your readers, who will probably be used to linear reporting, and who will be reading the work for what you have discovered or illuminated, not as a literary puzzle or game where you set them riddles.

Many research reports, particularly theses, are long, and the readers are unlikely to complete them in one sitting—time may elapse and important events may intrude in their lives between episodes. Therefore, give your readers plenty of landmarks—signposts to remind them of where you have come from and where you are going next. Suspense is not a good driver of research reading!

signposts for readers

Whether you are writing a thesis, a report on subsidised research or a scholarly paper, you have an absolute duty to do your utmost to ensure it is correct and free from errors, as we mentioned in Chapter 8 when discussing data analysis. This is first and foremost in your own self-interest. A paper that reads fluently and error-free allows the readers to concentrate entirely on your content. Moreover, they will not constantly be distracted by a careless or ignorant mistake, and have to stop to work out what you might mean, resulting in their becoming emotionally engaged in your writing in exactly the wrong way—with hostility! Total unblemished accuracy will of course be virtually impossible, and that is the function of copy editors and proofreaders. In the case of papers for publication, remember that most journal editors are unpaid, and that copy editing is very tiresome … and that lack of time is no excuse. We are all potential sinners: one of us recently had to make an embarrassed apology to an editor for a sloppily presented final draft of a chapter, where the proofreading fell between the cracks of two busy co-authors. Reputations as researchers suffer!

accuracy

copy editing and proofreading

For a thesis, there is even less excuse or tolerance. It is usually necessary to have somebody else cast their eye over your final draft. Your supervisor will certainly do this if you are a student. You should not presume on his or her tolerance and generosity, but do your very best first. The problem is that if the mistakes are ones you regularly make, you will probably not notice them in the first place. Inevitably, too, you become blind to others. When checking our text for errors, our eyes play tricks on us and will screen out an error that we would normally see in a moment, because we are already so familiar with it that it seems right. If you have difficulty with correct English, or it is not your first language, you would be very wise to get a proofreader for yourself, even if you have to find a way to pay for it. If possible, this should be a professional one, as they are trained to see what even the most literate amateur misses. To help you decide on whether you need to go to such an expense, here is a little list, not entirely random, of some of the most common errors that we come across (and commit) in draft work and even submitted copy:

outside eye

supervisors

professional proofreader

common errors

• inability to use paragraphs properly: either much too short, as if writing for a press release rather than allowing a flow of argument to build, or long, incoherent and turgid

paragraphs

• muddled or inconsistent use of tenses: always a minefield when reporting work in the present along with work and references in the past

tenses

• inelegant syntax often leading to grammatical error: particularly in overlong and complex sentences that lose themselves and their main clauses

syntax

■ punctuation

- incorrect punctuation which contributes to the above: in particular the separation of subject from main verb by a single comma, and the incorrect use of semi-colons and colons

■ spelling

- inability to spell key words that the spell-check doesn't pick up: the past tense of *lead* is *led*; the singular of *phenomena* is *phenomenon*; the adjectival form of *curriculum* is *curricular* and its plural is *curricula*.

If you confess to any of these as regular indiscretions and have difficulty in spotting them when checking, or if you don't know what we're talking about, you should certainly consider employing a proofreader.

Then there are the references to consider! But they are really worth a subsection on their own.

References and citations

■ referencing your report

■ referencing systems

■ American Psychological Association

■ Chicago style

■ Harvard style

■ Australian Government style

■ universities

■ publishers' style guides

■ appropriate referencing

Everything you have derived from a single and particular source must be acknowledged. Of course, direct quotations from the literature have to be fully referenced. Anything you have taken from interviews or other data collected must also be identified and referenced, though that may be encoded to protect the identities of participants. There are a number of standard referencing systems, mainly American: APA (American Psychological Association), Chicago and Harvard. This book was written using the Australian Government style guide (Snooks 2002), which has been modified to fit in with this publisher's standard format. You should choose a referencing style that suits you, if you can, though most journals and many universities will direct you to use the one they favour. Many book publishers, like Oxford University Press, have their own, somewhat variant forms, and you will encounter these when they send you their style guides. Whichever you choose, be consistent and use the same referencing system throughout.

■ primary audience

■ impressing examiners

This is where the universal precepts about quotes and references finish, and an element of intelligence and choice comes in, and where the rules for student research are actually different from those for publications or for official research reports, in one major respect. Again, it's a matter of your audience and your purpose. If you are a student, unless you are extremely altruistic, your main aim is to impress the examiners. Your erudition should be, at least to a degree, in their face. This means you need to indicate the breadth, depth and relevance of your reading, and the intelligent use you are making of it. Be careful not to endlessly reiterate the same references, and try not to spoil the flow of your argument by being too zealous. Remember too the places where erudition is inappropriate, such as when you are describing the fieldwork. It is a bit of a balancing act. You must, in summary, show:

- you are well read
- your reading is up to date
- your literature selection is judicious
- your acknowledgment is humble and assiduous
- your attribution (who said it) and citation (where) are meticulous.

If you are writing for a journal or book publication, you have a different primary audience. Your main purpose is to share new knowledge with peers and those who may be less knowledgeable, rather than to impress with your breadth of knowledge. You have to show your learning to your peers, but you do not have to thrust it in their face, try to one-up them or intimidate them. Your use of references should be sufficient to:

different audiences

- (modestly) indicate and back up your expertise, your school of thought and ideological or philosophical leanings
- acknowledge other people's direct and original influence on your ideas
- provide stepping-stones for your own argument and findings
- authenticate a statistic, a report or other objective evidence
- provide readers with a lead to further exploration of a relevant idea.

In a funded research report, you usually have considerably less space in which to convey your reading, and, moreover, an audience with limited attention span.

The contemporary use of referencing systems such as APA, where references are cited in the main text with an accompanying bibliography, rather than in footnotes or endnotes, provides a strong incentive not to lard your text with references, in order to avoid constant interruption for the reader in the flow of your argument.

in-text referencing
bibliography

Direct quotations should be as short and succinct as possible. Long, long quotes are tedious and suggest you lack confidence in your own ideas. You may have the reader wishing s/he was reading the quoted work and not yours! This is also usually true of footnotes; more so in fact, since these involve the reader leaving the main text and searching for the note. Carrying on an argument at length in a footnote, branching out into a new discursive path, or making lengthy asides, so characteristic of much scholarship of the past, are now regarded as self-indulgent practices, and can suggest you have not thought out your argument very carefully. If they are germane to your subject, they should be in the main text; if not, we suggest you leave them out and use them to start another paper. We have recently come across one counter-argument to this: a beginning researcher, Kim Senior (2008), who explicitly used footnotes, and lots of them, to indicate the relevant open questions, loose ends and unfinished business that she did not have the scope to follow up in that piece of research. However, that elegant device, if it becomes conventional and an excuse for the self-indulgence referred to above, will quickly lead to irritability in the reader.

direct quotations

footnotes

You may need to refer to your own previous work, or work in another allied field, but excessive self-referencing is also an extremely bad habit. Not only is it a vanity, but it suggests that you have probably already covered this territory, so raises the question of why *this* publication as well. We leave it to the reader to decide if we have been guilty of this sin in this book.

self-referencing

You do not need to reference ideas that are already in the public domain, even if you happen to have read them in a scholarly text. You may have noticed that we quoted Marshall McLuhan's phrase 'the medium is the message' earlier in this chapter, without further referencing it—everybody's heard it, and most people know who coined it and can find it if they need to. All writers use common knowledge and clichés anyway, and it

public domain

unnecessary referencing

clichés

does not validate them to attribute them to other writers who may have also used them. This is where some intelligence, common sense and general knowledge come in. You do not need to give a bracketed reference to a well-known quotation from Shakespeare, or cite '(Wittgenstein 1965)' when talking about a film based on his *Philosophical Investigations*, especially as the date of the edition referred to is anachronistic.

■ anachronistic references

In Wales's description of her research quoted earlier this chapter, she dutifully referenced Laurel Richardson's use of the metaphor 'a spine [to support the research]'. We removed the citation. While Richardson certainly used it, if you think about it, is there anybody writing in English who has not, when denoting a factor that gives strength to an argument? It's well and truly in the public domain, was so before Richardson used it, and as a metaphor, it's dead. In recent years, we have seen the claim that 'Eskimos have seven words for "snow"', frequently in academic and scholastic writing. Whether or not it is true, it seems to be treated as a plea for linguistic and semiotic sensitivity— even for relativity in truth (a contentious assumption)—and presented as a *commonly held* fact. But it may be neither commonly held nor a fact. Ideas can also be said to be in the public domain if where you encounter them is a long way away from the knowledge source. We question whether you need to reference Time/Life Publications when using a snippet picked up from *Time Magazine* on Taoism or neurology—unless you think the reader might be interested to track down that particular article. If it has led you to serious reading about Taoism or brain functions, then those are the references you quote, not *Time Magazine*.

Many of these practices contribute to blowing a bibliography out to unusable lengths. (This stricture does not apply to students, who need to maximise what they have read— albeit honestly, including only the reading that has genuinely been relevant.) It is more useful to provide a limited bibliography, containing the texts quoted, with perhaps a few other texts important to this research and your thesis, which will help other researchers. Remember, not only writers but readers too play games with bibliographies. They can cruise the bibliography, looking for the key influences or the books not cited: the over-reverential acolyte or the threadbare scholar. They can even spot the smarter egotist, who does not quote himself or herself in the main text, but ensures there are pages of self-references in the bibliography.

■ bibliography games

Appendices and attachments

The report itself may not be the end of it, of course. Research in education often incorporates student outcomes, artefacts and other products of fieldwork, and CD or DVD recordings may be a necessary corollary to be viewed along with the text or exegesis. There are usually other documents that would clutter up the main text, but are necessary for the reader to be able to refer to or check, such as tables, correspondence, or pieces of contrasting or particularly significant transcript. In deciding how much of this material to include as appendices, it is worth considering who your primary readership is. In general, we would give much the same advice as we did with footnotes—keep it minimal, and if you can leave it out, do so. Most of it is raw text, and your reader is above all interested in the substance of your processed and analysed data. If a table or a

■ CD/DVD
■ ancillary documents
■ tables
■ correspondence
■ raw data

letter, or a piece of vivid dialogue, is very pertinent to the argument, it ought to be in the main text anyway—and you could do worse at the end of your data analysis than comb through the whole lot once again, particularly your intended appendices, making sure that you have left out nothing really germane to the main report.

If your readership is likely to scrutinise the probity and authenticity of your data, then you will have to provide some elements of ancillary data. That is, of course, the case with any student research. This would include some longer extracts from interviews or journals, say, from which you have extracted material, to indicate that you are not quoting them out of context; some of those tangentially relevant or preliminary tables that you are not actually using; perhaps a particularly key piece of correspondence or two. However, do respect the *cri de coeur* of a not young examiner to whom a thesis was sent in one volume, with an appendix considerably lengthier than the hundred thousand word main text. The examiner complained not only that she could not hold it up in bed to read, but that it hurt her knees even supporting it when sitting in a chair. There is then one last effort of critical judgment to be made by the writer: only include those documents that are truly necessary, and not just indulgent or betraying your own insecurity. You may have thoroughly enjoyed some ethnographic witnesses' statements, for example, but you have already picked the eyes out of them (or should have) and the examiner or reader already has plenty to read without wading through all that again. Nor does the examiner need copies of all your letters of consent, invitations to schools or draft contracts. If the worst comes to the worst, bulky appendices and attachments should be bound and sent as a separate volume. But in theses, as in art, less is usually better.

> ▨ DYNAMIC REPORTING

Reporting research as conversation

Educators, especially in arts and humanities, have rightly been very taken by the metaphor of research as reflective conversation, or dialogue, as we discussed in Part A, and have emphasised since then, and some have even tried to subvert the genre *research report* in various ways. The simplest way is to provide the reader at least with a range of voices to listen to. This is easier to do in a book than a thesis or article, since chapters can represent different perspectives and even be written by different and conflicting authors. But it is also possible in a research thesis. For instance, in an ethnographic study the researcher must try through the inadequacy of print to give some flavour of the life of the community being studied. Live quotation from research participants can be highly articulate and vivid, particularly when they are speaking about matters of deep concern to their lives. On the other hand, raw and unedited they can be deadly dull and fragmented and muddled … full of ums and digressions and mumbles. Therein lies an unresolved issue of authenticity. How far can a transcript of a live conversation be edited before it ceases to become the respondent's own words? Is it even authentic in the first place, as it doesn't include all the emotional and relational subtexts, the non-verbal and paralinguistic elements of the original?

Margin notes:
▨ ancillary data
▨ interview transcripts
▨ journal entries

▨ conversation
▨ dialogue
▨ range of voices

▨ quotations

▨ authenticity

media of reporting   A further step to provide different voices is to provide a number of different media of reporting. Theses and even books can now contain CDs or DVDs. These put back a bit of that visual and aural subtext. One problem with this approach is that it is more demanding on the reader, who has to switch media, and supply a video player as required—not easy to do when reading the research on an aeroplane, for example.

arts-informed reporting   A quite different approach is taken by the arts-informed enquiry specialists. They bring art itself to compensate for the defects of the research report. We have already encountered a number of examples earlier in this book. A simple and clever way to ensure authenticity in the voices of respondents is to ask them, where possible, to respond in a literary genre.

> Drama is,
>
> 'Jesus Sal!'
>
> Good quotes from good texts
>
> Good years
>
> Good times
>
> Good friends
>
> GOOD SHIT!
>
> (Sanders 2003)

poetry

emotion in reporting   The poetry of a boys' class (see above) expressed not only a list of some of the qualities they identified in drama, but their emotional and relational understanding of it. The researcher may choose to do the same, for instance to convey the emotional timbre of a situation that cannot be coldly reported in print, like this extraordinary (as research writing) piece by David Wright:

> *Within this grief I connected with that grief and I found myself howling for me, howling for him and howling for her. I also found myself taking notes, writing things down, leaving myself messages and struggling with a pen and haphazardly gathered pieces of paper to find words that somehow did justice to my feelings. I wanted to feel it and know it. My growing fascination with my own feeling seemed also natural, right and real. Grief deserved my howl and it was a wonderful thing to howl at grief too.*
>
> This is not only my experience. Anyone who can identify with this piece of writing—relate to it emotionally and/or phenomenologically—can claim it equally. It is, however, an awareness that I discovered through creative exploration. The discoveries contained in the creative process are manifold and attested to regularly. (Wright 2005)

Creative writing can also do the reverse, and provide *more* emotional distance from the research site and subjects, and the researcher herself (as we remember from this extract from narrative research first quoted in Chapter 4, with the researcher re-christened 'Pip'):

> Lotte is on playground duty in the quadrangle. Andrea is heading for the slope, a preppie on each hand. ... There are games to be played, holes to be dug, buckets to be filled, and so little time ... Pip's passage through the playground is noted. (Sinclair 2005, pp. 262–3).

Art-making as research report

If you really want to wed your own artistry to your research reporting, and you have a good head for heights, you could always try an arts-*based* enquiry, where the artwork you produce will stand as at least a proportion of the research report itself. The concept of artwork *as* research, or as research *equivalence*, as discussed in Chapter 4, is an area of acute contemporary interest and debate, still being explored with rather more enthusiasm than illumination. The university sector is quite perplexed about it, and if you are considering it as a methodology, you should probably shop around, as there is a wide divergence among the programs that universities and colleges offer, from artwork-only qualifications like Doctor of Creative Arts to PhDs and master's degrees with varying or negotiable proportions of artwork and exegesis. It is a risky business, however, and the risk is in the reporting. You must marry the artistic demands and criteria of your 'artwork' with the demands and criteria of orthodox research. It is an area in which examiners themselves sometimes have little experience, and one where you will be exposing yourself on two very different fronts. What if the examiners like your exegesis but think the film is terrible? Are you confident enough both of your artistic prowess and your research skills to put them both up for scrutiny? If so, and you want to go the whole hog in terms of bringing your research to life, and your research topic is somewhere in the area of ethnographic enquiry, you might always try ethnographic performance. However, if you are attracted to that, go in with your eyes open. As we warned in Chapter 4, that's a roller-coaster.

In the end, the kind and amount of aesthetic input you can make into research reporting depends again on your audience and your positioning. As well as its findings, the style and the aesthetic and the subtexts of your research are in your report down to the last word, for all the people who may come across it in their paths. The medium is, indeed, the message.

art as research equivalent

Doctor of Creative Arts

PhD with artwork

master's with artwork

exegesis

ethnographic performance

positioning

↘ PUBLISHING RESEARCH

primary readership

Nobody does research in order to keep it to themselves. Whether you have been involved in a university study or a funded research project, you have a primary readership, which you must concentrate on. If you are a student, that readership is your eventual examiners, and more immediately your supervisors (who will themselves be acutely aware of those examiners and what they will be looking for). In the case of a funded research project, whoever commissioned it will want to read and be able to understand the results. Both will want to be engaged by it, which can work in your favour with both those audiences, but both are in a sense a captive audience, who will read it anyway.

publishing pre-completion

We have, earlier in this chapter, referred to another dilemma that student researchers face—one that is becoming an increasingly significant factor in contemporary Australian universities: whether or not to publish before the research is complete and if so, what. Some research can generate very valuable findings en route. You might be carrying out pilot studies that can stand by themselves, and which would be of interest to the scholarly community, or to others with a stake in your discipline. Sometimes, the thorough literature review which you may have been the first person to carry out on your topic (especially if the study is interdisciplinary) can be a valuable addition to that literature itself. Maybe your fieldwork, or the methodology of your project in itself, can be so interesting that a running commentary can arouse the interest of journal readers.

co-publication

In these cases, we are strongly in favour of *co-publication*, where your thesis supervisor or lead researcher can, as it were, ride in the side-car. Your name should come first, in authorship order, but the more prominent name, which follows it, may well open readerships and publications to you, and in any case, sharing in a joint writing task will teach you a lot about scholarly conventions in print, in your Education specialism. Some universities even insist that student or associate researchers co-publish with the supervisor or lead researcher.

transforming for publication

However, there are very good reasons for being cautious about publishing anything at this stage. Your study should be your primary concern, and take up the bulk or all of your energy and time, and writing for publication means an extra job. You cannot just send the publisher completed bits of the project, or your thesis. The audiences for an academic journal or a book are very different from an examiner. The readers are not interested in how learned, clever or meticulous you are, but in what you have to offer them—and they are usually fully fledged professionals in their fields. They are, in other words, a different primary audience.

premature publication

There are other dangers. If your research is a single-focused or a holistic study, especially if it involves open-ended action research or some other kind of intervention, publishing may be a very bad idea: metaphorically speaking, half-baked. By the end of your research, you may have reached quite different conclusions and insights from halfway through, and if so, you will just be obscuring these later findings by premature exposure, and, what's more, laying yourself open to being cited on something you no longer believe to be true. Furthermore, in this kind of study, until you are finished, you probably won't have much to offer, so you will have to talk up what you have done, which is a dangerous temptation. And finally, you could be doing a disservice to yourself, by imposing on others. Academic journal editors and reviewers are very busy and distinguished scholars, usually unpaid, whose job is to ensure that their journals present the best and fullest in research and praxis. More and more, they are finding their time taken up with giving editorial advice to fledgling researchers with good ideas half-conceptualised or projects half-realised. This is helpful to the researcher, but really the job of your supervisor, and at its worst can give you a bad name with the journal editor. We realise that sometimes you cannot avoid this pressure towards premature publication, but do be aware of these dangers, and as we say, consider co-publication. The better place to give your ongoing research its first public airing is usually at a scholarly conference preferably in your own field (where you might be lucky and have it published in the proceedings).

imposition

pressure to publish

However, particularly when it is over, you should be considering how you can disseminate and publicise your research to be of use in the promotion of your work and your field. Once your research is completed, advocacy is no longer taboo, and with luck your project has given you something to shout about. You will need to think about making it both pertinent and engaging to other audiences who are not captive, so it will certainly need some adaptation. You will need to identify who you want to read your research—what kind of audience or audiences are they; even more important, why should they bother to pick up your work to read in the first place—what is in it for them? Different publication types—scholarly books, textbooks, conference presentations, refereed articles, non-refereed articles—all have different readerships with different demands (and sometimes different constraints) on approach, length and style. The following sections give you some help in identifying these distinctions.

dissemination

identifying readership

Academic journals

First, there are our own academic, scholarly and practical journals; there are many well established here and overseas. We listed some of these in Chapter 6 for you to read in your literature review, and earlier this chapter we warned against the dangers of rushing into journal writing before you are ready. Well, now you *are* ready to join this community of scholar-writers yourself, and that list is a good place to start. If you are keen on establishing your research credentials, you must look for journals that are peer-reviewed by a panel of research scholars. These research journals are usually the only ones that 'count' in university contexts, and represent the top of the trade. This is unfortunate for those of us who are interested in practice and conveying our research discoveries directly to our fellow teachers and education workers, who tend to read journals of practical advice rather than research. Refereed journals, and research books published by firms and organisations that have an accountable system of peer manuscript review, are the only ones that university gatekeepers are interested in, the only ones that give brownie points and financial inducements, by the decree of the Department of Education, Employment and Workplace Relations. To appear in a refereed journal does also confer more status on your paper, as it will have passed the peer scrutiny of distinguished scholars in the

peer-review

university performance indicators

peer-reviewed books

peer scrutiny

field. Few of the refereed journals in arts and many other areas of education, even such standard fields as educational assessment, have yet broken through the gatekeepers of the science and social sciences indices of research journals, such as the ISI (Index of Scientific Information), and it is becoming progressively harder to persuade universities to accept journals that have not. This means that if your education field is one of these, you might have an agonising and really unfair decision to make: whether to communicate your research, as you should, to your own scholarly community—your peers—or to the largely different, and lay, audience of a prestigious and ISI-ranked journal … which will demand writing and authenticating your paper in quite a different way.

▪ journal indices

One thing to remember about refereed journals is that it is not acceptable to submit papers to more than one of them at a time, though it is very tempting—their processes may mean considerable waiting time before you know whether your paper has been accepted, or might be accepted after revision. Nor should you send papers to journals if the same paper might be accepted as a chapter in a book, or refereed conference proceedings. Both these strategies involve those overworked reviewers and editors in duplication of their work with perhaps no reward. In their invitation to you to present, conferences often now include a sentence that precludes any publication of your paper without the organisers' permission.

▪ referee process

If you are meticulous and lucky, you may get your paper accepted in a journal without changes. More often than not, the reviewers and editor will ask you to revise your work. There are many reasons for this: to take account of some of the stylistic differences between a thesis or formal research report and a journal article; because it fits in better with the focus and scope of the journal; because there are some gaps that the reviewers would like to see filled. You will probably be given quite a tight timeline for the revision. You should not take issue with the reviewers, even if you do not like what they say. Accept it, or look for another publication more suited to your approach. Try to address most of their concerns, and if possible find a critical friend to check whether you have done so. If a major requirement by any reviewer really is against your principles, then defend it in your response to the editor, but don't waste the editor's time splitting hairs on minor points. Then make sure you get it back to the editor by the deadline. Nothing infuriates journal editors more than chasing up overdue copy. Remember that you might want to use this journal again, so it's best not to acquire a reputation for lateness.

▪ revision

▪ critical friend

▪ deadlines

If you are interested in going beyond your own discipline's backyard, think more broadly about the people and associations who might benefit from the products of your research: other possible primary audiences. Historically educators, especially in 'marginal' or specialised disciplines, have not very cleverly addressed the problems of our lack of visibility and esteem in the broader educational community. Overwhelmingly we publish the results of our research in discipline-specific journals (history education, geography education, philosophy of education, music education, science education), and at their linked conferences—subject associations. We have often feared being misunderstood or undervalued by, say, generic education audiences, which we see as potentially hostile or at any rate less supportive than our own tightly knit community. However, to cheer particularly the arts practitioners among the readers, in recent years

▪ non-discipline journals

there has been a major wind-shift in education. *Creativity, imagination, innovation, interactivity* and *teamwork*, which are our core business, are now buzzwords in corporate life, in the world of new technologies, and in education systems. Yet these stakeholders are looking bewilderedly around to find where they can be located. In the practice of all of those buzzwords, artistic educators actually have an enviable record of achievement, and now quite a lot of evidence-based research. We can best help the corporate and systemic leaders to know of these achievements by publishing in the journals they read. Best of all, many of the standard educational and social science journals are recognised by the scholarly indices, which will give your work added prestige. For those readers, that's a thoroughly positive motive to publish in the prestigious journals of others!

▪ buzzwords

Scholarly books

If the research is really substantial and has a potentially wide audience, you should be thinking of trying to find an appropriate commercial publisher, either for a book or in an edited collection. There is some skill needed here, and there is even the beginning of a helpful literature on the subject. Royce Sadler (1992) will give you a helpful *précis* in thirty-four pages, or Robin Derricourt (1996) a comprehensive tour of the territory in over two hundred; and more up-to-date help from authors' and publishers' websites is easily sourced. The biggest problem is which publisher to choose, of the thousands available, from local, restricted distribution and 'vanity' publishers, to international giants like Oxford University Press, Routledge and Springer. Consulting a colleague who has had some prior success in your particular area is probably the best first bet. Then you should carefully consider your audience, and try to be realistic.

▪ commercial publications

▪ vanity publishers
▪ international publishers

▪ targeting audiences

- First of all will it be predominantly local, Australian or international? (Remember, try to be realistic …)
- Who is the book aimed at: teachers, educators and workers in your discipline, students, postgraduates; or specialists in literacy, adult education, assessment, etc.?
- Who will actually ensure the book is bought in quantities large enough to merit a preliminary print run? That is usually not less than one thousand copies, and bigger publishers expect more. Will it be purchased and recommended by the readers themselves, or their teachers, their lecturers or their employers?
- Some major publishers are increasingly producing books with a very small initial print run, and then a 'print on demand' policy. This tends to lead to very expensive books that can only be afforded by major libraries and extreme specialists, so will your text be significant enough to attract those libraries?

▪ print runs

All publishers have particular profiles they are looking for, so the next step is to look at the publications you have used in your own research, and ask the people with whom you have been working. Spend some time surfing publishers' websites and product lists on the internet, getting a feel for what their strengths and emphases might be.

▪ publishers' profiles

When you have decided on a publisher, you will need to fill out a book proposal. Although the publishers are basically all looking for the same information, each has its own format for the proposal, partly at least to discourage would-be authors

▪ publication proposals

from sending proposals and manuscripts simultaneously to several publishers. As with journals, that habit is really to be frowned upon, though it might be acceptable sometimes to test the waters by submitting to a couple of likely publishers with differing focus of interest (at least their editors and readers are usually paid). The book proposal will want to know:

- what the book will be about
- its likely structure; some will ask for lists of contents or chapters
- its exact audience, and the likely numbers. Don't just write 'teachers' or 'postgraduate students' but indicate which groups of these will be motivated to buy the book, and why
- what there is to appeal to that audience, and what new knowledge otherwise unobtainable will be contained in your book
- what competition there already is in the market in the field, and why will those readers be disposed to read your book as well as or instead of the others; it is wise to be candid here, as the publishers or their reviewers are sure to check up for themselves
- who you are, and what credentials you have for writing in this area.

■ manuscript samples

The publishers may also want a sample chapter or a draft introduction, to get a sense of your approach and writing style. Some ask for this in the next round of negotiations. Don't send a complete or half-complete manuscript at this stage unless they ask for it.

■ publishers' referees
■ publishers' readers

They may also ask for the names of referees to contact to verify your credentials or the importance of the research results. They may even ask for names of potential readers for the manuscript, and for people and journals that they could send inspection copies to for review or for recommendation, assisting with publicity or distribution.

■ publishers' rejections

Be careful not to get your hopes up unduly about publication, or to be too upset by knock-backs—particularly if the rejection is more than just a pro-forma response. Read and note carefully the reasons for rejection: these may be helpful in reconceptualising the book, or looking for a more appropriate publisher. One problem that scholars in our areas face is that we are often dealing with more than one discipline, for example, cultural studies and literacy, physical education and community studies. Interdisciplinary studies often fall into the cracks between publishers. Each has its own known readership, and few are willing to venture into the unknown.

■ publishers' contracts

■ royalties

If you are among the lucky few who get a positive response and a draft contract, take a deep breath and take stock of it. Your aim will probably go no further than seeing your work in print, and giving as many people as possible access to your research. In any case you will not make more than petty cash in royalties from a research publication, or even a textbook for teachers or drama workers. The only educational books that bring their authors substantial royalties are student texts that are bought in class sets. Anyway, read the small print and, almost every time, refuse the first contract. Publishers run on the profit principle, and will certainly offer a low percentage, with the implication that this is the standard and only rate. Invariably it is not, and you will not lose the contract by at least suggesting to them that you deserve more. Publishers also demand a very different

■ other income

share of the Copying and Public Lending revenue, varying at the time of writing from around 50 per cent up to 90 per cent or more, and this may well be buried in the small print. This is administered in Australia by the Copyright Agency Limited (CAL), and is quite likely to be the major source of ongoing income from your book, if it is aimed at a university or teaching market, so it is worth making a pitch for a fair share. The publishers want the book enough to have made you an offer, and will not want to lose their investment, so at least they will discuss both this and the royalties. Check too that the manuscript delivery date is possible and acceptable, and that the arrangements for copyright and sub-licensing, if the book is a success, are suitable. If your work is the result of university study, such as a PhD, you need to check on intellectual property and royalty provisions, as these vary among universities.

▦ Copyright Agency Limited (CAL)

▦ sub-licensing
▦ intellectual property

Conferences and proceedings

It is usually most sensible to give your research its first outing in a small-scale conference of your own community, say a state subject association conference or a research seminar at your university. For university degrees, this is becoming a common requirement of the course. This way you will get your research out immediately to the people who matter most, your peer colleagues, and you will also get their feedback on it, usually fairly gently and supportively. But you need not stop there, if you think the research has a wider currency. If you work in a university, you will gain brownie points (i.e. money for the university) for making a research presentation at a fully refereed conference.

▦ refereed conferences

The same publicity and advocacy advantages apply for conferences as for journals, certainly those that have their papers refereed and published as conference proceedings. Those Education discipline-based scholars (such as in history, music, philosophy) who have ventured to put their works above the parapet, in conferences of generic education, new technologies, literacy, adult education and so on, have usually been very surprised at how positively their presentations are received. One of us (Beckett) has as many refereed publications in adult education as in his core discipline, philosophy of education, and many more again, which are non-refereed, in the very generic 'education policy' area. You may well be underwhelmed in other academic conferences (even, occasionally, in Education) by the presentational abilities of some of your fellow presenters. Many of them will just read their prepared papers word for word, without even a PowerPoint presentation. But as practice-proficient educators we would not make that mistake, would we? Even if we are reading a paper, we know about connecting with the audience through eye-contact and ad-libs, don't we? Social science conference workshops can disappoint too, which unlike our embodied and interactive group encounters often just mean more talks by presenters where the participants may join in the discussion a bit at the end. So be confident that you are offering a valuable product that is likely to be valued, especially if, on the way through, you let the process of presenting give rein to your practical skills. The audience will thank you for that, at least!

▦ conference proceedings

▦ presentational skills

Non-refereed publications

We have so far only discussed refereed journals and research books. This does not mean that you should neglect those that don't confer this kind of status. You may wish to get your research results straight into the hands of teachers and community and corporate workers, who tend not to read the academic and refereed journals as enthusiastically as they read practical journals published by their professional associations, for example, the Australian Council for Education Leaders, the Australian Institute of Training and Development, the Australian Human Resources Institute, the Australian Evaluation Society and so on.

▪ practical journals

If your research is substantial and can contribute signally to the world of practice, you should consider adapting the study for a publication of a practical kind. Again, you will need to consider carefully your intended audience. A first port of call for research that is of use to teachers might well be a professional teachers' association. Many teachers' national and state associations—'subject' or discipline-based—are quite active in the publications of monographs and books that suit their membership. This pathway to publication also gives a very clear focus to write to, and a pretty reliable if narrow distribution network.

▪ professional associations

▪ monographs

You will need to apply exactly the same procedure to publishers of textbooks and practical handbooks as we described above for scholarly books. Textbooks may confer more financial reward, as teachers' textbooks and especially class sets sell many more copies than scholarly ones, whose main purchasers are often libraries. The commercial educational book market is if anything tougher than that for research publication, and you will need to demonstrate that your book has currency for larger numbers of purchasers (usually at least three thousand for a first imprint) and lengthy life expectancy. However, publishers will want to hang on to a manuscript that they have identified as sellable, so you can probably be tough in your negotiations. If you are intending to convert your research into a publishable textbook or handbook, remember that you will have to give it an even more thorough makeover than for a research book, and find an entirely different style and presentation.

▪ textbooks

If your research will be helpful as advocacy to the general public, you should not turn up your nose at those even more popular avenues of dissemination like newspapers, magazines, radio shows or internet blogs. After all, a feature in a newspaper will reach many more thousands of people than a scholarly article, and provide useful information to parents, teachers, other allied professionals and workers, as well as those countless people who have never heard of or never think of your specialisation. The same advocacy principle that we mentioned in connection with refereed books and conferences applies to informal magazines too. General educational magazines and newspapers are usually crying out for copy, and an article in the education department's magazine, or the newsletter of the independent schools association, parent teachers' association or teachers' union journal will reach real stakeholders who did not know, hitherto, that they had a stake in your branch of education. Now they do, through your wonderful and research-based, timely piece on 'creativity', 'innovation', 'team-building' or 'generic skills': it's partly about how you badge yourself!

▪ popular outlets

▪ lay audiences

▪ advocacy

? REFLECTIVE QUESTIONS

1   If I were to read my own writing closely, what would be attractive about it (or, let's face it, is it like treading through hot tar)?

2   Does my reporting of research do justice to the participants, to the kind of data I collected and to the purposes with which I started?

3   Metaphors abound! Have I used them in a controlled and insightful way, or do they merely muddy (oops!) the reporting?

WIDER READING

Conrad, C. and Serlin, R. 2006. *The Sage Handbook for Research in Education.* Sage, Thousand Oaks, California. Section 6: Challenges in Writing, Voice and Dissemination of Research.

Dunne, M., Pryor, J. and Yates, P. 2005. *Becoming a Researcher: a Companion to the Research Process.* Open University Press, Maidenhead, UK. Part 3: Data with Destiny: Reconstructing Text.

Moss, J. (ed.) 2008. *Researching Education: Visually — Digitally — Spatially.* Sense Publishers, Rotterdam.

POSTSCRIPT TO PART B: A VALEDICTION

After so much talk about the cognitive and logistical elements of research, and now the communication and possible commercial implications, we hope that you have not forgotten the reasons you wanted to start research, or picked up this book in the first place. To rekindle the excitement, sense of risk and joy that are entirely proper and necessary to a researcher, we will finish on a metaphorical note as you get back to the rough ground. What gives your topic the friction to move forward—the traction?

To change the metaphor slightly into another variant of the 'journey' cliché, you are setting sail on a research voyage that D.H. Lawrence (1957) manages to describe in a fresh and eloquent way; we think it's a lovely analogy, though he's not actually talking about research (except in an extreme arcane sense), so if you look the reference up you might be sorry. The Education research community, who you have now joined, wishes you (especially if this is your first trip into the dark sea of the unknown), *bon voyage*, as you …

> Now launch the small ship … launch out, the fragile soul
> in the fragile ship of courage, the ark of faith
> with its store of food and little cooking pans
> and change of clothes,
> upon the flood's black waste …
> where still we sail darkly, for we cannot steer and have no port …

And it sometimes feels like that, certainly! But hang in there …

> … And out of the eternity, a thread separates itself on the blackness …
> wait, wait, the little ship
> drifting, beneath the grey of a flood-dawn.
> The flood subsides, and the little ship wings home,
> faltering and lapsing on the pink flood
> and the frail soul steps out, into the house again,
> filling the heart with peace.

Show us what you've found when you get back.

EPILOGUE TO PART B

THE Agony Column
Part 2—Getting it done

Dr Sophie answers your questions about research degrees. This month: *Getting it done*

Two questions this week about rules, and the first is quickly dealt with.

Q Must do research for something called capstone subject in my Master's—seem to be an awful lot of stupid rules—how carefully must I read them? @*innocencepersonified (received on Twitter)*

A Capstone subjects are both a culmination of your undergraduate studies, and a new beginning as a researcher, so to answer your question in your own style: very carefully, stupid. Uni rules and regulations are there for two good reasons: to protect you against others (and sometimes yourself), and to protect the university too. I'll come back to that, because the most essential rules—often the most bewilderingly complicated, and certainly the most frustrating—are to do with protecting what you are doing, and, when you've done it, what you have produced. My column in a couple of weeks will be about gaining human ethics clearance—these are some of the most important rules, so you'd better read that column too, or you might end up in deep trouble. Next to the ethics rules and procedures are their close cousins, the rules and procedures about intellectual property ... and if you don't know and follow those, you could end up in very expensive trouble.

Q I really want to do my PhD at a university some distance away, but I live up country and it has strict residency rules: moving would impose real hardship for me as I have children at school and my partner has an important job. *Anonymous—name supplied, Swan Hill*

A You'll have read my answer above about rules—but don't despair: I've got more sympathy with you than for that last twitterer. I have sometimes found that rules can be bent, because they do not always reflect our needs or our history (in your case, obviously). Universities are mostly built on scientific traditions, and are often run by scientists, and besides, changing the rules in a university is a very slow process. For instance, in one university not a million miles away from where you live (it might even be the one you want to attend), there is a rule that PhD students must permanently live in the city of that university. In the past, when the institution was a local university and immediate communication was face-to-face or not at all, this was entirely necessary. Even today, for science departments, local residency is mostly still a good idea, where a PhD student is likely to be a twenty-something, still very raw in the ways of research, needing regular access to the lab and personal mentoring from experienced profs ... and handy, too, to have around for emptying the petri dishes on Christmas Eve.

It is not like that in Education (even science education). As I mentioned in a previous column, it is perfectly feasible to study at a distance from your university, and often essential to be in close proximity to your research site. A new music colleague of mine and I had arrived fresh at that university, each with a number of new students who had nominated my colleague and me as their chosen supervisor, and who were eager to take advantage of the fine education reputation of this university. To our astonishment not one of them could be accepted. Just to take one example: Chan was a middle-aged male academic, an associate professor already running a university department in Taiwan, with a growing family to boot, and with his research site based in his own university up there. There was no way he could spend three years in Australia even if it had made sense (or even one year, as the rule has subsequently been amended to). I was forced to say goodbye to Chan, and watch him accepted with alacrity by a rival university. My music colleague was smarter, and learnt quickly that in such cases, 'residency' can be quite a creative term. Since then, she and I, and many of our other colleagues, have supervised a range of candidates in two universities with this rule who were in reality based afar off, but could present themselves as necessary to the university authorities. [Note, this is for readers' eyes only, and must not on any account fall into the hands of my associate dean of research—eat this page after reading it.]

Two questions this week on the same subject:

Q **A few months ago your column dealt with half my question, about relationships with supervisors, but quite ignored the other half, about problems of distance. Last week too you talked about studying at a distance, but you didn't say how. Can you please finish the job?** *(Getting impatient) Dr Chen, Melbourne*

A Yes, I'm sorry, Chen (sorry, Dr Chen), my editor's word limit stopped me from the second bit of your very complex question, but see below.

Q **I'm an adult teacher finishing the first year of my PhD in a good Australian university with a wonderful supervisor, but I am moving to Kenya with my partner. It's on NGO training in developing countries, so it'll be good for my fieldwork, but should I transfer to my local university?** *Gayleen (Obdhyerambo), Eldoret, Kenya*

A As for you, Gayleen, it's up to you, and whether your local university has a good faculty, with an appropriate supervisor—in your subject area, they might well do.

Now to answer both your questions: if you decide to stick with what you know and trust, the logistics of distance are never insuperable, if the spirits are willing (and if the university regulations permit or can be bent). Thanks to electronic and cyber-technology, you can have a strong, regular, immediate and ongoing supervision relationship remotely. I am currently supervising four students based in another Australian city, two of whom are doing their fieldwork in China. We enjoy our monthly skype, and from one of them, my co-supervisor and I get long emails full of queries and insecurities, both of which can be answered at length online, or by a phone, skype or face-time call. The personal relationship that we discussed last week can also reinforce this remote correspondence: I sustained a long-running email correspondence with a Kiwi through a ritual based on the fact that she was a passionate Silver Ferns national netball team supporter, and we never failed to start our emails by baiting each other on the latest cross-Tasman sports news. After that start, any critical comment by me about the direction, variable commitment or quality of her PhD work, and any unease or problems she was having and needed sorting out, seemed like mere trifles.

Face-to-face contact is still valuable, of course, and she and I also took advantage of a characteristic of my specialised field of study that you too may be able to use: we are quite a small community, with a finite number of conferences and congresses that we tend to attend where possible. She and I would arrange to attend the same conference, at least once a year, and put aside at least half a day (as well as drinking and yarning time) for a thorough supervision, eyeball to eyeball.

I do this wherever possible with students from whom I am physically separated—and with two others it proved a boon for quite a different reason. Both these students were good candidates, but during the second half of their degree were removed quite a distance from the stimulus and fieldwork that had been the mainspring of their PhD. They had both moved internationally to new and demanding jobs, and downgraded their PhD to part-time status. That was further reduced within the context of their jobs, where completing the PhD was neither a priority nor specially encouraged, and they were given other fierce priorities and timelines. Each of these fine candidates had a further weakness too: one was very easily distracted—quite the party girl—and as far as her PhD was concerned, it was mainly out-of-sight, out-of-mind. The other was more dedicated, but had a very deep insecurity about her writing (which was fine, actually), that blocked her from putting pen (or keyboard) to paper. Our annual conference meetings thus turned into quite essential rev-up sessions— where my main (quite hard) task was to breathe life back into the moribund near-corpses of both projects. In this I was sustained in both cases by our strong personal friendship and my own respect for the candidates' abilities—I knew both of them were entirely capable and would get there in the end. They did.

Q I want to start my action research fieldwork in social psychology this term. I have a marvellous chance to work with a group of Macedonian senior citizens, all elderly women, helping them deal with a lot of inter-generational tensions and prejudices about their Australian grandchildren by storying their experiences and dramatising them. However, I've been told that I must fill in an ethics procedure and lots of rigmarole that could take months. Is there any way round this? After all, they are not kids. *Aphrodite, Wanneroo*

A Not a chance. If you are working with other people, and especially children and minors, and members of special groups like you are (with minors too—those grandchildren?), you have to navigate the human ethics process. There is no way round, and nor should there be, and I guarantee that this will almost drive you mad, and your supervisor too. The energy, passion, inspiration and hard graft that you put into designing your fieldwork will be leached out remorselessly by the seemingly endless questions that demand obvious answers (Are you using radioactive isotopes or prohibited substances?) or detailed and unanswerable responses (How can you know exactly how your research participants will respond to your storymaking until you try it?).

You and your supervisor will do the best you can and send the form in hopefully, trying to second-guess the panel, and then get back a whole new set of questions that you hadn't even considered, which will depress your supervisor even more than you, because he or she should have thought of them. If you are very unlucky, the assessment panel will be chaired by somebody with a purely quantitative research background, who will be uncomprehending as to why you have such a small and unrepresentative research sample from which no control groups could be set up or firm conclusions drawn; or worse, somebody coupling that with their own mythical baggage about drama (probably from a cognitive psychology background) who is convinced that applying drama strategies to either children's learning or immigrant stories is at best dangerous social engineering, and most likely child abuse …

Then to get the thing through the second time you will have to convince that prejudiced sceptic incontrovertibly that they are wrong—not easy with academics, and especially cognitive psychologists, in my experience. The downside of this is that it will probably occupy all your energy and time for up to six months when you wanted to get stuck into the research. The upside is that this is actually very good training, not only in saintly patience and soul improvement, but in covering all your bases and examining the minutiae of your actions and words for any possible sub-textual or subliminal meaning or ambiguity. The research and data analysis should no longer hold terrors for you, as you've already been through the fire—you will have become a far more sophisticated survey designer and scrutineer, a master of second-guessing, a much improved interviewer and as Pecksniffian a vigilante as that Panel Chair.

Two grumbles this week, which again I'll answer together for obvious reasons:

Q What is the right amount of time between supervisions? My supervisor expects to see me every week and show exactly what progress I've made, and I feel like a naughty schoolgirl—in my opinion a PhD is an independent study and I need the space to think for myself, and have the supervisor there just when I need help—which isn't often. If these are the rules, they should be relaxed. *Autonomous Learner, Adelaide*

Q My supervisor is never around for a supervision when I need one, and when I get one as often as not she cancels. She hasn't shown any interest in introducing me to other supervisees, and even on my floor I can't work out who to ask for IT advice, or how to access travel funds. Not only that, but she will be away having a baby next year and what do I do then? I really admire her and need her expertise. In my Master's I saw my supervisor weekly, which made me feel really good and we became good coffee mates. What can I do about this? There should be some rules. *Disgruntled, Bald Hills*

A I think you are both pretty unlucky, by the sound of it (and perhaps you should swap supervisors!). In both cases, have you talked to your supervisor about how you feel, and to find out how they view your progress and the frequency of supervisions? If you have done so, and this letter is the result of your continuing frustration, you should contact your faculty dean of research studies, and without whinging, talk your situation over to see what can be done by the university. There are no rules about this, and really there can't be, though this is one of the trickiest areas of negotiating and managing a PhD, demanding great sensitivity from the supervisor and often some flexibility from the student.

Let's look at it both from your needs and those of the study. Each study is different, and each student more so. You have come with a particular level of research expertise, of being up-to-date in your field, of being familiar with your research topic, site and participants, and being *au fait* with the literature … or not, in any of those areas. Each of these demands a different spot on the regularity dial. Your research site, topic or participants may need especially careful handling for some reason, or might present you with risks or the need to make decisions quickly and wisely, where another more experienced head can be essential.

Then there are your own study habits and proclivities: I notice that one of you signs yourself as 'Autonomous Learner'—fine, and I was too, and you should be allowed to spread your wings and use your professional judgment. Unlike you, I was allowed to get on much as I wanted, which in my PhD was a great boon, but in my Master's degree was a real pity, since I was also arrogant enough to think I knew more about my subject (true) and research design (culpably false) than my supervisor did. I ended up putting together a really soggy piece of research that discovered far less than it should have or could have if it was properly handled. Moreover, even though I did know more about my subject than my supervisor, instead of ignoring and despising his limitations and prejudices against my approach, I could have used this to test out and marshal my opinionations into more coherent thoughts—if only to teach the teacher.

Furthermore, you may know you are a genuinely autonomous learner, but your supervisor probably doesn't. I can tell you that as a supervisor I have spent many anxious moments wondering whether a long silence from a student means he or she is deeply engrossed in the research, squirreling away confidently and independently, or whether it means he or she has just gone walkabout for an indefinite period, lost interest in the whole shebang, had something come up in his or her personal life that has temporarily derailed the study, or just got confused, lost confidence and is too embarrassed or guilty to admit it.

As for you, 'Disgruntled', you certainly have a right to regular and reliable supervision, but not just to make you 'feel really good'. Embarking on a PhD does demand fortitude and stamina, and a lot of that independent learner. There will probably be times when the study, or your personal or professional life beyond it, hits a crisis, and you genuinely need a wise shoulder to cry on, or some pastoral advice. But that is not every week; even if you are a good mate of your supervisor, just consider whether your desire for that regular cosy chat comes from the needs of your study or your own psychological neediness—and perhaps caffeine addiction! Supervisors are also very busy people, and however interested they are in your study, they only have limited time. Except for emergencies, your meetings should be focused on providing you with academic input and critique that you can't get elsewhere.

I am a little surprised that your university has not provided either of you with a backup— most nowadays demand a second supervisor, and some even require a panel of three or more. Mind you, apart from increasing two- or three-fold the total work required from the supervisors, that does not necessarily guarantee a better service for you. Second and third supervisors also need to be in sync with each other, as well as you. If you have a supervisor you admire and trust, that person must be your major mentor. It is useful to turn to another more disinterested or distant eye at difficult times, or if you find yourself at loggerheads with your supervisor, and also when you have an almost complete draft of the thesis. Whatever you do, don't send both of them everything you write and a schedule of everything you do, and expect a full response from both. If they are in sync you will just be giving them both a bigger workload. Moreover, you may well find that they don't give exactly the same response (especially if they don't have time to talk to each other about your latest offering), and you will suddenly find yourself confused by apparently different or conflicting advice—as often as not just a difference of emphasis, but you probably won't see that. I have also known students who play games with their supervisors, and play off one against the other, if they don't like what one of them says (but I'm sure you are not at all like this!).

Q My university tells me that in order to pass the PhD they expect me to have published at least six refereed papers, but I am already running late with my data analysis, I don't have any coherent findings yet, and I have never written a paper before. I am panicking. Can I just send some chapters of my thesis to journals as articles? *Alice, Sydney*

A Alice, I am deeply sympathetic with you and understand your anxiety. Your university is asking you to do what the Red Queen suggested to your namesake, six impossible things before breakfast, and as that tyrannical ruler also observed, it takes all the running you can do to stay in the same place. However, as usual, there are two sides to this question—just as, in a way, there are two different kinds of study—as well as several different reasons for publishing your research.

Put aside your panic for a moment, and look at your thesis to see whether any of your study might be 'detachable'. If you have done a pilot project, or generated some early results that will stand the test of your ongoing investigation, you might have something worth publishing. Have you done a literature review which would itself add usefully to the literature? Even perhaps your fieldwork or the methodology you are using might be so interesting that a running commentary can arouse the interest of journal readers.

However, you do sound as if you are involved in a holistic study that is only going to give up its pearls of new knowledge slowly and late. If so, you are in a pickle, and I don't have any advice, other than to plead this as an excuse to your faculty assessment panel or supervisors. Point out to them that the money you will earn for the university on your graduation is many more dollars than it will get for your publication quantum ... and that you'll be only too keen to publish under the university imprimatur after you've finished!

Whichever of these situations you are in, remember two complementary, not necessarily contradictory, things. First, while you are engaged on your research project you are involved in a dynamic, changing learning environment, and need to be able to concentrate on that. Second, it is not a solitary environment—you are also engaged with a community of scholars, and can and should communicate with this community as you go. Your study is probably important enough to have a public conversation about your ongoing work, and get useful input yourself, besides reporting to others. Traditional refereed journal publication is a horribly slow form of conversation, but you can and probably should take your work to a conference—or several—and give it an airing in a paper or poster presentation, where perhaps it will be published as part of the proceedings. Alternatively, you could go online and find one of the new electronic academic platforms, which often have a much quicker turn-around.

To answer your specific question about submitting thesis chapters to journals: not exactly, no, definitely not. If you refer to Chapter 9 of that excellent book *Educational Research: Creative Thinking and Doing*, you'll find that the authors spell out clearly the differences between how you write for a PhD thesis and how you write for a journal—to satisfy the two quite different audiences. So, even if some of your chapters can stand as discrete pieces of complete research, valuable to your field, then you are going to have to spend some of your precious time revising them accordingly. There is a long-term benefit, if you can think that far ahead: any articles you do get published will give you the invaluable asset of a publication profile, without which, if you are working in a university environment, you will be lost … quite besides the warm glow of satisfaction of knowing that strangers are reading and quoting your work as an authority! Anyway, the best of luck with your thesis …

That reminds me, I've decided to say goodbye to all you brave new researchers, as I'm off to improve my own publication profile, instead of sitting here giving free advice to the likes of you.

[Editor: Dr Sophie's column will not be appearing in subsequent editions, as she appears unaccountably to have disappeared, without leaving a forwarding address. Her column will be replaced next week by our new cartoon feature, 'Alex in Wonderland: a dummy's guide to phenomenology'.]

BIBLIOGRAPHY

Ackroyd, J. and O'Toole, J. 2010. *Performing Research: Tensions, Triumphs and Trade-offs of Ethnodrama*. Trentham Books, London.

Adams, D. 1978. *The Hitchhiker's Guide to the Galaxy*. BBC Publications, London.

Anderson, T. 2001. Casualties of Contingency: Nurses' Professional Development in Postmodernity. PhD Thesis, The University of Melbourne.

Au, Y-M. 2013. Changing Practice?—Exploring the Potential Contribution of Applied Theatre Training to Capacity-building for NGO Workers in China. PhD Thesis, The University of Melbourne (in progress).

Austin, H. 2003. *Schooling the Child: The Making of Students in Classrooms*. RoutledgeFalmer, London.

Babbie, E. 2002. *The Basics of Social Research*. Wadsworth Thomson Learning, Belmont, California. Part 2, The Structuring of Inquiry; Part 4, Analysis of Data.

Bagley, C. and Cancienne, M. 2000. *Dancing the Data*. Peter Lang, New York.

Barba, E. 1995. *The Paper Canoe*. Routledge, London.

Barone, T. 2001. *Touching Eternity*. Teachers College Press, New York.

Barrett, M. and Smigiel, H. 2003. 'Awakening the Sleeping Giant: The Arts in the Lives of Australian Families.' *International Journal of Education and the Arts* 4 (4).

Bateson, G. 1989. *Mind and Nature: A Necessary Unity*. Hampton Press, Creskill, NJ.

Beckett, D. 1998. 'Management Learning Research Survey', in D. Boud (ed.) *Current Issues and New Agendas for Workplace Learning*. National Centre for Vocational Education and Training, Adelaide.

Beckett, D. 2010a. 'Adult Learning: Philosophical Issues', in B. McGaw, P. Peterson and E. Baker (eds) *International Encyclopaedia of Education* (3rd edn). Elsevier, Oxford, UK.

Beckett, D. 2010b. 'Learning to Be at Work', in L. Scanlon (ed.) *Becoming a Professional*. Lifelong Learning Book Series: Springer, Netherlands.

Beckett, D. 2012a. 'Ontological Distinctiveness and the Emergence of Purposes', in P. Gibbs (ed.) *Learning, Work and Practice: New Understandings*. Springer, Netherlands.

Beckett, D. 2012b. 'Of Maestros and Muscles: Expertise and Practices at Work', in D. Aspin (ed.) *International Handbook of Lifelong Learning* (2nd edn). Springer, Netherlands.

Beckett, D. and Hager, P. 2002. *Life, Work and Learning: Practice in Postmodernity*. Routledge, London.

Benjamin, W. 1973. *Understanding Brecht*, trans. A. Bostock. NLB, London.

Bertram, D. 2013. *Likert Scales are the Meaning of Life*. Retrieved March 2013 from http://poincare.matf.bg.ac.rs/~kristina//topic-dane-likert.pdf.

Blackburn, S. (ed.) 1996, *Oxford Dictionary of Philosophy*. Oxford University Press, London.

Boomer, G. 1982. *Negotiating the Curriculum*. Falmer, London.

Bruner, J. 1977. *The Process of Education*. Harvard University Press, Cambridge, Massachusetts.

Bruner, J. 1990. *Acts of Meaning*. Harvard University Press, Cambridge, Massachusetts.

Bundy, P. 2006. Cited in J. O'Toole, *Doing Drama Research*. Drama Australia, Melbourne.

Burton, B. and O'Toole, J. 2005. 'Enhanced Forum Theatre: Where Boal's Theatre of the Oppressed meets Process Drama in the Classroom.' *NJ: Journal of Drama Australia*.

Burton, D. and Bartlett, S. 2005. *Practitioner Research for Teachers*. Paul Chapman Publishing, London.

Byrnes, J. 1999. We Don't Need Another Hero: An Action Research into Effective Leadership Development in Adults within a Non-profit Organization. DEd Thesis, The University of Melbourne.

Camm, J. 2012. Learning in the Franchise Panopticon: Competency, Foucault and new Franchise learning. DEd Thesis, The University of Melbourne.

Capra, F. 1996. *The Web of Life: A New Scientific Understanding of Living Systems*. Anchor Books, New York.

Carr, W. and Kemmis, S. 1986. *Becoming Critical: Education, Knowledge and Action Research*. Falmer, London.

Carroll, J. 1996. 'Escaping the Information Abattoir: Critical and Transformative Research in Drama Classrooms', in P. Taylor (ed.) *Researching Drama and Arts Education: Paradigms and Possibilities*. Falmer, London.

Carroll, J., Anderson, M. and Cameron, D. 2006. *Real Players? Drama, Technology and Education*. Trentham Books, London.

Carroll, L. 1865. *Alice's Adventures in Wonderland*. Variously published.

Carroll, L. 1871. *Through the Looking-Glass, and What Alice Found There*. Variously published.

Charmaz, K. 2005. 'Grounded Theory in the 21st Century: A Qualitative Method for Advancing Social Justice Research', in N. Denzin and Y. Lincoln, *The Sage Handbook of Qualitative Research*. Sage, Thousand Oaks, California.

Chase, S. 2005. 'Narrative Inquiry: Multiple Lenses, Approaches, Voices', in N. Denzin and Y. Lincoln, *The Sage Handbook of Qualitative Research*. Sage, Thousand Oaks, California.

Chinyowa, K. 2005. Manifestation of Play as Aesthetic in African Theatre for Development. PhD Thesis, Griffith University, Brisbane.

Chipp, H.B. (ed.) 1968. *Theories of Modern Art: A Source Book by Artists and Critics*. University of California Press, Berkeley.

Clandinin, J. and Connelly, M. 2000. *Narrative Inquiry: Experience and Story in Qualitative Research*. Jossey-Bass, San Francisco.

Clarke, D. 2013. International Centre for Classroom Research; available at www.iccr.edu.au.

Clemans, A. 2005. Community Education Work: So Close to Home! PhD Thesis, The University of Melbourne.

Collins, A. 1992. 'Towards a Design Science of Education', in E. Scanlon and T. O'Shea (eds) *New Directions in Educational Technology*. Springer-Verlag, Berlin.

Conrad, C. and Serlin, R. (eds) 2006. *The Sage Handbook for Research in Education*. Sage, Thousand Oaks, California.

Cowen, J. 2006. Corporate Curiosity: The Learning Trajectory of a Global Chief Executive Officer. MEd Thesis, The University of Melbourne.

Creswell, J. 2008. *Educational Research: Planning, Conducting and Evaluating Quantitative and Qualitative Research* (3rd edn). Pearson Education Inc., Upper Saddle River, New Jersey.

Creswell, J. 2009. *Research Design: Qualitative, Quantitative and Mixed Methods Approaches*. Sage, Thousand Oaks, California.

Creswell, J. 2012. *Educational Research: Planning, Conducting, and Evaluating Quantitative and Qualitative Research*. Pearson, Boston.

Csikszentmihailyi, M. 1990. *Flow: The Psychology of Happiness*. Rider, London.

Cutcher, A. 2004. The Hungarian in Australia: A Portfolio of Belongings. PhD Thesis, University of Sydney.

Damasio, A. 1999. *The Feeling of What Happens: Body and Emotion in the Making of Consciousness*. Harcourt Brace, New York.

Damasio, A. 2010. *Self Comes to Mind: Constructing the Conscious Brain*. Pantheon, New York.

Davies, A. and Dart, J. 2005. *The Most Significant Change (MSC) Technique: A Guide to its Use*. Retrieved January 2013 from www.mande.co.uk/docs/MSCGuide.pdf.

Davis, S.H. 2008. *Research and Practice in Education: The Search for Common Ground*. Rowman & Littlefield Education, Lanham, Maryland.

Davis, S. and Ambrosetti, A. 2012. Digital Tools for Dramatic Engagement: Transforming Sustainability Education for the Digital Age. Grant Submission, University of Central Queensland.

Daye, C. 1998. Designing an Art Program for Adults with an Intellectual Disability: An Innovative Approach. PhD Thesis, The University of Melbourne.

de Freitas, S. and Maharg, P. (eds) 2011. *Digital Games and Learning*. Continuum, London.

de Landsheere, G. 1999. 'History of Educational Research', in J.P. Keeves and G. Lakomski (eds) *Issues in Educational Research*. Pergamon, Elsevier Science, Oxford. Chapter 2.

Denzin, N. 1997. *Interpretive Ethnography: Ethnographic Practices for the 21st Century*. Sage, Thousand Oaks, California.

Denzin, N. 2003. *Performance Ethnography: Critical Pedagogy and the Politics of Culture*. Sage, Thousand Oaks, California.

Denzin, N. and Lincoln, Y. (eds) 2005. *The Sage Handbook of Qualitative Research* (3rd edn). Sage, Thousand Oaks, California.

Derricourt, R. 1996. *An Author's Guide to Scholarly Publishing*. Princeton University Press, New Jersey.

Deshler, D. and Selener, D. 1991. 'Transformative Research: In Search of a Definition.' *Convergence* 24 (3).

Dewey, J. 1938. *Experience and Education*. Macmillan, New York.

Dewey, J. 1956. *The Child and the Curriculum, the School and Society*. University of Chicago Press, Chicago.

Diamond, P. and Mullen, C. 1999. *The Post-Modern Educator: Arts-Based Inquiries and Teacher Development*. Peter Lang, New York.

Dodds, M. and Hart, S. (eds) 2001. *Doing Practitioner Research Differently*. Routledge, London.

Donelan, K. 2005. The Gods Project: Drama and Intercultural Education. PhD Thesis, Griffith University, Brisbane.

Drew, C., Hardman, M. and Hosp, J. 2008. *Designing and Conducting Research in Education, Part III, Data Analysis and Results Interpretation*. Sage, Thousand Oaks, California.

Dunn, J. 2002. Dramatic Worlds in Play. PhD Thesis, Griffith University, Brisbane.

Dunn, J. and O'Toole, J. 2008. 'Learning in Dramatic and Virtual Worlds: What Do Students Say about Complementarity and Future Directions?' *Journal of Aesthetic Education* 42 (4).

Dunne, M., Pryor, J. and Yates, P. 2005. *Becoming a Researcher: A Companion to the Research Process*. Open University Press, Maidenhead, UK.

Eisner, E. 1979. *The Educational Imagination: On the Design and Evaluation of School Programs*. Macmillan, New York.

Eisner, E. 1985. *Learning and Teaching: The Modes of Knowing*. University of Chicago Press, Chicago.

Eisner, E. 2008. 'Persistent Tensions in Arts-based Research', in M. Cahnmann-Taylor and R. Siegesmund (eds) *Arts-Based Research in Education: Foundations for Practice*. Routledge, New York. See also Chapter 1, 'Arts-based Research: Histories and New Directions'.

Elam, K. 1980. *The Semiotics of Theatre and Drama*. Methuen, London.

Engestrom, Y. 2003. 'Cultural-historical Activity Theory, the Activity System.' University of Helsinki. Retrieved 7 January 2013 from www.edu.helsinki.fi/activity/pages/chatanddwr.

Esslin, M. 1987. *The Field of Drama: How the Signs of Drama Create Meaning on Stage and Screen*. Methuen, London.

Ewing, R. 2006. In correspondence with John O'Toole, during the preparation of *Doing Drama Research* (2006). Drama Australia, Melbourne.

Ewing, R. and Smith, D. 2004. 'Creating New Epiphanies', in A. Cole, G. Knowles, G.L. Neilson and T. Luciano (eds) *Informed by Practice*. Backalong Books, Canada.

Ezzy, D. 2006. 'The Research Process', in M. Walter (ed.) *Social Research Methods: An Australian Perspective*. Oxford University Press, Melbourne.

Ferres, K., Buckridge, P., Bundy, P., Ellison, D., Alexander M., Keys, W., O'Toole, J. and Woodward, I. 2006. *Sustaining Culture: The Role of Performing Arts Centres*. ARC Linkage Project in association with Queensland Performing Arts Centre, Sydney Opera House, Victorian Arts Centre and Adelaide Festival Centre. Griffith University, Brisbane.

Finley, S. 2005. 'Arts-based Inquiry: Performing Revolutionary Pedagogy', in N. Denzin and Y. Lincoln, *The Sage Handbook of Qualitative Research*. Sage, Thousand Oaks, California.

Flanders, N. 1970. *Analysing Teaching Behaviour*. Addison-Wesley, Reading, Massachusetts.

Floden, R.E. 2006. 'What Knowledge Users Want', in C. Conrad and R. Serlin, *The Sage Handbook for Research in Education*. Sage, Thousand Oaks, California.

Foreman-Peck, L. and Winch, C. 2010. *Using Educational Research to Inform Practice: A Practical Guide to Practitioner Research in Universities and Colleges*. Routledge, London.

Foucault, M. 1970. *The Order of Things: An Archaeology of the Human Sciences*. Tavistock, London.

Foucault, M. 1972. 'The Discourse on Language.' Appendix in *The Archaeology of Knowledge*. Pantheon, New York.

Foucault, M. 1980. 'Truth and Power', in C. Gordon (ed.) *Power/Knowledge: Selected Interviews and Other Writings 1972–1977*. Pantheon Books, New York.

Freebody, K. 2006. Social Justice and Drama in the Classroom: Socioeconomic Status as Interactional Topic and Resource. PhD Thesis, The University of Melbourne.

Freebody, P. 2003. *Qualitative Research in Education: Interaction and Practice*. Sage, London.

Freire, P. 1974. *Pedagogy of the Oppressed*, trans. A Ramos. Continuum Books, London.

Freud, L. 2006. *Freud at Work/Photographs by Bruce Bernard and David Dawson; Lucian Freud in Conversation with Sebastian Smee*. Alfred A. Knopf, New York.

Gadamer, H-G. 1960, trans. 1975. *Truth and Method*. Sheed and Ward, London.

Garfinkel, H. 1967. *Studies in Ethnomethodology*. Prentice-Hall, Englewood Cliffs, New Jersey.

Geertz, C. 1973. *The Interpretation of Culture*. Basic Books, New York.

Geertz, C. 1983. 'Blurred Genres: The Reconfiguration of Social Thought.' *The American Scholar* (29) 2.

Glaser, B. and Strauss A. 1967. *The Discovery of Grounded Theory: Strategies for Qualitative Research*. Aldine Publishing, Chicago.

Gleick, J. 1987. *Chaos: Making a New Science*. Viking, New York.

Golding, C. 2010. That's a Better Idea: Philosophical Progress in Philosophy for Children. PhD Thesis, The University of Melbourne.

Gottdiener, N., Boklund-Lagopolou, K. and Lagopoulos, A. (eds) 2003. *Semiotics*. Sage, London.

Graue, B. 2006. 'Writing in Education Research', in C. Conrad and R. Serlin, *The Sage Handbook of Research in Education*.

Grbich, C. 2004. *New Approaches in Social Research*. Sage, London.

Habermas, J. 1987. *The Theory of Communicative Action*, trans. T. McCarthy. Beacon Press, Boston.

Habibis, D. 2006. 'Ethics and Social Research', in M. Walters (ed.) *Social Science Research Methods: An Australian Perspective*. Oxford University Press, Melbourne.

Haseman, B. 1981. 'Five Workshops: Drama from Practice to Theory.' Convenor's Report, Brisbane South Region Drama Resource Project, Mt Gravatt College of Advanced Education, Brisbane.

Haseman, B. 1991. Beyond a Grounded Theory for Teacher Education in the Arts. MA Thesis, Sussex University.

Hassall, L. and Hogan, B. 2003. *Touchmetypeyou.org.asm*. Ethnodrama performed at Drama Australia Conference, Brisbane.

Hatton, C. 2004. Backyards and Borderlands: Transforming Girls' Learning through Drama. PhD Thesis, University of Sydney.

Heathcote, D. 1971. *Three Looms Waiting*. 36mm film directed by R. Eyre. BBC Films, London.

Heathcote, D. 1997. In interview with John Carroll, 'Drama as Radical Pedagogy: Agency and Power in the Classroom.' *Teaching Education Journal* (9) 1.

Holland, C. 2009. 'Reading and Acting in the World: Conversations about Empathy.' *Research in Drama Education*, 14 (4).

Holstein, J. and Gubrium, J. 2005. 'Interpretive Practice and Social Action', in N. Denzin and Y. Lincoln, *The Sage Handbook of Qualitative Research*. Sage, Thousand Oaks, California.

Hopkinson, W. 2012. We Don't Do Macramé: A Case Study of the Adult Learning Possibilities in an Inner City Uniting Church in Australia Arts and Spirituality Mission. PhD Thesis, The University of Melbourne.

Howell, G. 2009. Beyond Words: Newly-arrived Children's Perceptions of Music Learning and Music Making. MEd Thesis, The University of Melbourne.

Husen, T. 1999. 'Research Paradigms in Education', in J. Keeves and G. Lakomski (eds) *Issues in Educational Research*. Pergamon, Elsevier Science, Oxford.

Hussain, W. 2008. Perceptions of Teacher Evaluation in Pakistan: A Case Study from Peshawar District. DEd Thesis, The University of Melbourne.

Hutchinson, S. 1988. 'Education and Grounded Theory', in R. Sherman and R. Webb (eds) *Qualitative Research in Education: Focus and Methods*. Falmer Press, London.

Jabeen, S. 2013. Evaluating Unintended Outcomes: A Case Study of a Social Development Programme in Pakistan. PhD Thesis, The University of Melbourne (in progress).

Janesick, V. 2000. 'The Choreography of Qualitative Research Design: Minuets, Improvisation and Crystallisation', in N. Denzin and Y. Lincoln (eds), *The Sage Handbook of Qualitative Research* (2nd edn). Sage, Thousand Oaks, California.

Johnson, B. and Christensen, L. 2012. *Educational Research: Quantitative, Qualitative, and Mixed Approaches*. Sage, Thousand Oaks, California.

Johnston, S. 2007. New Cars, New Work, New Learning: Productive Workplace Learning at a Lean Manufacturing Site. DEd Thesis, The University of Melbourne.

Jones, R. 2006. *Visual Literacy in Prisons Pilot Project*. Department of Community Cultural Development, Victoria College of the Arts.

Kaehler, S. 2006. 'Introduction to Fuzzy Logic', *Encoder, Newsletter of Seattle Robotics Society*. Retrieved 3 June 2006 from www.seattlerobotics.org/encoder/mar98/fuz/fl_part1.html.

Keeves, J.P. and Lakomski, G. (eds) 1999. *Issues in Educational Research*. Pergamon, Elsevier Science, Oxford.

Kelly, A. 2004. 'Design Research in Education: Yes, But is it Methodological?' *Journal of the Learning Sciences* 13 (1).

Kerlin, B. 2002. *Why NUD.IST?* Retrieved 12 January 2006 from http://kerlins.net/bobbi.research/nudist (site no longer current).

Kervin, L., Vialle, W., Herrington, J. and Okely, T. 2006. *Research for Educators*. Thomson Social Science Press, Melbourne.

Knowles, M. 1970. *The Modern Practice of Adult Education: Andragogy versus Pedagogy*. Associated Press, New York.

Lapsley, D.K. 2006. 'Challenges in Formulating and Framing Meaningful Problems: Introductory Essay', in C. Conrad and R. Serlin, *The Sage Handbook for Research in Education*. Sage, Thousand Oaks, California.

Lather, P. 1992. 'Critical Frames in Educational Research: Feminist and Post-structuralist Perspectives.' *Theory into Practice* 31 (2).

Lawrence, D.H. 1957. 'The Ship of Death', in *D.H. Lawrence: The Complete Poems*, vol. 3. Heinemann, London.

Leavis, F.R. 1975. *Revaluation: Tradition and Development in English Poetry*. Greenwood Press, Westport, Connecticut.

Lee, A. (dir.) 2012. *Life of Pi*. 20th Century Fox, Los Angeles.

Leedy, P. and Ormrod, J. 2001. *Practical Research, Planning and Design* (7th edn). Merrill Prentice Hall, Columbus, Ohio.

Lewin, K. 1952. *Field Theory in Social Science*. Tavistock Press, London.

Lindeman, M. 2006. Emerging Identities: Practice, Learning and Professional Development of Home and Community Care Assessment Staff. PhD Thesis, The University of Melbourne.

Lockhart, S. 2008. Of Secrets, Sorrows and Shame: Undergraduate Nurses' Experiences of Death and Dying. MEd Thesis, The University of Melbourne.

Lockhart, S. 2013. Terror, Taboo and Transformation: The Undergraduate Nurse's and Midwife's Experience of Patient Death. PhD Thesis, The University of Melbourne.

Lovesy, S. 2003. Drama Education Secondary School Playbuilding: Enhancing Imagination and Group Creativity in Group Playbuilding through Kinaesthetic Teaching and Learning. PhD Thesis, University of Western Sydney.

Macdonald, J. 2006. Cited in J. O'Toole, *Doing Drama Research*. Drama Australia, Melbourne.

Macintyre, A. 1982. *After Virtue: A Study in Moral Theory*. Duckworth, London.

McTaggart, R. and Kemmis, S. 2005. 'Participatory Action Research', in N. Denzin and Y. Lincoln, *The Sage Handbook of Qualitative Research*. Sage, Thousand Oaks, California.

Mangeni, P. 2006. Negotiating Gender Equity through Theatre for Development. PhD Thesis, Griffith University, Brisbane.

Martel, Y. 2001. *Life of Pi*. Knopf, Toronto.

Marton, F. 1997. *Learning and Awareness*. Erlbaum, Mahweh, New Jersey.

Maturana, H. and Favela, A. 1987. *The Tree of Knowledge: The Biological Roots of Human Understanding*. Random House, Boston.

Mette, H., Mjoen, L., Mostad, H. and Petrusdottir, T. 2002. *Rosenborg Religion: Stories of the Kjernen*. Ethnodrama performed at Rosenborg FC Fan Club, Trondheim, Norway.

Millett, T. 2002. The Understudy: The Embodiment of Life on Stage. PhD Thesis, Griffith University, Brisbane.

Morris, G. 2004. Embodied Identities: Somali Women 'Doing' Adult Literacy. PhD Thesis, The University of Melbourne.

Moss, J. (ed.) 2008. *Researching Education: Visually—Digitally—Spatially*. Sense Publishers, Rotterdam.

National Research Council 2003. *Scientific Research in Education: Committee on Scientific Principles in Educational Research*. National Academy Press, Washington, DC.

Newsom, J. 1963. *Half Our Future*. Central Advisory Council for Education, UK.

NVivo 2013. Home Page. Retrieved 7 February 2013 from www.qsrinternational.com/products_nvivo.aspx.

O'Brien, A. 2006. Cited in J. O'Toole, *Doing Drama Research*. Drama Australia, Melbourne.

O'Connor, P. 2009. 'Editorial: Special Edition—Everyday Conversations About Everyday Theatre.' *Research in Drama Education* 14 (4).

O'Donoghue, A. 1999. Specific Learning Difficulties Through the Eyes of Parent, Teacher, Support Teacher and Child: A Case Study. Master of Teaching Honours Specialist Study, University of Sydney.

O'Loughlin, M. 2006. *Embodiment and Education: Exploring Creatural Existence*. Springer, Dordrecht, The Netherlands.

O'Toole, J. 1977. *Theatre in Education: New Objectives for Theatre, New Techniques in Education*. Hodder and Stoughton, London.

O'Toole, J. 2006. *Doing Drama Research*. Drama Australia, Melbourne.

O'Toole, J. and Burton, B. 2005a. 'From DRACON to Cooling Conflicts to Acting Against Bullying', in H. Löfgren and G. Malm (eds) *Bridging the Fields of Drama and Conflict Management: Empowering Students to Handle Conflicts Through School-Based Programs*. Studia psychologica et paedagogica series Altena CXXX, Malmö University, Malmö, Sweden.

O'Toole, J. and Burton, B. 2005b. 'Action against Conflict and Bullying: The Brisbane DRACON Project 1996–2004—Emergent Outcomes and Findings.' *Research in Drama Education* 10 (3).

O'Toole, J. and Burton, B. 2006. *Countering the Bullies: Action Research on Policy Change and Teacher Re-education through Innovative and Pro-active Techniques in Schools*. ARC Linkage project in association with Education Queensland, Griffith University, Brisbane.

O'Toole, M. 2011. *The Language of Displayed Art*. Routledge, London.

Orwell, G. 1946. 'Politics and the English Language.' *Horizon*. April.

Pietzner, J. 2013. Hermeneutics and Philosophy for Children (working title). PhD Thesis, The University of Melbourne (in progress).

Plunkett, A. 2003. The Art of Cooling Conflict: Using Educational Drama and Peer Teaching to Empower Students to Understand Conflict. PhD Thesis, Griffith University, Brisbane.

Polanyi, M. 1958. *Personal Knowledge: Towards a Post-Critical Philosophy*. Routledge, London.

Popper, K. 1980 [1935]. *The Logic of Scientific Discovery* (4th edn). Hutchinson, London.

Power, A. 2004. Moving On Through Drama: A Study of the Developing Drama Skills of Trauma Victims. BA in Applied Theatre Honours Thesis, Griffith University, Brisbane.

Provalis Research. Available at http://provalisresearch.com/products/qualitative-data-analysis-software.

QDA Miner 2013. Home Page. Retrieved 7 February 2013 from http://provalisresearch.com/products/qualitative-data-analysis-software.

Ramanathan, V. and Morgan, B. (eds) 2007. 'TESOL and Policy Enactments: Perspectives from Practice.' *TESOL Quarterly*, 41 (3) (Sept. Theme Issue).

Raphael, J. 2003. Theatre of Daylight: Drama, Disability and Empowerment. MEd Thesis, The University of Melbourne.

Richardson, L. 1997. *Fields of Play: Constructing an Academic Life*. Rutgers University Press, New Brunswick, NJ.

Richardson, L. 2000. 'Writing, a Method of Enquiry', in N. Denzin and Y. Lincoln (eds) *The Sage Handbook of Qualitative Research* (2nd edn). Sage, Thousand Oaks, California.

Sadler, R. 1992. *Up the Scholarly Publication Road: a Guide to Publishing in Scholarly Journals for Academics, Researchers and Graduate Students*. HERDS: A green guide series, Higher Education Research and Development Society of Australasia, Sydney.

Saldaña, J. 2005. *Ethnodrama: An Anthology of Reality Theatre*. Altamira Press, Walnut Creek, California.

Sanders, T. 2003. Where the Boys Are: The Experiences of Adolescent Boys and their Female Teachers in Two Single Sex Drama Classrooms. PhD Thesis, Griffith University, Brisbane.

Sanjakdar, F. 2006. Revelation versus Tradition: Beginning 'Curriculum Conversations' in Health and Sexual Health Education for Young Australian Muslims. PhD Thesis, The University of Melbourne.

Schön, D. 1983. *The Reflective Practitioner: How Professionals Think in Action*. Maurice Temple Smith, London.

Schön, D. 1987. *Educating the Reflective Practitioner: Towards a New Design for Teaching and Learning in the Professions*. Jossey-Bass, San Francisco.

Schön, D. 1995. Reflective Practice: Its Implications for Classroom, Administration and Research. Public lecture given for the Department of Language, Literacy and Arts Education, The University of Melbourne. Retrieved 9 June 2006 from www.edfac. unimelb.edu.au/ace/pdfs/Reflective%20Practice_270905.pdf (no longer current).

Senge, P. 1990. *The Fifth Discipline: The Art and Practice of the Learning Organisation*. Doubleday, New York.

Senior, K. 2008. Indelible Stains: Researching Pedagogy within the Spaces and Tensions of an Ethnographic Study of Learning to Teach. PhD Thesis, The University of Melbourne.

Sinclair, C. 2005. Giving Voice and Being Heard: Searching for a New Understanding of Rehearsal Processes and Aesthetic Outcomes in Community Theatre. PhD Thesis, The University of Melbourne.

Singh, P. and McWilliam, E. (eds) 2001. *Designing Educational Research: Theories, Methods and Practices*. Post Pressed, Flaxton, Queensland.

Smigiel, H. 1996. The Place of Educational Drama in Workplace and Vocational Training. PhD Thesis, University of Tasmania.

Smith, L.T. 1999. *Decolonising Methodologies: Research and Indigenous Peoples*. Zed Books, New York.

Snooks & Co 2002. *Style Manual*. John Wiley, for the Department of Finance and Administration, Commonwealth of Australia, Canberra.

Snow, C.P. 1963. *The Two Cultures and the Scientific Revolution*. Cambridge University Press, Cambridge, UK.

Somekh, B. and Lewin, C. (eds) 2005. *Research Methods in the Social Sciences*. Sage, London.

Song, R. 2013. Cross-cultural Communication in Chinese-Western Business (working title). PhD Thesis, The University of Melbourne (in progress).

South Australian Department of Education and Child Development 2012. *Most Significant Change*. Retrieved January 2013 from www.learningtolearn.sa.edu.au/learning_workroom/pages/default/msc/?reFlag=1.

Stake, R. 1995. *The Arts of Case Study Research*. Sage, Thousand Oaks, California.

Stake, R. 2005. 'Qualitative Case Studies', in N. Denzin and Y. Lincoln (eds) *The Sage Handbook of Qualitative Research*. Sage, Thousand Oaks, California.

Stewart, I. 1989. *Does God Play Dice? The Mathematics of Chaos*. Blackwell, Oxford.

Stinson, M. 2009. '"Drama is Like Reversing Everything": Intervention Research as Teacher Professional Development.' *Research in Drama Education* 14 (2).

Stinson, M. and Freebody, K. 2005. *Drama and Oral Language: Impacting Oral English Language Performance with Process Drama and Normal Technical Sec 4 Students*. Research Report, National Institute of Education, Singapore.

Taylor, E. 2000. 'Role-play without Tears', in J. O'Toole and M. Lepp (eds) *Drama for Life*. Playlab Press, Brisbane.

Taylor, P. 1996. 'Doing Reflective Practitioner Research in Arts Education', in P. Taylor (ed.) *Researching Drama and Arts Education: Paradigms and Possibilities*. Falmer Press, London.

Timma, H. 2004. Ontology, Assessment and the Worker: Constructing Worker Identities through Assessment. PhD Thesis, The University of Melbourne.

Tyler, R. 1949. *Basic Principles of Curriculum and Instruction*. University of Chicago Press, Chicago.

Usher, R., Bryant, I. and Johnson, R. 1997. *Adult Education and the Postmodern Challenge: Learning beyond the Limits*. Routledge, London.

Usher, R. and Edwards, R. 1994. *Postmodernism and Education*. Routledge, London.

Vaughan, D. 1992. 'Theory Elaboration: The Heuristics of Case Analysis', in C. Ragin and H. Becker (eds) *What is a Case? Exploring the Foundations of Social Inquiry*. Cambridge University Press, Cambridge, UK.

Vygotsky, L. 1962. *Thought and Language*. MIT University Press, Cambridge, Massachusetts.

Vygotsky, L. 1978. *Mind in Society: The Development of Higher Psychological Processes*. Harvard University Press, Cambridge, Massachusetts.

Wales, P. 2006. Circus Acts: Performative Subjectivities of Women who Teach Drama. PhD Thesis, University of Melbourne.

Walter, M. 2006. 'The Nature of Social Science Research', in M. Walter (ed.) *Social Research Methods: An Australian Perspective*. Oxford University Press, Melbourne.

Wang, Y. 2008. Reading Chinese Literature or Reading China? An Intercultural Thematic Approach to the Reading of Chinese Literature in the TCFL (Teaching English as a Foreign Language) Curriculum. PhD Thesis, The University of Melbourne.

Watson, D. 2003. *Death Sentence: The Decay of Public Language*. Random House, Sydney.

Watson, D. 2004. *Watson's Dictionary of Weasel Words: Contemporary Clichés. Cant and Management Jargon*. Knopf, Sydney.

Winston, J. 2006. 'Researching through Case Study', in J. Ackroyd (ed.) *Research Methodologies for Drama Education*. Trentham Books, London.

Winter, R. 1996. 'Some Principles and Procedures for the Conduct of Action Research', in O. Zuber-Skerritt (ed.) *New Directions in Action Research*. Falmer Press, London.

Wise, R. 2000. Deepening Australian Democracy: What Can Schools Do? PhD Thesis, University of Melbourne.

Wittgenstein, L. 1953. *Philosophical Investigations*. Blackwell, Oxford.

Wolcott, H.F. 1999. *Ethnography: A Way of Seeing*. Altamira Press, Walnut Creek, California.

Woods, P. 1994. 'Collaborating in Historical Ethnography: Researching Critical Events in Education.' *International Journal of Qualitative Studies in Education* 7 (4).

Wright, D. 2005. 'Reflecting on the Body in Drama Education.' *Applied Theatre Researcher/IDEA Journal* 6.

Wright, D. 2006. Cited in J. O'Toole, *Doing Drama Research*. Drama Australia, Melbourne.

Yates, L. 2004. *What Does Good Education Research Look Like?* Open University Press, London.

Yeats, W.B. 1939. 'Long Legged Fly' from *Last Poems*, variously published.

Yin, R.K. 1989. *Case Study Research: Design and Methods* (2nd edn). Sage, Newberry Park, California.

Yin, R.K. 2003. *Applications of Case Study Research* (2nd edn). Sage, Thousand Oaks, California.

Zuber-Skerritt, O. (ed.) 1996. *New Directions in Action Research*. Falmer Press, London.

INDEX